D0759948

THE MOZARTIAN HISTORIAN

The Mozartian Historian

ESSAYS ON THE WORKS OF

Joseph R. Levenson

Edited By
MAURICE MEISNER
and
RHOADS MURPHEY

UNIVERSITY OF CALIFORNIA PRESS
BERKELEY LOS ANGELES LONDON

University of California Press
Berkeley and Los Angeles, California

University of California Press, Ltd.
London, England

ISBN 0-520-02826-0
Library of Congress Catalog Card Number: 74-82849
Printed in the United States of America

CONTENTS

PART TWO
Levenson as Historiographer

PART THREE
The Levenson Legacy

PART FOUR
The Choice of Jewish Identity

CONTRIBUTORS

JAMES CAHILL is Professor of History of Art at the University of California, Berkeley

RALPH CROIZIER is Associate Professor of History at the University of Rochester

JOHN K. FAIRBANK is Francis Lee Higginson Professor of History at Harvard University

HAROLD KAHN is Associate Professor of History at Stanford University

DONALD KEENE is Professor of Japanese Literature at Columbia University

J.C. LEVENSON is Edgar Allen Poe Professor of English at the University of Virginia

ROSEMARY LEVENSON is Project Director, Regional Oral History Office at the University of California, Berkeley

ANGUS MCDONALD is Visiting Assistant Professor of History at the University of Minnesota

MAURICE MEISNER is Professor of History at the University of Wisconsin, Madison

RHOADS MURPHEY is Professor of Geography at the University of Michigan

FRANZ SCHURMANN is Professor of History and Sociology at the University of California, Berkeley

BENJAMIN SCHWARTZ is Professor of History and Government at Harvard University

JONATHAN SPENCE is Professor of History at Yale University

LYMAN P. VAN SLYKE is Associate Professor of History at Stanford University

FREDERIC WAKEMAN, JR., is Professor of History at the University of California, Berkeley

CONTRIBUTORS

EDITORS' INTRODUCTION

Maurice Meisner and Rhoads Murphey

The idea for this book was first discussed when a small group of us who had attended the memorial service for Joseph Levenson in Berkeley on April 13, 1969, gathered afterward, as people will do, to share, primarily in wordless ways, our sense of loss and shock. We spoke of him, of course, and we talked rather haphazardly about possible memorials, but our thoughts, then as now, were not easily put into words. Such words as we managed at the time only tended to magnify the grief over his sudden and terribly premature death. We felt that the richness and significance of his historical work had been neither sufficiently appreciated nor sufficiently understood. More than anything else, it was this feeling that moved us to undertake the work for this volume. As Levenson himself once put it in a personal letter, too few of his readers had "sprained eyeballs" in attempting to understand the meaning of his writings. We felt there remained an intellectual need and a moral obligation to encourage ourselves and others to explore further some of the many human and historical problems which he had treated so creatively and humanely. The problems he raised and the themes he pursued are matters of enduring and universal concern; his writings have a message for the present and the future, and should not be allowed to pass into the "silence of the museum."

After the numbing effect of his death had eased a bit, many of his friends and colleagues were able to think about more specific plans. At the end of April of 1969, The Joseph Levenson Memorial Scholarship Fund (to which all royalties from this book will go) was founded at the University of California at Berkeley, with the help of many elsewhere. At the same time, we began to explore the possibility of assembling in book form reflective and critical essays on the significance of his work as an historian. We were determined not to produce the usual *festschrift* of miscellaneous and usually unrelated essays and articles, but rather an interpretive study focusing on Levenson's work itself and the historical problems with which he wrestled. Our purpose has been to add something of intrinsic as well as of extrinsic value for those who are concerned with history and with ideas, in the form of essays directed at what Levenson was trying to do, how he did it, what his work has to offer to other scholars, and what new lines of scholarly inquiry might be derived from that work. We invited contributions of this sort from over sixty people, beginning in the summer of 1969.

This book has been long in the making, for the usual reasons of competing demands on busy people, but also for another reason. Although it is not difficult to find richly varied meaning and significance in Levenson's writings, the prospective commentator or critic tends to hear (as Brahms, the symphonist, of Beethoven) the steps of a giant behind him. For many who were close personal friends of Levenson's the prospect of evaluating the work he left behind seemed also too cold and calculating a task; it was a problem which only the passage of time could alleviate.

Contributions came in over some four years, with the understanding that they might not be judged appropriate for the kind of book we had in mind. Accordingly, many essays were returned because we did not find them adequately related to the focus of the volume: the significance of Levenson's work and its impact. For the same reason, we discouraged other prospective contributors once they had sent us a title or outline. Still other essays were lost to us because we felt we should not wait longer for them. This volume appears more than six years after his death, much longer than we had anticipated, but perhaps not too long to permit a degree of perspective on the scholarship without losing the nearness to the scholar and the man which is an appropriate and indeed essential part of this undertaking.

We believe that we have succeeded in assembling an integrated collection of critical scholarly studies which manages also to convey something of Levenson's notable humanity as it informed his work. This volume is neither basically exegetical nor is it an attempt to systematize the corpus of his writings. It certainly does not aim to establish any "Levensonian cult." Indeed, there is much in this book which is explicitly critical in nature. We assumed from the beginning that this would and should be the case when we asked for samples of the different ways in which scholars have understood, used, and reacted to what he wrote. The collection provides, we believe, a representative set of such samples, critically exploring, analyzing, and pursuing further some of the major themes and modes with which Joseph Levenson was concerned, evaluating the work of a scholar who treated universal human problems in a uniquely stimulating way.

The essays are grouped in sections which focus on particular aspects of Levenson's career, personal style, and writings. His scholarly impact extended far beyond fellow historians of China, and if we have a regret about this volume, it is that we were not able to include more essays from the many people outside the discipline of history or the field of Chinese studies who have been influenced and stimulated by his work. Part One presents pictures of Levenson as a human being evolving through a professional career; Part Two deals in greater detail with his work as an historian; Part Three offers critical and evaluative reviews of two of his major themes; and Part Four brings the volume back to a more personal plane in the form of a previously unpublished essay on Judaism, intended as the beginning of a larger work which Levenson had mentioned to some of us in earlier years. It may strike some readers as incongruous with the rest of his writings—indeed it appears incongruous to us—but we have not attempted to edit it in any way and reproduce it here exactly as he left it, though not necessarily as he would have left it had he lived. Despite its fragmentary and unfinished form, the essay deserves to be printed, partly because it has already had some circulation and is referred to in several of the essays in this book as well as in Frederic Wakeman's Foreword to *Revolution and Cosmopolitanism,* and partly because it reflects Levenson's deep involvement with his own religious and cultural tradition. His widow Rosemary has provided a thoughtful introduction which sets the essay in context.

By its nature, a volume such as this, the work of many people writing independently about the same set of themes, must sound many of the same notes more than once. Yet each essay is distinct and, where the same themes are discussed, the treatment is nevertheless different. It is not to be expected, however, that even two people writing about the significance of his career or his work would produce wholly nonparallel results, any more than a multi-author volume on the meaning of Mozart to music could or should somehow manage to mention the C-Minor Mass only once. Indeed, an important part of the value of this book, we believe, is its demonstration of the extent to which a score of scholars have responded to many of the same ideas in Levenson's work, and at the same time responded to them in different ways.

When Levenson's first book, *Liang Ch'i-ch'ao and the Mind of Modern China,* was published in 1953, it was greeted with a scathing review by Dr. Arthur Hummel, then widely considered "the dean" of American Sinology. Writing in *The Far Eastern Quarterly,* Hummel charged that Levenson lacked sympathy for the subject of his study, that he had set out to "debunk" an important figure in modern Chinese history, and that he (Levenson) was "out to get his man" (Liang). In addition to various complaints about Levenson's style, Hummel accused Levenson of approaching his subject with perspectives "alien to the spirit of (Chinese) civilization" and failing to assess "the ethical values, the timeless truths" which Liang wished to preserve. Nor was Hummel pleased that Levenson found social class differentiations in Chinese society; Levenson was taken to task for the sin of reasoning "dialectically" to "postulate" a landlord literati against an illiterate peasantry and for having characterized the Confucian tradition as a gentry class tradition. And Hummel concluded that,

> A book purposely written, as the author admits, to put "the searchlight's glare on Liang" can hardly be taken as a work of objective, historical scholarship. It really tells us more about the wayward, corrosive thinking of our time than it does about the figure whom, in a moment of true illumination, the author characterizes as "the first mind of the new China."[1]

Other reviews of *Liang Ch'i-ch'ao*—and later of the three volumes which now comprise the trilogy *Confucian China and Its Modern Fate*—were not to offer such harsh judgments, and indeed some were highly laudatory. But, on the whole, the critiques were bland and the intellectual response was feeble. With very few exceptions, his work was never adequately dealt with in the reviews that appeared in scholarly journals. Levenson felt this too, not because

1. *Far Eastern Quarterly,* vol. XIV, No. 1 (November 1954), pp. 110-112.

he wanted praise, or lacked professional scholarly recognition, but because it is disappointing to any author not to provoke a response commensurate with the scale and scope of his work. Few appreciated the significance of his books when they were published—and many dismissed their significance. There remained widespread suspicions, echoing some of the criticisms first leveled by Hummel, that Levenson was writing more about his mind than about "the mind of modern China," that he was imposing alien concerns on the Chinese historical record, that he ignored "the facts," or that he was a clever stylist who sacrificed historical substance to a fancy turn of phrase. If Levenson's scholarly career was no ordinary career but rather the record of "genius at work"—as John Fairbank characterizes it on page 39 of this volume in a judgment we share—then we find it both remarkable and distressing that his works received so little in the way of either serious criticism or critical acclaim, at least in the published scholarly record.

Why was the intellectual response so feeble? Why was it that so few understood and appreciated the significance of his writings when they first appeared? In large measure, we would suggest it was because the radical implications of his work had a profoundly unsettling effect on scholars who remained intellectually tied to the dominant (and predominantly conservative) assumptions of the Western Sinological tradition. Levenson, to be sure, was not a political radical, and indeed had little taste for political activism of any kind. But he was intellectually radical as an historian—radical in how he conceived historic processes, radically unconventional in the manner in which he wrote about them, and perhaps most profoundly radical in what he wanted from history and hoped it might yield. As Levenson gained scholarly standing and professional recognition, few of his Sinological friends and colleagues denied his brilliance and many valued his historical insights, but most thought his writings too unconventional and perhaps a bit heretical; his historical judgments were widely questioned and the way he arrived at them was widely misunderstood. It was partly a matter of style and approach that made his writings suspect in some professional eyes. In the realm of style and structure, he was deliberately iconoclastic in defying the conventional canons of historiography which dictate that the historian deal with unique phenomena in concrete detail and narrative style. To achieve depth and interpretive integration he was quite willing, as he once put it, to "take sudden dips of a few centuries or so . . . at whatever cost to the narrative ideals of smooth progression and never looking back."

Confucian China and Its Modern Fate, for example, does not begin with Confucius and end with Mao, although a great deal is said about both Confucianism and Maoism. The first volume begins with heterodox Confucian "empiricists" of the seventeenth century while the final volume finishes with an Hasidic parable, concluding a lengthy analysis of the failure of Confucianism in the modern Chinese historical environment and its passing into the "history" of the contemporary Chinese Communist museum. And there is much that comes between. The lines of historical inquiry extend from the classical age of Confucius and Mencius to Marxist interpretations of the Confucian classics. Events, men, and concepts are drawn from all eras and ages—from Chou to Ch'in to Han, through the great and small "middle" dynasties to the "early modern" Ch'ing, the Republic, and the People's Republic—but they do not appear one after the other in the usual chronological fashion. The thread weaves back and forth throughout Chinese history and the lines of inquiry go out to other histories as well. They reach back to Moses and Aristotle—and the ideas of Voltaire, Rousseau, Herder, Francis Bacon, Croce, Hegel, Tagore, Swift, Marx, and Lenin (to mention but a few) flow into an analytic synthesis of a distinctively Chinese process of modern intellectual and social change. Alexander the Great, Louis XIV, and Russian Czars appear alongside the names of Chinese emperors. And a discussion of bureaucracy in Prussia (and elsewhere) merges into an analysis of the particular nature of bureaucracy in Confucian China.

There was method in what seemed to some so bewildering a way to write about Chinese history. The method was a highly sophisticated and often subtle form of comparative historical analysis which revealed the unique characteristics of Chinese historical phenomena by placing them in the universal perspective of the whole of human history. For Joseph Levenson believed that the more histories an historian knew, the better he would be able to recognize what was significant about the particular history he studied. Thus, for example, in using medieval European, Islamic, and Byzantine points of comparison for an exploration of the traditional Chinese conception of monarchy, he observed that while what Confucianists made of monarchy was something particularly Chinese, "we can hardly understand what they made of it unless we recognize in monarchy what is potentially universal."[2] It was this appreciation of the universal immanent in the unique that permitted Levenson to move the writing of Chinese history from the confines of its Sinological sanctuary to the realm of world historical discourse. Having mastered all the professional tools of "the China specialist," he was not content to use them simply to dissect a self-contained Chinese history of interest only to other China specialists. Rather the aim was to relate what was significant in Chinese history to the broader concerns of those interested in the significance of the whole human historical experience. And it was because he had a deep and wide-ranging knowledge of non-Chinese histories that he knew what in Chinese history was of more than purely Chinese historical significance and what was comparable with the histories of other cultures. But what was comparable was not necessarily analogous. Levenson drew and explored many analogies, but mostly to show their historical untenability. Precisely by demonstrating the failure of analogies he demonstrated what was distinctive about traditional China and what was distinctively modern about modern China. China had a separate history, to be sure, but not one that should be separated from universal historical concerns. For understanding Chinese history, China was not all; and for understanding history in general, China was not peripheral.

The style and structure of *Confucian China* is unconventional; chronological lines are more than a bit "irregular," and this rubbed against some conventional historiographical grains. But what rubbed even harder, against some conventional Sinological grains, was the radical content of Levenson's analysis of the modern Chinese historical condition. The thrust of his argument and the conclusion of his inquiry was that various kinds of socio-intellectual change and various kinds of departures from tradition in modern times had culminated in a fundamental and radical break with the past. For the makers of modern Chinese history, the values and institutions of the past had become (at best) "merely *historically* significant," no longer part of a living tradition offering genuine inspiration for the present but rather a culture "dead to modern

2. Joseph R. Levenson, *Confucian China and Its Modern Fate: A Trilogy* (Berkeley: University of California Press, 1968), vol. II, p. 3. All references to the three volumes of this study are taken from the above-mentioned combined edition, hereafter referred to as *Confucian China*.

man." The great Confucian tradition, long sinking, departed from the modern historical scene; its intellectual substance was exhausted and its outworn institutions had come down with "a dying fall." Long-term processes of social change and intellectual alienation had resulted in a qualitatively new Chinese historical situation, a situation where "finally the tie is snapped."[3] Various intellectual balms might be applied to soothe the emotional strain, but the historical-intellectual break was beyond repair.

Levenson did not celebrate the snapping of ties to the past. Indeed, his own feelings about modern abandonments of tradition were profoundly ambiguous. But, as he put it, "an historian has to assume the authenticity of change," and as an historian of China his view was clear and unambiguous: ". . . to put it flatly, traditional Chinese civilization has not been renewed in modern times but unravelled."[4] This interpretation of modern Chinese history as a history characterized by a radical and fundamental break with the past did not suit the usual historiographical preference for the gradualness of historical change within tradition, the impulse to experience any given historical present in terms of stable and persisting elements firmly anchored in the past. Nor did Levenson's analysis conform with the Western Sinological predisposition to explain modern Chinese thought and society in terms of the survival of traditional cultural and institutional patterns. Questions and objectives were raised and most of the questions revolved about the problem of "continuity" between contemporary China and the Chinese cultural-historical inheritance.

Joseph Levenson was centrally concerned with the problem of the relationship between the past and present of China, and perhaps even more concerned with modern Chinese concerns about what he called a cultural situation of "fractured continuity." One way to understand the work of Levenson, and perhaps to understand some misunderstandings about his work, is to examine how he treated the problem of "continuity" in his conception of the varieties of processes of historical change.

"Historical continuity" is a problem, in part, because the term is so historically ambiguous. As Alexander Gerschenkron has remarked, "one cannot suppress the suspicion that it is the very uncertainties of the term which have made it flow so readily from

3. *Confucian China*, vol. I, p. xxxii.
4. *Confucian China*, vol. III, pp. 63 and 47.

pens and tongues."[5] Rather than dwelling on the semantic obscurities involved, one might briefly take note of the conceptual ambiguity reflected in the customary distinction between "change" and "continuity," a familiar dichotomy which has proven so convenient for titles of books and articles. What is often implicitly suggested or understood by this conventional distinction is the view that continuity is the opposite or absence of change. Although few would agree with Schopenhauer's "law of continuity," according to which nothing essential changes except "names and dates," it would seem that there are many who believe that it is possible for some historical phenomena to change while others remain stable. But it has yet to be theoretically explained or empirically demonstrated how certain elements of socio-historical order remain in stasis while others are changing; if the elements of a society are structurally interrelated, then change in any one or more parts of the structure necessarily influences the nature and function of other aspects of social life and affects the historic process as a whole.

Despite the easy acceptance of the dichotomy between "continuity" and "change" in contemporary historical discourse, perhaps few historians actually mean what they seem to imply—that continuity is simply the opposite of change. When the term continuity does not merely refer to the obvious relationship between past and present as a temporal sequence, it generally refers to gradualness in the rate of change. There is no reason to quarrel with the notion that continuity in history describes a certain kind of change that is relatively gradual in nature. What becomes historically questionable is the tendency to place a normative value on gradual change and to see gradualness, in the form of virtually imperceptible movement, as a more or less universal characteristic of history. Here continuity as gradual change is perceived as historically desirable as well as historically natural. And this too often becomes a convenient way to deny the possibility, or the reality, of revolutionary change and to morally condemn it at the same time. It also precludes a conceptual framework which distinguishes between different kinds of historical change. If the concept of continuity is to have any real analytic utility, it must be part of a general theory of historical change

5. Alexander Gerschenkron, *Continuity in History and Other Essays* (Cambridge, Mass.: Harvard University Press, 1968), p. 11.

which allows for the possibility of discontinuities and radical modes of change as well as for continuity in terms of gradual change.

It was with such a broader conception of the varieties of historical change that Joseph Levenson approached the problem of continuity in Chinese history. Radical departures from the past did not preclude continuity but implied it, for he conceived continuity to be a category of change, not the antithesis of change. For Levenson, all history was a constant process of change and development, never a nonprocess of timeless realities; he viewed history in terms of dialectic process, not in terms of unchanging essences or "timeless truths." His concern was not with the functional interrelationships of society at any given moment in time, but rather with historical phenomena which were changing and developing or had the potential to develop into something different from what they were. And when that potential was not fully realized, or proved abortive, he felt the need to explain why. No historical situation could ever be static, in Levenson's historical world view, and he was drawn to the elements of tension in history which were potential sources of change and which held dynamic possibilities. He was less interested in what was at any given time or place than in how it became what it was and what it was in the process of becoming, or what it might have become. He saw change inherent in even the most tradition-bound histories, for while taking into account the social context, he took it as a universal historical truth that men make history and that they do so by their own ideas and efforts.

> A completely binding traditionalism would keep a people forever at the post, never moving into history. Some tempering of traditionalism by judgment must occur, or histories would be frozen by the law that nothing can be added to a way of life, if it seems a departure from what has gone before. Absolute traditionalism is a completely hypothetical, self-destructive concept; a sense of the past can never develop if an original unmitigated reverence for "what is" precludes its ever becoming past.[6]

This dialectical conception of history precluded the conventional mechanistic distinction between "change" and "continuity." At the same time, it allowed for a distinction between quantitative and qualitative historical change, between the nature of the history of

6. *Confucian China*, vol. I, pp. xxxi-xxxii.

traditional China and the changes which brought about the posttraditional history of modern China.

Levenson did not see Confucian China as the land of petrified tradition; on the contrary, he saw and described it as a constantly changing historical world, a world full of human drama and historical tension. And although it was not his world, he had the deepest admiration for what was best and most humane in the tradition of that world—and especially for the Confucian ideal of the amateur and the generalist; he was drawn not to the Confucian as bureaucrat but to the idea of the Confucian "all-round" man who did not impoverish his personality in specialization. But the Confucian world was not a world of radical change; it was a history of gradual change in terms of the continuity of a viable and developing tradition.

Yet other kinds of historical changes were possible in China, radical social and intellectual changes which no longer permitted Chinese to develop tradition but forced them to abandon it. Levenson knew that radical change had come to China in modern times and had to come, that modern Chinese radically changed China, and that this had resulted in a qualitatively new historical situation. He both accepted the authenticity and necessity of revolutionary change in the modern Chinese historical environment and recognized the historical logic of its Communist outcome. This was not a denial of continuity between China's past and present, but rather a recognition that the historian's concept of continuity as denoting gradualness in the rate of historical change, while appropriate for dealing with change in traditional China, was inadequate for understanding revolutionary change in modern China. Indeed, it was precisely by demonstrating radical and traumatic breaks with the traditions and values of the past that Levenson posed continuity as a special problem in modern Chinese history and raised that problem to a new and higher level of historical discourse. And no Western historian of modern China had a deeper understanding of (and empathy with) the special concerns of Chinese intellectuals caught up in a situation of massive cultural and social disintegration and searching for viable links to a Chinese past which they could relate to their present and to their visions of the future. What Levenson denied was not continuity (which, as an historian, he necessarily assumed) but the notion of the persistence of allegedly unchanging traditional Chinese "essences." The persistence of tradition, it might be noted, requires historical explanation as much as change. And perhaps the burden of explanation rests with those who view the Chinese tradition as immutable.

The question of continuity in the modern history of China is, of course, posed most sharply by the Chinese Communist revolution. Joseph Levenson's scholarship did not deal primarily with the history of Chinese Communism. He preferred to write an essay on Liao P'ing, "a small Confucianist" who was "really unimportant;" he would not have been inclined to write an article about the mystery of Lin Piao, a matter most Pekinologists think really important. But if his research did not focus primarily on the history of Chinese Communism as such, he was nevertheless centrally concerned with the larger historical question of the place of Chinese Communism in Chinese history, and his writings in general had important implications for understanding the historic significance of Marxism and Communism in China. They were implications which posed incisive challenges to the dominant views in Western scholarship on the relationship between Communist China and the Chinese cultural-historical heritage. Many scholars of modern China found those implications uncongenial, especially the passages where Levenson deals explicitly with the place of Chinese Communism in Chinese history (as in chapters 3 and 4 of the third volume of the trilogy). For what he wrote about Chinese Communism was in part a critical reaction to what he called the principle of "Sinological determinism" in what others wrote about the subject; in part his views on Communist China were the logical culmination of his general analysis of the passing of traditional China into "history."

Levenson did not ignore the problem of the survivals of the past and it is not our intent to dismiss the question here. Almost a century before his Chinese disciples were to confront the problem, Karl Marx warned that the new society produced by a socialist revolution inevitably would be a society "still stamped with the birthmarks of the old society from whose womb it emerges," and that this would be the case "in every respect, economically, morally and intellectually."[7] This revolutionary truism applies with particular force to modern Chinese history, where a modern

7. Karl Marx, "The Eighteenth Brumaire of Louis Bonaparte," Marx and Engels *Selected Works* (Moscow, 1950), vol. I, p. 225.

revolutionary vision triumphed in a country still largely dominated by an archaic social and value structure. Contemporary Chinese society remains deeply stamped by the traditions and burdens inherited from old China. It is thus hardly surprising that Western scholars of the Chinese Communist revolution should emphasize the survival of traditional institutional forms and traditional patterns of thought in interpreting the results of that revolution, that they should stress the importance of the birthmarks stamped on the new society more than the fact of the birth. The general assumption, although it is by no means a universal one, is that something of the "essence" of traditional Chinese civilization has survived the upheavals of modern times to mold the nature of the Communist present. What is really essential about Chinese Communism, it is suggested, is that it is essentially Chinese—and Chinese in some traditional sense. What constitutes the traditional Chinese "essence" that has persisted is, of course, a matter of interpretation, and there are many different interpretations. There is no need to catalogue them here; they range from simplistic notions that Communist China is another dynasty in a long line of Chinese dynasties to more serious and sophisticated arguments which attempt to explain contemporary historical phenomena in terms of more or less immutable patterns of traditional thought, culture, and behavior. The reader of Western writings on modern China is presented with an endless number of perceived historical "continuities" between the Confucian past and the Communist present. What is conveyed, on the whole, is a rather deterministic picture of Chinese Communists as either the carriers of traditional modes of thought and socio-political behavior or as prisoners of their millennial cultural-historical inheritance.

This emphasis on the persistence of the past is by no means monopolized by historians. It is reinforced by much of contemporary social science theory, and especially by the old anthropological bias which stresses the resilience of cultural traditions. Even practitioners of "modernization" theories lend their support to "continuity" arguments. In the literature of this very different kind of determinism, where the impersonal forces of "the modernization process" presumably dictate movement toward some universal socio-historical end, one frequently finds references to traditional behavior being carried on under the cover of modern forms. David Apter informs us, for example, that "Quite often modernizing societies, under some indigenous brand of nationalism or socialism, will disguise a deep connection with traditional practices."[8] The notion that a new form merely conceals an old content is characteristic of a strong Western predisposition to interpret contemporary Chinese history in terms of the survival of tradition. And modern Chinese are even more firmly tied to their past by the growing influence of structuralist theories; if there are in fact unalterable "deep structures" of language and culture which basically determine thought and behavior, then certainly there cannot be much really new under the Chinese sun.

Perhaps there is something comforting in a picture of Chinese Communists doing little more than pouring old Chinese wines into new Marxist-labeled bottles. Westerners long have been attracted to the notion that non-Western societies are characterized by unique and unchanging cultures. Cultural determinism suits the Western taste to see non-Western societies as exotic and to keep them exotic, just as cultural and historical relativism can be employed (as Peter Worsley has observed) "to keep backward societies backward in the name of preserving their cultural 'uniqueness.'"[9] Both cultural relativist and cultural determinist arguments have been used to deny a distinctively modern Chinese historical process, in the first case by emphasizing the uniqueness of traditional Chinese culture, and in the second by emphasizing its permanence. In an age when the dynamic forces of historical change have come to reside largely in the non-Western areas of the world, some in the Western world can find political and psychological satisfaction in explaining—and explaining away—distant revolutionary changes as repetitions of old cultural patterns merely cloaked in modern dress. There long has been a widespread feeling in the West that history is no longer "going our way,"[10] and thus Westerners are attracted to culturalistic interpretations to seek compensation for this sense of loss, compensation gained by denying the reality of historical changes we can only observe and by denying the validity of revolutionary hopes we cannot share.

The old Western Sinological tradition is well suited to satisfy the contemporary Western conservative response to revolutionary change in China, for it is a scholarly tradition which not only dwells on the uniqueness of traditional Chinese patterns of culture

8. David Apter, *The Politics of Modernization* (Chicago: Aldine, 1965), p. 81.
9. Peter Worsley, *The Trumpet Shall Sound* (New York: Schocken Books, 1968), p. 259.

and social behavior but also conveys the view that those patterns are fixed and eternal. Western political anxieties can be eased by the belief that there is a traditional Chinese cultural "essence" which is perennial and that, therefore, Chinese are "always Chinese." It is precisely this notion that Sinology has bequeathed to scholarship on contemporary China and it lends support to the comforting conclusion that Chinese Communists have merely provided new revolutionary forms to conceal an old Chinese content and that nothing fundamentally has changed to disturb the timeless "continuity" of traditional Chinese civilization. The same conclusion is sometimes arrived at by a variation on the theme: Chinese Communist use of traditional forms and language is taken as a sure sign that they are carriers of an equally traditional content.

The influence of the Sinological tradition on contemporary scholarship is problematic and we shall not attempt to deal with it. Here it need only be noted that Joseph Levenson worked in a scholarly milieu dominated by a strong disposition to emphasize the survival of tradition to explain the nature of modern and contemporary thought and society. Old Sinological images of an "unchanging China" mingled with new modes of historical and social science determinisms to paint a general scholarly picture which portrayed modern Chinese more as products of an old history than as the producers of a new one.

Joseph Levenson was often harsh in dealing with "continuity" arguments which suggested that the Chinese Communist revolution merely provided superficial forms for the persistence of eternal Chinese essences. It was one thing for nineteenth-century Chinese to misuse the old *t'i-yung* formula as a rationalization for Western borrowing and to believe that they were still preserving the essence of traditional civilization, for at the time that reflected a real social process and met a genuine intellectual need. But when contemporary Western observers dredged up similar old formulae to explain contemporary history, it was no more than "a bit of easy phrase-making."[11] Levenson sometimes mocked those who saw Chinese Communism as Confucianism with another name: "Canonical

10. For a critique of contemporary Western historiography, and the "wave of pessimism and ultra-conservatism" which has overtaken much of it in recent decades, see E.H. Carr, *What is History?* (New York: Vintage Books, 1967).

11. Levenson, *Confucian China*, vol. I, p. 69.

texts and canonical texts, bureaucratic intellectual elite and bureaucratic intellectual elite—nothing has changed, allegedly—except possibly, everything."[12] Or, more charitably, he playfully attributed "a taste for paradox" to Western observers with Sinologically-deterministic predispositions.[13] It was not simply that the prevailing analogies between Confucian and Communist China were often irritatingly simplistic, or that reasoning by analogy—even when the analogies were argued in sophisticated fashion—was no substitute for serious historical investigation. He explored and exploded most such analogies with an historical incisiveness that no one else has matched and cerainly cannot be matched here. What was really irritating was that "continuity" arguments and analogies ignored genuine continuity in history by implying "a timeless, noumenal version of continuity" where "past was related to present not by sequence but by essence."[14] To Levenson this seemed no less than a denial of history itself and an attempt to deny that modern Chinese could make their own modern history.

Levenson's own view of Chinese Communism started from the fundamental premise that Chinese history (like all histories) was a process made by men, that Chinese Communists were real revolutionaries who made a real revolution which marked a fundamental departure from the past, a revolution which culminated a long historical process of departures from traditional China in various areas of social, economic, and intellectual life. This did not deny continuity between past and present, at least not as long as continuity is not equated with persistence. The Chinese Communist intelligentsia, after all, did not emerge full-blown from the old Confucian order; they were the Marxist heirs of the iconoclastic May Fourth generation who had already decisively rejected traditional values and beliefs, a generation that was itself the product of a century-long erosion of the traditional social structure. It was precisely this long and agonizing process of the decay of traditional society and the attrition of traditional culture—and of "men thinking" in a rapidly changing socio-historical environment—that established the historical connection between Confucian and Communist China. The Chinese Communist revolution was the logical (but not necessarily the inevitable) historical outcome of the failure of Confucianism in

12. Ibid., p. 162.
13. Levenson, *Confucian China*, vol. III, p. 62.
14. Ibid., pp. 62-63.

modern Chinese history. Critics who charged Levenson with ignoring the social context whereby new ideas replaced old ones would do well to ponder the paragraph which concludes the first volume of the trilogy:

> the continuity of Chinese history, including its current communist phase, can be affirmed without our explaining the latter as the Confucian eternal return. Revulsion against the landlord system, the family system, the Confucian education system has been building up for a long time in China, certainly not just since yesterday in doctrinaire directives. Though communists in power have helped such ideas along, their sources are deep in a century and a half of unplanned western action on the earlier social structure that was offered up to the contact. And what of the intellectual side of Chinese continuity? Old forms with genuinely new content (like the *t'i* and *yung, t'ien-hsia* and *kuo, ching* and *shih* dichotomies) establish continuity convincingly, at least as well as new forms with allegedly old content would do—and convey the reality of change better. If, as I have meant to do throughout this narrative, one interprets intellectual history as a history not "of thought", but of men thinking, one will not see a bloodless Confucianism imposing itself by identity on a similarly abstract communism, but Confucian generations giving way, living, feeling, and easing the strains. The Confucian tradition, transformed and abandoned, has led directly to the communist version of Chinese change of mind, not by preserving itself immanent in communist doctrine, but by failing in self-preservation, leaving its heirs bereft and potentially strange in their own land, and commending that latest doctrine as an answer to a need.[15]

By demonstrating that the Communists are the products of an intellectual milieu that had broken with the traditions and values of the past, Levenson compels us to distinguish between anti-traditional Communists committed to radical change and the "objective" Chinese social situation which the Communists inherited. Some of the economic, social, and intellectual traditions of old China may have survived the Communist revolution—what Levenson referred to as the "fragments" or "bricks" of the old structure, not the structure itself—but it is not necessarily the case that it is the Communists who are perpetuating them.

Levenson's general analysis of the relationship between past and present also compels observers of Chinese Communism to consider,

15. Levenson, *Confucian China*, vol. I, pp. 162-163.

in more sophisticated fashion than is usually the case, the question of the relationship between the form and content of modern revolutionary history. Cultural determinists have been disposed to have it both ways on this matter. On the one hand, they dismiss Chinese Marxist forms as just so much icing on the old Confucian cake; on the other hand, we are told that Communist use of traditional Chinese forms indicates that Chinese Communists must be the carriers of some profoundly important traditional "essences." Levenson discussed both assertions. On the first, he perhaps put it best in his analysis of the significance of the disappearance of monarchical symbols in the Revolution of 1911: "Radical depreciation of the significance of 'form' in comparison with 'content' (a depreciation involved in suggestions that things are 'really' the same as ever in what is merely formally the Republican era in Chinese history) is both trite and misleading. If form has any 'mereness', it is not in its unimportance when it changes; it is in its failure to hold a specific content when it, form, remains the same."[16]

On the matter of Communists reviving and utilizing traditional Chinese forms, Levenson saw a tendency for scholars to confuse a nationalistic display of tradition with the genuine persistence of tradition. In part, it reflected a failure to appreciate the antitraditional origins and nature of modern Chinese nationalism, a failure to distinguish between the "traditional" and the merely "traditionalistic," and a failure to understand the nature of Marxism and the role it has played in a post-Confucian age. In part, Levenson also argued, it reflected a failure to distinguish between the political and intellectual needs of "iconoclasts struggling for power" and "iconoclasts in power." For the former, tradition still seemed a mortal enemy because elements of it were identified with conservative political and social causes. But Communist iconoclasts in power could, Levenson argued, "adopt the relativism of their bested foes, and turn from blasting the old with hatred to explaining it coolly away."[17] And more than just explaining tradition away, they could use it for their own social and political ends. Levenson was especially incisive in demonstrating how traditional forms could have a profoundly nontraditional significance in a Communist setting, how the Confucian classics (as

16. Levenson, *Confucian China,* vol. II, p. 125.
17. Levenson, *Confucian China,* vol. III, p. 96.

objects of historical study) could be used not to revive Confucian values but rather to document a Marxist concept of historical progress, and how Communists can praise ancient Taoist "science," for example, to support their own claims to be the carriers of modern (and very non-Taoist) scientific values.[18] Neither the use of traditional forms nor their absence is sufficient to demonstrate the persistence of tradition, and neither, by themselves, reveals much about the problem of continuity in modern Chinese history.

Levenson discussed the problem of continuity between Confucian and Communist China (and discussed it more fully) in yet another sense—in the sense of the psychological need for revolutionaries, and especially for revolutionaries who also are nationalists, to come to terms intellectually with a past they have rejected. If revolutionaries must attempt to destroy the survivals of the past which bar the realization of their vision of a new future, they must also tie themselves to their historical-cultural heritage, they must learn to inherit, appropriate, and appreciate the historical accomplishments of their predecessors. The two tasks are psychologically conflicting, and especially so for Chinese Communist revolutionaries whose nationalism also demanded iconoclasm. Levenson saw Marxist historical theory as the intellectual vehicle which resolved this conflict—and resolved the longer-term tension between "history" and "value" in the history of the modern Chinese intelligentsia. Through Marxist historicism and relativism, he argued, the Communists were able to adhere to their own modern values while sympathetically viewing the Chinese past in terms of universal and progressive stages of social evolution, thereby appropriating their heritage while keeping it a matter of "merely historical" significance.

If the wholesale assault on the heritage of the past in the Cultural Revolution casts doubts about Levenson's analysis of how successful Chinese Marxists were in resolving the agonizing tension between "history" and "value"—and raised problems which he himself recognized and attempted to confront in his last writings[19]—perhaps his analysis seems less questionable when one views China in the aftermath of the Cultural Revolution. Whatever deficiencies one may find in aspects of his argument, his general analysis of the role and uses of Marxist historical relativism still makes explicable,

18. Ibid., pp. 98-99.

19. See Joseph R. Levenson, *Revolution and Cosmopolitanism: The Western Stage and The Chinese Stages* (Berkeley: University of California Press, 1971).

without recourse to the dubious assumptions involved in most analogies drawn between Confucian and Communist China, how the Communists can prize the historical accomplishments of traditional China while at the same time retaining their own modern and fundamentally antitraditional values. It makes historically understandable how Chinese Communists can violently condemn the feudal past without surrendering their nationalist claim to be the true heirs of that past. The analysis holds as long as one recognizes that it is contemporary political and ideological needs which determine what elements of the past are to be celebrated.

In the end, what is perhaps most noteworthy about Joseph Levenson's writings on Chinese Communism is a deep empathy for Chinese striving to create their own modern Chinese future. Like Lu Hsun, whom he so much admired and frequently quoted, Levenson did not want China to remain an antique for foreign observation. His own political and intellectual values were far different from those held by the Communists, and he was highly critical of many of the practices of Chinese Communists in power. But, unlike many of his contemporaries, he approached the study of modern China with an historical world view that allowed for a revolution that was real and one which appreciated the historical significance of the revolution that was made. His writings were not addressed to Chinese who were making their modern history, but to Western observers who might not have recognized that this was really the case. As he put it in one of his last essays: the ends of Chinese history are open, and thus Western minds should not be closed.[20]

THE MOZARTIAN HISTORIAN

We know that many readers found Levenson's writing style difficult and even irritating. He did not write in accordance with the conventional canons of "good historical writing," and no doubt his idiosyncratic style was one factor which limited his audience and limited appreciation among the audience he had. He clearly loved to use his imaginative literary powers, but the style that was so uniquely his own was not intended for exhibition nor did it serve

20. Joseph R. Levenson, "Marxism and the Middle Kingdom," *Diplomat*, XVII, No. 196 (September 1966), p. 51.

that end. It did not intend to obscure historical reality but to illuminate the nuances and complexities of the historical process and to bring new insights and deeper meanings to old facts. Levenson wrote history much as a novel or symphony is composed, scoring many themes more than once, and in different ways and contexts, until they culminated in the grand historical themes which his work announces in such textured fashion. Indeed, the structure and style of *Confucian China and Its Modern Fate* reflect his own description of Proust's "overture" and "Combray," where "bits of themes crackle, mingle, flicker into new ones; until finally a single long-breathed tune, swirling out of the rich tone that founded it and announced it, leads into *Swann's Way* and the great theme of search."[21]

Levenson's love and appreciation of music had much to do with the uniqueness of his historical style. He was an accomplished musician and his sensitivity to music is evident throughout his writings. One recalls from a 1953 essay that briefly eloquent sentence, carrying (typically) a deep double meaning: "An audience which appreaciates that Mozart is not Wagner will never hear the eighteenth-century Don Giovanni."[22] Like Mozart, he made of his craft an art which stood apart from the professional standards of his day. Levenson was a virtuoso with language, but he used his technical mastery to create something more significant than virtuosity, producing new and important visions of complex reality and transmitting these to his readers in a manner at once profound, intriguing, and delightful. One does not easily, if ever, forget his great themes, his development of them, or his artful embroidery and vivid illustration. He is less often as felicitous as Mozart in using technique, manipulating an in itself sparse set of basic materials (notes, words) so magnificently that an audience listening to Mozart forgets the technique as it is overwhelmed by the impact of what technique allied with genius has wrought. Words do sometimes get in the way of what Levenson is trying to say, although one suspects that this is less a failing of the writer than of the reader who cannot fully share Levenson's sparkling mental and verbal facility. As Mozart was said to shake music out of his sleeve, so Levenson shakes words and images. The language

21. Levenson, *Confucian China*, vol. III, p. 85.

22. Joseph R. Levenson, "'History' and 'Value': The Tensions of Intellectual Choice in Modern China," in *Studies in Chinese Thought,* ed. Arthur F. Wright (Chicago: University of Chicago Press, 1953), p. 146.

of music is more nearly universal and does not require in its hearers the same apprenticeship. Levenson had the problem of many gifted intellects in assuming too generously that others shared his own immense command of literature and language. As a result he may sometimes appear obscure, or even trapped by words. But the meaning is there, for those with the wit, the learning, and, sometimes, the patience to find it.

Historians who may find Levenson an inspiration are unlikely to produce work like his. Mozart was Tschaikowsky's self-confessed God, although it is not easy to find Mozartian parallels in Tschaikowsky's music. For Tschaikowsky, Mozart showed what could be done with music. For historians, Levenson shows what can be done, not with a particular and idiosyncratic style, but with history. Like only a very few historians, Levenson makes of the problems of a particular time and place a paradigm of the human problem, and yet, without ostensibly or specifically trying to do so, the universalist thrust of his work is inherent and the point makes itself, or catches the reader up in its sweep as if by self-discovery. This was certainly what Levenson intended, but it is not easily done. If the best history is that which holds up a mirror to the human condition and transcends the specifics of time and place of which it is constructed, then Levenson has created a model from which future historians will appropriately take inspiration.

As listeners with some musical training and experience value Mozart more highly, so may readers of Levenson who are themselves literate historians find more to admire. This is so not only in respect of technique, which other technicians can best appreciate, but in terms of the scope and profundity of Levenson's work. Where to some it may appear that he is playing with words and ideas in their multi-meanings and combinations in sheer virtuosity, to others it will be evident that, like Mozart, he is only incidentally a virtuoso, and more importantly an historian whose intellectual and verbal gifts are so great that he uses them effortlessly, perhaps sometimes even distractingly, in whatever he does. But what he is after is deeper meaning. He is not just playing, but probing, finding new meaning in old problems, illuminating with often dazzling clarity matters where one thought the facts were already available but where the full implications had been only dimly perceived before.

He takes the reader into a sometimes confusing world of language and metaphor where the seemingly artificial or cryptic paradox, the deceptively simple or merely epigrammatic phrase, prove as his exposition develops to yield rich meaning. His rhetoric does not trick; it is carefully planned, like Mozart's musical virtuosity, to construct a total edifice. Like Mozart also, he uses tension to deepen meaning and to heighten its impact. His writings are in all these respects conceived and executed as works of art, although as often pointed out they can be read—as Mozart's music can be listened to—on several levels. His themes and explorations are woven into a grand design, coherent and dynamic intrinsically rather than extrinsically.

What helps to make Levenson's writings a delight as well as a revelation is, however, certainly a matter of virtuosity in part. This is far from being merely technical competence. His agile and effervescent mind as well as his wide mastery of literature and the arts keep asserting themselves, but always with coherent effect. Where others walked or plodded, he flew, as one is tempted to characterize Mozart in comparison with so many other musicians. Reading his work, as listening to him in life, one is often left faint but pursuing—pursuing nevertheless, in large part because he was able to intrigue as well as to illuminate, and to leave periodic rewards, clues, or come-ons along the trail for his inevitably slower followers.

His immense learning was used to delight and to enlighten, not to impress. His allusions and comparisons may sometimes be overwhelming to some readers, like his occasionally involved sentences, double-entendres, bracketed words or phrases, and structured paradoxes. They are not there for display but in an effort to extract, refine, and transmit meaning. He often flatters his readers by taking too much for granted, as if they could follow as effortlessly as he could lead.

It is appropriate that his writings can so readily be labelled humanistic, for he was quintessentially a humanist in life, endlessly excited by the range of manifestations of the human spirit, from the droll to the sublime. His personal sweetness, unlike his involvement with humanity in the large, is not perhaps directly recognizable in his writings, but the same themes worked by other hands (if such a thing is conceivable) would surely have been different, at least in part because they would have lacked that notable aspect of his humanity. It was also his easy and instinctive identification with what lay outside himself which enabled him to recreate the past so vividly and to allow his readers to enter, as he had entered, the very minds and souls of the host of fellow wrestlers with the modern world who people the intellectual landscapes about which he wrote. His work is both intensely personal and genuinely universal, in the sense that his vision and his insight made the struggles, perplexities, and joys of mankind his own.

It is tempting to borrow for him one's favorite epitaphs of great men, especially Sir Thomas More's ". . . angel's wit and singular learning . . . marvelous mirth and pastimes and sometimes . . . as sad a gravity." But however appropriate such words are for Joseph Levenson, the Mozartian analogy seems more compelling, especially as a commentary on his writings. As already suggested, they are unlikely to be followed by a school, partly because it is the nature of style and even of form and substance to change. Future scholars will follow different paths. But they will, we think, continue to see Levenson's work as a monument, a pinnacle of the historian's art. G.B. Shaw summed up much of what we feel about Levenson, writing in his role as a music critic in December of 1891 on the centenary of Mozart's death:

> Many Mozart worshippers cannot bear to be told that their hero was not the founder of a dynasty. But in art the highest success is to be the last of your race, not the first. Anybody, almost, can make a beginning; the difficulty is to make an end—to do what cannot be bettered.

PART ONE

Levenson as Man and Historian

J.R.L.—GETTING STARTED

John K. Fairbank

As all teachers know, one learns from one's students. When a student happens to be one of the creative spirits of the age, his teacher will learn a great deal.

Having been born thirteen years earlier than Joe Levenson, I had the fortunate experience of being his undergraduate tutor in Kirkland House when he was a sophomore and junior at Harvard in 1938-1939 and 1939-1940. He was of course a vivacious and spirited undergraduate, full of wide-ranging interests, and our tutorial activity was not especially focused on China, but rather on history in general, which at that time was Europocentric. Joe, as an undergraduate, was not particularly oriented toward what was then called the "Far East." His six years of basic education in the Boston Latin School, 1931-1937, had moved him toward the mainstream of Western learning. In the summer of 1939 he spent some time at the University of Leiden.

World War II changed all that. Joe graduated magna cum laude in June 1941. By February 1942, he was in the United States Navy's Japanese Language School, under which he spent a year at the University of California and the University of Colorado before going to the Pacific. This was his wartime induction into Japanese language as a practical tool. He saw action with the New Zealand Army and the United States Navy in the Solomon Islands and the Philippines. Enlisted as a yeoman second class in March 1942, he was discharged in March 1946 as a lieutenant senior grade.

Having finished his B.A. just in time for the war, he returned to Harvard in the fall of 1946 just in time for the inauguration of the Regional Studies Program on China. He did not enter this program, however, but took his M.A. in history in 1947 and his

Ph. D. in February 1949, moving fast to make up for lost time. Yet along the way he participated in the Regional Studies program and got the best of these two small worlds. The History Department made use of his talent as a teaching fellow and tutor in the two years 1946-1947 and 1947-1948. He was then chosen as a Junior Fellow in the Society of Fellows at Harvard for three years beginning in July 1948. During this period he joined me in lecturing in the course on modern China while also developing his thesis into a book, *Liang Ch'i-ch'ao and the Mind of Modern China.* Thus we had him with us at Harvard for five years, 1946-1951, and witnessed his growth from graduate student to lecturer, teacher, and writer.

In the following pages I have tried to trace from old correspondence files the transition that Joe made from graduate student at Harvard to professor at Berkeley. This kind of correspondence is of course mainly administrative, recommending him for his first job, getting his first book published, and it by no means does justice to his intellectual growth in this period. Yet any exchange of correspondence with Joe, even on the most mundane matters, was a test of wit, in which he usually came out ahead with spontaneous ease. A brief summary of this correspondence may have some value for the graduate student of today. Anyone who feels mired in problems of self-training, general examinations, thesis writing, and job hunting, may take comfort from this evidence that even the most eminent scholars were once, in fact, graduate students.

Here we see a case study of the problems involved in moving from the graduate student phase into a faculty position. As in most cases, it involved for Joe Levenson an active program on at least three fronts: first, getting experience in the field, in his case in Hong Kong, and developing linguistic proficiency; second, completing his book manuscript; and third, pursuing job openings and having interviews and letters of recommendation sent from his instructors. Readers of today will perhaps note the rudimentary state of the China studies field in the late 1940s and early 1950s, as well as the political state of the nation.

Job openings appeared quite soon. In December 1947, Conyers Read of the History Department of the University of Pennsylvania wrote inquiring for a competent man to teach the history of China and Japan. I replied recommending Joe. "Having studied Japanese during the war, he has since his return specialized in Chinese and is doing his thesis on a leading figure of modern China, with reference to the mixture of Western and Confucian ideas which he represented." I suggested that his book would "be a major contribution in due time," and added "he gave us a session last month on Toynbee's interpretation of Far Eastern history, followed by his own comments on Toynbee, which was brilliantly presented as well as exceedingly interesting." At this same time, however, we in the History Department were recommending Joe for a Junior Fellowship: "Given the nature of his field of interest, Chinese intellectual history in the modern period, he needs most of all an opportunity for steady application and development which a Junior Fellowship would afford."

Before this had eventuated, however, a query had come in from Brainerd Dyer, Chairman of the Department of History at Berkeley in February 1948: "We are looking for a man young enough to be happy to start as an Instructor and able enough to remain with us and rise to the top" in Far Eastern History. I replied, "Mr. Levenson is a brilliant young man with excellent prospects of making a major contribution to the field of modern Chinese intellectual history . . . He has an excellent background in European history and uses Japanese easily as well as Chinese . . . We have no other student here in history who is at present so far advanced."

In the meantime and parallel to all these beginnings, Joe also applied to the Social Science Research Council for an Area Research Training Fellowship, and Professor Donald C. McKay of Harvard wrote of him in March 1948: "He moves with a good deal of ease in the higher regions of intellectual history and political theory and still manages to keep his feet pretty firmly planted on the ground . . . a man of very agreeable personality . . . a man of great promise." Even if he should obtain a Junior Fellowship, it was suggested that he would still need a trip to China and SSRC support for that. I also wrote to the SSRC supporting the idea of such a trip: "I should expect him in China to work with Professor T.S. Ch'ien, Dr. Hu Shih, Professor Fu Ssu-nien, and others at Peking University."

By May 1948, Joe had received his Junior Fellowship and was no longer interested in Pennsylvania. At the end of the year we had Joe's curriculum vitae available for inquirers and sent it to Yale in response to a History Department query from there. I urged Joe to offer a paper at the 1950 meeting of the Far Eastern Association, writing him in July 1949, "This is advance notice that the FEQ will soon announce that Professor Arthur Wright of the History Department at Stanford University will be in charge of the program for the 1950 meeting of the FEA. If you wish to present a paper at that time . . . write to him in the near future."

In November 1949 the Berkeley Department was still expressing interest and we sent to Professor John D. Hicks the Harvard Appointment Office file containing confidential appraisals from Joe's instructors. My own contribution stated that he had concentrated as an undergraduate on modern Europe, showing "a very wide-ranging curiosity and intellectual enthusiasm in the field of the humanities and especially of European culture. During the war his study of Japanese and his practical experience evidently provided the stimulus for a steady development." He had "an effective personality as a lecturer . . . great natural talents . . . pertinacity and ability for hard work. He will make his own distinct contribution and probably prove to be a pioneer and leader in the undeveloped field of intellectual history of the Far East."

Professor Hicks had written, "we need someone at California who will enliven the teaching in the Far Eastern field particularly in the survey course . . . We are hopeful that the man we employ will also be an excellent research man, but he must be a good teacher." I replied that "Levenson has a real flair for the presentation of a subject and is on the whole the best prospect among the men I have seen since the end of the war in this respect. My belief is that he will prove able to interest and attract a large undergraduate audience. He has a flair for words, a vigorous voice and manner, a lively sense of humor, and a feeling for the dramatic. In one of his lectures two years ago to our graduate seminar on China, he brought down the house with a characterization of the Gee Whiz School of History as opposed to the Spenglerians and others, and this phrase is still current locally among students. I cite this not as a contribution to scholarship but as indicating a certain genius for presentation."

Members of the Berkeley department arranged to see Joe at the post-Christmas meeting of the American Historical Association in Boston. The Cold War was just setting in, and one of the senior and more European-oriented of these interlocutors raised a question as to whether Joe had a susceptibility to Marxist ideology. In January 1949 I wrote a reassurance on this score. "One of his merits as an historical worker is that while he is tremendously interested in theory, he is totally uninterested in a personal dogma for himself. Everything is grist for his mill." In any case the Berkeley Department decided to make no appointment in 1950, much to the regret of Professor Woodbridge Bingham.

By August 1950 Joe had got his manuscript on Liang into the Harvard University Press and was about to spend the fall months in England and go to Hong Kong in December. In October the Director of the Press, Thomas J. Wilson, forwarded the evaluation of "one of the real authorities in the field of Chinese intellectual history," which opined that the Liang manuscript was definitely worth publishing. The reader also raised the question whether the "mind of modern China" was a proper title since it received rather marginal treatment. Joe replied to this reader's suggestions in extenso as follows:

> The reader states accurately certain limitations of this work,—thus, the biographical parts are, as he says, rather terse. They do, however, give a generally thorough account of the materials available, and I don't believe that further excavation will be particularly rewarding until the Liang family releases his correspondence, etc. I plan to write something about this in the conventional "author's preface". The biographical sections of my manuscript, as they stand, make up a considerable bulk of closely documented data, more than yet exists in print in a western language, I would guess, concerning any modern Chinese figure but Sun Yat-sen, Yuan Shih-k'ai, or Chiang K'ai-shek. And stylistically, the seeming dehydration of the chapters about Liang in action sets off rather well, I believe, the richer accounts, in the alternate chapters, of the vital dramatic and exciting inner life which Liang was simultaneously leading. For, as the reader divines, and as I have indicated in the manuscript and will state again in the preface, I have been interested here mainly in the working of Liang's mind.
>
> And yet, I would question the reader's judgment that this work is mainly a psychological study of Liang. I am by no means wedded to my title, but I do believe that there is a lot of news about the "mind of modern China" in the book, about history as well as biography, about the way a culture and a society, not just a personality, change and develop. The hard core of my book is, I agree, a sort of psychoanalysis of Liang (by a method akin to that which Harry Wolfson uses in his "Philo" and which he calls "hypothetico-deductive"), but my intent is, by finding out what worried Liang, to establish what his milieu expected of him and could offer him.

When we find Liang using European ideas which in Europe agitated people in a different way, or when we find him putting a different construction on Chinese ideas from that which earlier Chinese had put on them, we learn something not only about Liang but about how and why China differs from Europe, and Ch'ing Dynasty from Han. Continuously throughout the book I have, I believe, maintained an interplay between history and individual, bringing historical analysis to bear on Liang's writings and returning with what Liang's writing reveal to throw more light on history. One can consider the "mind of modern China" to be given marginal treatment only if one expects this work to be a portrait gallery of worthies, with Liang sketched in most prominently. As the reader indicates, it is not that. And, as he indicates too, the question of Liang's influence, although rather fully treated, is not emphasized. I have been more interested in Liang's significance, in what his thought signifies for Chinese history, than in his influence.

I have used Liang's major works as generally as his minor ones (and I do not recognize the deficiency which the reader sees in my treatment of "Liang and science"). But a long and scholarly work may be based on no more elaborate a premise than a short essay, and I mean rather to deduce Liang's premises than to copy on one piece of paper what has been written on another. Analysis, no summarization in extenso, seemed to be the best way to organize the tremendous mass of material.

I repeat that I am not really happy with the tentative title either. Perhaps *The Crumbling of Tradition: A Study of the Chinese Thinker Liang Ch'i-ch'ao, 1873-1929* would be better. This is what it really deals with and the title suggests the supra-biographical and non-parochial aspect, the concern with how ideas change, which I would like to see emphasized.

My own comment to Tom Wilson was to ask if "the reader who commented could indicate some of the pertinent references to which he refers vaguely . . . A lot of junk, of course, can be put in footnotes, but it is still junk . . . I do not particularly like Levenson's suggested title about the crumbling of tradition. Perhaps they could be put together in the forms of 'Liang Ch'i-ch'ao and the Crumbling of the Chinese Tradition', but this rather suggests that Liang was a crumb."

As to the subsidy desired for the Liang book, Professor Crane Brinton suggested in November 1950 to the Press that it be published in the Harvard Historical Studies. "We've never printed a book about the Far East, I believe, and I think the Department would accept the manuscript. Then the Society [of Fellows] might chip in $500 or so to help the Department . . . . We are sending Levenson to Hong Kong to soak up Chinese in direct contact and that is going to cost us nearly $2000."

By January 1951 I was writing "Dear Bud [Joe's nickname in youth],—We note that the local authorities of our government in Hong Kong foresaw your arrival and announced the desirability of all Americans leaving, two days before you reached the island. I trust that you are now established in a pleasant house on the Peak with the necessary servants. We eagerly await the first word of you, as to your impact upon China and the Chinese response."

This crossed a long letter of January 25:

> Confounding skeptics, we're really installed in Hongkong, or rather Kowloon, just to make our absorption into the New China a shade easier. The city seems almost complacent, especially if one has just seen demoralized Manila. The British announce construction plans and are keeping a pile-driver throbbing in the center of town to convince the pop. that there'll always be a Crown Colony, and scorn the U.S. for advising its citizens to vanish, but the latter advice has done the Levensons a great good turn—after bleeding for a couple of days in the Gloucester [Hotel] at $66 HK per diem (the best that Frillmann [Public Affairs Officer in the U.S. Consulate General] could find for us), we were taken in by Joe Yager [U.S. Consulate General], who had just shipped away wife and kids—thus, we live in a spacious rent-free flat, complete with servants who are very solicitous and testify, I hope, to the Canton Commandant that we are democratic personalities. I think Joe may have to break camp here soon and move to Hongkong—if so, I think we can move into a flat at the disposal of an old navy friend of mine whom I find at the head of an oil company here. Lubrication is dying in Hongkong. The strangling of HK business foreshadowed by the American sanctions campaign is, of course, a big factor in forming the amazingly virulent anti-American attitude among the British community here. There seems to be among many of the English a kind of subterranean and self-consciously perverse enthusiasm for the Chinese Communists—this from the business community—just because of the American noise against them. And yet, the taipans don't really mean to cut off their noses—I recall a vivid scene of last Saturday which was almost a caricature of an Asiatic Communists's anti-imperialist cartoon—an elaborate magnificent course-after-Peking-duck-type-course banquet on the Peak for about 30 English, American, assorted European, and wealthy Chinese (one of whom explained to me in impeccable Oxonian that the Chinese CP would fail because it was flouting tradition!),

followed by liqueurs in the lovely garden, and the toast. "Mort á Staline et Mao Tse-Toung."

I'm to have a long talk next Saturday with an old scholar named Ma Kiam (or so it was romanized by his son), an intimate, I'm told, of Liang Ch'i-ch'ao, K'ang Yu-wei, Chang T'ai-yen et al—and I hope through him to meet scholars and perhaps get a tutor who can talk to me firsthand about the twentieth century and tour through some earlier intellectual history with me in the texts. His son, Ma Meng . . . has, however, led me to what seems to be a good thing in the book business [Joe was buying books for Harvard], the "Willing Book Co.," merely an attic front office, impossible to find without lead, which gets books from the mainland—They are sending to Mr. Chiu [the Harvard-Yenching librarian] a list, with prices, of $100 US worth of 1945-to-the-present non-Communist publications (same to Mary Wright [then at Hoover]), and will, I think, be able to procure the Manchurian list and other items which he mentioned in his recent letter. I have found for Mary, and will list in a forthcoming letter to Harvard-Yenching, quite a few recent Hong Kong and Formosa-published anti-Communist works on history and social studies.—brief and rather pamphleteering—some by reputable scholars such as Ch'ien Mu.

What is the latest news from embattled U. of Cal. [this refers to the struggle over the state requirement of a special teacher's oath, to which faculty members objected]—I think a court decision on tenure was due soon after we left. I left Berkeley with the impression that though Kerner, for one, ascribes to me guilt by association with JKF, an asst. prof. would be offered to me (he had just made a speech which the papers headlined, "Professor Says War Brings Peace".) Did the AHA recommend any policy toward U. of Cal? Rumor was that Bill Holland would head their institute. Good. One HK rumor is that attack on Formosa comes with Chinese New Year. Bad. Who knows what shells may be hidden here among the fireworks? Wayne Altree boarded our ship in Honolulu and is here now too as a student—we've had very good times together. Rosemary sends her very best. *Yours, Bud.*

Since the above was all on one page of an air letter, I replied offering to buy Joe a typewriter in the interests of legibility. On the date of March 1, 1951, I noted that the Institute of Pacific Relations "is now being attacked by the McCarran Committee. There is much interest in the forthcoming Far Eastern Association meeting in Philadelphia. . . . The latest excitement is that neither Wittfogel, Lattimore, nor Eberhard were willing to join together in a session on Oriental society. The University of

Washington crew are highly miffed by the proceedings and feel persecuted as usual. They are therefore striking out against the encirclement which they feel surrounds them." Two weeks later on April 2 I reported "the Far Eastern Association meeting occurred without incident, although not without the presentation of 92 papers . . . . There are many projects afoot for writing memoranda back and forth among various committees. Locally, we will set up a project in which everybody has sometime to be director. The only requirement is that everybody must finish his thesis and be offered an $8000 job in Washington. We are also forming a Committee on Chinese Thought, which Arthur Wright will take over from me so as to inject the thought after I have formed the committee . . . . We have large schemes afoot, like the professors of two score other universities, and if the money all comes in we will be so busy in handling it that nothing will be done except by the second year graduate students."

This is in response to Joe's letter of March 22 from Hong Kong:

Dear Wilma and John,

The Red Tide, as they say, threatens to Engulf All Asia! and Rosemary and I have taken to the hill and a little white eyrie that once was Standard Oil. And I wait for them here, with my Winchester 44 and my Pimm's No. 1, and cook and amah and ½ gardener (another squire claims a leg and a wing), and our own running dogs—an Alsatian bitch and a (west-German) Dachshund. Now I think this is an entirely adequate situation, and what I want to know is, why do they say the people of Asia are discontented? Rice isn't everything, and they can always eat Mandarin duck. I get it myself, and I can't even speak Chinese.

I'm just back from a "discussion group" meeting at the University —Gene Boardman, Wayne Altree, George Cressey, a young Fulbright-fellow geographer yclept Norton Ginsburg, a student named Wang who wants to write something about Chinese history and asks what he should be interested in, and the presiding genius, Professor of Economics Stuart Kirby, who strikes me as being one of the most muddly nice people I've ever met. He favors the old order in Eastern Asia and I suspect the very old order in eastern America—civilization must be preserved out here, of course, but it is ludicrous to believe that the United States is well-bred enough to qualify for the task. Oh, the predicament of the Bowling Alley Bar—as symbolized in Kirby's answer (reported by Altree) to a student who gave the Communist critique of U.S. post-war policy in China: "It's not that I disagree with you, but that answer just doesn't make sense."

There are professors here more rewarding to know, such as the Taiping historian Jen Yu-wen, who is extremely nice, thoughtful, honestly puzzled about the position of Western-oriented Chinese intellectuals, full of lore, and narrow in interpretation. He much admires "The United States and China" but wonders whether Dr. Fairbank may not have been taken in by the Reds since he finds an agrarian question or something like that as an issue in the Taiping rebellion. In all Jen's years of study of the rebellion, he has never found, he says, an expression of class-consciousness in it. Just Chinese vs. Manchus. Oh well. But he has showed me a lot of modern Chinese art and discussed with me the swirling currents of traditionalism and eclecticism and westernism in China's modern art history, and it's around this subject that I'm trying to organize some thoughts about modern Chinese intellectual history in general . . . .

During this period the McCarran Committee continued to make twice-weekly headlines with revelations in Washington, while in Berkeley there was considerable ferment concerning the hiring practices of the administration, and Joe's appointment there continued to hang fire. On May 1, 1951, I wrote him a general reassurance that there was so much going on in American studies of China that many places would certainly be interested in his services, supposing an offer from California did not materialize. "Current discussions for the development of research programs in research centers during the coming year are so far advanced that by the summertime there is likely to be a very vigorous scramble and competition going on for personnel like yourself. Probably somebody will want to make you a director of something."

By May 21, Joe was replying, in response to our concern about the legibility of his letters,—"I'll try to write loud and clear, since my overweighting typewriter had to be jettisoned at the Boston Airport last December. Just think of my letters as a series of bluebooks and resign yourself to the test . . . . Your stipendiary idea is a very kind thought. And the 'Research Agency' plans are very interesting. Bingham has written two letters assuring me that only the state legislature, probably good Associated Farmers and true, may seek to repair the damage inflicted by the communistic courts and slap a bill of attainder or something on the budget resolution, setting Ed Shafer, et al., on their ears again and Levenson on the road."

May 28: "I have heard from Van Nostrand, Acting Chairman at Cal. In this best of all possible looking-glass worlds, he sends me not a contract but a withholding tax form (and an oath form) with the following letter: 'It gives me pleasure to confirm the statement made to you by Woodbridge Bingham. My regret is that I cannot make this note much more official than the preceding one. I do enclose two blanks which will bring you a step or two nearer the goal when they are filed here. The budget for the coming year is being printed for the benefit of the Regents, to whom it will be presented at the next meeting. Instead of your name, there will appear in the printed budget a line which reads 'Provision for Assistant Professor of History'. You know, the University administration knows, the Senate Budget Committee knows, Dean Davis knows, and I know that 'Provision 4' means you'.

"What do you make of all this melodrama? If the Regents actually are duped into making provision for me, I am asked to teach the following courses: A) History of Modern China, 3 hours a week, full year, B) Intellectual History of Modern China, 2 hours a week, first semester, C) Chinese Historiography, two hours a week, second semester, D) Seminar on Modern China, two hours a week, full year. This sounds very good to me."

By this time, as some readers will recall, we were deeply involved in the McCarthy era with all its tensions and uncertainties. I was expecting to go to Japan for the year 1951-1952, but would find myself held up and diverted to a year of self-investigation in preparation for defensive testimony. The Berkeley department were doing what they could to put through the Levenson appointment, but the formal action was delayed. On June 1 Joe wrote from Hong Kong, "I have no further word from California. However, I am sending personal effects there from Hong Kong, have sworn their lovely oath before one of our consuls (but have not mailed it yet) and will feel extremely ruffled indeed if the comedy gets any more complicated." On June 13, 1951: "We're in flight at last from HK after a wonderful and profitable stay. But ultimate destination is still unknown. I wrote you of Cal's assurances, as far as the university authorities are concerned; the Regents and state legislature, however, have yet to pass on it and to my amazement and consternation, because I didn't believe a university could operate in this way, I have had to leave Hong Kong without any decision having been communicated to me, no word at all in several weeks.

"Can you outline specifically what you see as an alternative for me? Is Harvard opening a research organization? Does the History

Department or Gen Ed need any time-tried tutor? Can the football team use a water boy? Arthur Wright, in a recent letter, referred noncommittally to the carbon copy of your letter to me about future prospects. He hopes to see me in Berkeley. I really must see a definite proposition—time, place, tasks, figures, prospects, not pie in the sky . . . *Yours ever, De Profundis (low altitude, this BOAC), Bud* At home, July 17, 1951. Mrs. Levenson will pour."

As it turned out, Joe began teaching at Berkeley in September 1951. *Liang Ch'i-ch'ao and the Mind of Modern China* was finally published in 1953 with a preface dated in April and a glossary of eighteen pages providing Chinese characters for names, terms, and book titles. By this time Joe had advanced on another project that would eventuate in 1959 in the publication of *Confucian China and Its Modern Fate.* In this development he had presented a paper at the first of the five conferences on Chinese thought, held at Aspen, Colorado, in September 1952. The kernel of his thinking was briefly summarized in an application to the Social Science Research Council to support a summer's work at Harvard in 1953 (the requests were modest in those days). Joe's description of his project was a succinct statement of his history-and-value approach to modern Chinese thought:

> Testing and documentation of the following original hypothesis:
>
> In nineteenth-century China, claims of "history" (predisposition toward the offerings of one's own particular culture) begin to intrude on judgments of "value" (quests for universal truths), and ideas which are losing their philosophical command continue to be espoused by thinkers who are compelled by history, emotionally, as their intellectual convictions falter, to attribute value to these ideas. As the motivations of the thinker change, i.e. as change occurs in the questions he asks and the alternatives he denies, loyalty to Confucianism is gradually transformed from a primary, philosophical commitment to a secondary, romantic one, and the "meaning" of Confucianism changes correspondingly. This inner change in a persisting idea furthers the trend to the other type of intellectual change in time, alienation from hitherto accepted ideas. Increasing failure in the effort to bring value to history (i.e. to retain the conviction that the Chinese heritage is valuable according to universal criteria) leads to the effort to bring history to value (i.e. to devise rationalizations whereby intellectual choices no longer governed by precedent may yet appear to be in the natural stream of an autonomous Chinese history, so that even a westernized China may seem culturally equivalent to the West).

> The impact of the modern West has intensely stimulated the conflict between Chinese commitments to value and history. Modern Chinese intellectual history, which is the decay of traditional Chinese civilization (i.e. two corollary processes: Progressive abandonment of tradition by iconoclasts and petrifaction of tradition by traditionalists) may be analyzed as a sequence of intellectual expedients to make these commitments seem to coincide. The relationship between eclecticism in the field of native Chinese choices, the *"t'i-yung"* and *"chin-wen"* rationalizations for innovation, nationalism, and communism is conceived to be such that a principle of explanation of the sequence, though impossible to prove valid for each case from the facts of that case alone, may be accepted as meaningful because consistent with the facts of all the cases together . . .
>
> . . . the subject demands that I range as widely as possible through the sources and scholarly literature of the nineteenth and twentieth centuries (with frequent reference to earlier sources). For this breadth of reading, in the manner of an uncharted survey, a summer at Harvard would be invaluable . . .

Meanwhile, the Harvard History Department, to its discredit, made the egregious error of not only letting *Liang Ch'i-ch'ao and the Mind of Modern China* go out of print, but took the further step of economizing by breaking up the plates. The initial sale of this pioneer work had not broken records in the small China field, but the demand, of course, persisted and grew. Joe therefore arranged for a British revised edition to get the book back into print. Joe also contributed to the symposium that derived from the second conference on Chinese thought, held at Steele Hill near Laconia in New Hampshire in September 1954. By 1956 he had his manuscript on "Confucian China and Its Modern Fate" moving along toward publication.

Since Joe had now become a leading figure in the modern China field, this sketch of correspondence can no longer illustrate the problems involved in a young man getting started on his career. Joe's was no ordinary career—its record is that of genius at work. The following excerpts represent efforts to keep in touch with him. In November 1959, I wrote: "I much appreciate receiving the new edition of *Mind of Modern China*, which I sometimes think of as the mind of modern Levenson and never cease to enjoy reading. It seems to me the local boys are still very much on the faceless end of their relations with you, and this publication puts you not only one up but gives us of the Orient a useful talisman with which to intimidate future Occidentals." In August 1961, "By writing so far ahead, like the ladies who sign one up for addressing the annual meeting twelve months hence, I am obviously attempting to establish a claim upon your hospitality which will be difficult to avoid except by leaving town and will give us both something to look forward to with whatever emotions may arise. Our brief encounters are usually so hectic and gastronomic that I think we might make another effort."

Let me conclude with a couple of items. In August 1968, I wrote Joe—"Your ear tingling is only the result of my doing a pamphlet on *New Views of China's Tradition and Modernization* for the History Service Center series [of the American Historical Association]. It will be on all the news stands before the election. I enclose a copy of a passage referring to your *Modern Fate*, wanting you to be the first to have it. You will see that your famous style has seduced the author into following in your footsteps, not stepping on the feet of his followers. I have enjoyed it and I pass it along on the theory that praise is not libelous."

The passage in my bibliographical pamphlet, trying to parody Joe's style, was as follows:

> Professor Joseph R. Levenson's *Confucian China and its Modern Fate* is a three-volume study subtitled: (1) *The Problem of Intellectual Continuity,* (2) *The Problem of Monarchical Decay,* and (3) *The Problem of Historical Significance* (University of California Press, 1958, 1964, 1965). This trilogy is extraordinarily wide-ranging in both references and referents. Mr. Levenson has a contagious way with words and poses more paradoxes than the *Tao Te Ching* (thus the Ming scholar-painters' "routinization of intuition" was part of an "academic anti-academicism"). Yet this is not a pose. His points have substance. If they often point in both directions ("milestones to the present . . . gravestones from the past"), like the double-ended posers of a Zen master (clapping hand against hand: Do you hear it?; clapping with one hand only: Do you hear that? Listen until you do!), still his invocation of a Confucian *Yin* and Marxist *Yang* is only an avocation, writing what comes naturally. It is not the main intent nor even content of these volumes. The author's inveterate awareness of multiple ambiguities —"We may describe an item in the human record as historically (really) significant, or as (merely) historically significant. The distinction is between an empirical judgment of fruitfulness in time and a normative judgment of aridity in the here and now"—may

make the reader wary, even weary, of the ambience of opposites surrounding every word. This Levensonian dialectic discerns the alternatives implicit in ideas and courses through them in both directions, an alternating current. The result is electric. Some may feel burned. Yet this is no private dialect but a doctrine for us all: "To resist the taxonomical zeal for precision, the literalist's restriction of one phrase to one concept, is both an intellectual and moral requirement for the historian. For as a whole man he stands on shifting sands, yet he must take a stand—and the tension implicit in "historical significance," the strain between neutral analysis and committed evaluation, must be acknowledged and preserved if history, the records men make, and history, the records men write, are to come close to correspondence" (Levenson, III, 85).

Visible from phrase to phrase within this verbal verdure are a host of ideas on every aspect of China's intellectual and institutional modernization: the disparity between science and Ch'ing empiricism, Ming aesthetics and the use of Buddhist attitudes in gentry painting, Tseng Kuo-fan's need for eclecticism, Chang Chih-tung's misuse of "substance" (*t'i*) and "function" (*yung*), K'ang Yu-wei's manipulation of the New Text school to reinterpret the classics, the struggle of nationalism against culturalism, the failure of Christianity to survive Confucianism: "when Christianity alone is Confucianism's opposite number, then a surrender of Confucianism to industrialism need not seem a surrender of China to the West—if Christianity only surrenders too" (Levenson, I, 122).

In addition to the theme of China's proud search for equivalence with the powerful West, Mr. Levenson illustrates the Taiping rebels' many departures from Chinese tradition, the confusion over old values under the Republic, and various ways in which the Communists have reappraised their past and fallen amid contradictions. Much in these essays is challenging, and all of Mr. Levenson's writing is graceful and provocative—not for him the pussyfoot-in-mouth approach. He plays upon words until they are all actors, but readers who follow carefully will come to praise and not to parry his insights. His virtuosity preys upon phrases and leaves them lying where his reader picks and chews among them.

I am still proud of the last line, but my attempted parody of the Levensonian style achieved no more than bits and pieces of word play; it lacked the sustained flow of concepts and images that informed Joe's writing and made his word-play just an embellishment, sometimes even a distraction.

Joe's reply on September 9:

> A weak little ribbon with which to thank you for your luxuriant exuberance. I mean gosh. Where can you be promoted from Lee, Higginson & Co. Professor, but just the same I'm going to send Up a chit recommending you for St. John the Divine. Then you can give all souls the logos that CCMF is now (or soon) available as three-in-one and one-in-three, a single paperback vol, at a lousy $3.25 (no stamps).
>
> I'm really very pleased and grateful for getting into the John Kingdom. It should be the most rousing pamphlet since Tom Paine. Analyzes all possible Confucian and post-Confucian positions. Plain wrapper.
>
> First lectures are looming up, and I suppose I should ready the oral ordure. How great to be not teaching this year. Why not come to Berkeley, at least for a while, and not teach here? You'll fit right in. All best, *Yours, Joe.*

On the final item let me offer these background notes: (1) The great Sung historian Ssu-ma Kuang (1018-1086) wrote a comprehensive summary called *Tzu-chih t'ung-chien* "The Comprehensive Mirror for Aid in Government." (2) It was in the tradition of edifying chronicles that ran back to the *Ch'un-ch'iu* or "Spring and Autumn Annals" of the era 722-481 B.C. (3) The *Shih-ching* ("Classic of Songs" or "Book of Poetry") may be referred to simply as the *Shih*. (4) I had sent Joe a volume (a syllabus?), evidently without an index; an index to the "Comprehensive Mirror" would be a book in itself. (5) Kuang and Chou spell the name for Canton. Joe's reply:

> *Dear Sumatra Kuang,*
>
> Many thanks indeed for your latest opus. As it says in the *Shih*
> Mirror mirror on the wall
> You have much more on the ball
> Than that boring *Spring and Fall*
>
> I'm delighted to have the volume. Next, please, do write an index to it.
>
> *Yours, Java Chou*

REMARKS AT THE MEMORIAL SERVICE IN BERKELEY, APRIL 13, 1969

Donald Keene

What Joseph Levenson meant to the world of scholarship, what he meant to us his friends, can surely not be summed up in a set of well-turned phrases. The tragedy is still too close for me to comprehend it yet, much less to describe my sense of loss. But there is another problem, one that all but ties my tongue on this solemn occasion: my memories of Joe, from our first meeting here in Berkeley in February 1942, are happy memories, and many are hilariously funny. Even his scholarly writings, a marvelous fusion of interpretative criticism and solid learning, are graced with the wit and virtuosity of expression that marked his conversation and his letters. Surely none of us will ever know again so captivating a friend.

Joe's conversations were brilliant, at once serious and funny, always intensely exciting, and listening to him, I for one thought and said things that had never occurred to me before. It was impossible to be bored when with him, though sometimes I sensed his ideas were soaring far beyond my range. He possessed, of course, an immense amount of information, the product of his omnivorous reading, but the acquisition of the hard facts of history or art or literature, the goal of many eminent scholars, was only incidental to him. Instead, Joe sought always to discover the central meanings of the facts, in all their mutability, for what they told us of the total experience of mankind. A visit with him to even a mediocre exhibition of paintings was likely to prove an illuminating experience, for he could describe not only the subject matter, or the quality of the artist's techniques, or the traditions to which the works belonged, but what each work probably meant to the artist, and how different that might be from what it meant to us.

Joe brought to his study of Chinese thought an incredibly wide knowledge of Western writing. The notes of any of his books reveal the staggering range of sources, and none was included merely for display. The absolute relevance with which Joe selected each quotation or reference for the light it, probably better than any other source, could throw on the matter at hand, suggests what was perhaps his greatest gift, his ability to grasp instantly meaningful connections. This same uncanny aptitude was surely a clue also to his wit. Perhaps I may be pardoned if I recall a frivolous memory. I once went with Joe to a performance of Puccini's *Manon Lescaut*. At the end of the third act, when Manon (portrayed by the stately Miss Tebaldi) is dragged by the armpits up the gangplank of a waiting ship, Joe turned to me and whispered, "That's Intourist for you." It did not take a trip to Russia for me to see the connection.

In his writings he often referred to books totally unrelated to his subject, finding in them exactly the evidence he needed to clinch his analysis of, say, a particular conflict facing Chinese intellectuals in the twentieth century. Undoubtedly, even as he read the varied books that provided such apt illustrations, he was discovering in them the hidden connections with his work that he would later exploit. He knew even when it was effective to quote Gilbert and Sullivan, and he did not hesitate to do so.

His knowledge of the West enabled him to write of China with a distinctive authority. At the same time, his exceptional knowledge of China gave him insights into Western culture that make his books as important to students of the Occident as of the Orient. For example, there is a section in his *Confucian China and Its Modern Fate* which I would like to quote as typical of his work:

> Historians of the arts have sometimes led their subjects out of the world of men into a world of their own, where the principles of change seem interior to the art rather than governed by decisions of the artist. Thus, we have been assured that seventeenth-century Dutch landscape bears no resemblance to Breughel because by the seventeenth century Breughel's tradition of mannerist landscape had been exhausted. Or we are treated to tautologies, according to which art is "doomed to become moribund" when it "reaches the limit of its idiom," and in "yielding its final flowers" shows that "nothing more can be done with it"—hence the passing of the

> grand manner of the eighteenth century in Europe and the romantic movement of the nineteenth.
>
> How do aesthetic values really come to be superseded? This sort of thing, purporting to be a revelation of cause, and answer to the questions, leaves the question still to be asked. For Chinese painting, well before the middle of the Ch'ing period, with its enshrinement of eclectic virtuosi and connoisseurs, had by any "internal" criteria reached the limit of its idiom and yielded its final flowers. And yet the values of the past persisted for generations, and the fear of imitation, the feeling that creativity demanded freshness in the artist's purposes, remained unfamiliar to Chinese minds.

This is the kind of passage I find most illuminating in Joe's writings, and its importance is suggested by the fact that the two writers on European art with whom he takes exception—so convincingly, it seems to me—were not straw men set up to afford him an easy victory, but Kenneth Clark and C.M. Bowra.

Even this brief extract should indicate that his writings have an originality and maturity of judgment not often encountered in the works of earlier Western authorities on Chinese history. I say this not to denigrate the arduous labors of those scholars who established the foundations of Western understanding of China. But they were often satisfied to ascertain the facts, and Joe chose instead to deduce from the facts his perceptive observations on how Chinese tradition changed and persisted, and what its meaning has been not only for China but for the West. His field was immense and could have provided even so brilliant a mind with the themes for a lifetime of study. How terrible to think that we are denied this wisdom. My own field is different, but again and again his writings have provided me with insights I could not otherwise find. But I leave to scholars of China a more adequate description of his attainments than I can make.

As I said, I met Joe in 1942, when we were in a group of college students entering the Navy Japanese Language School. From our first conversations I was dazzled by his wit and learning. But more than that, I felt the irresistible attraction of his warmth and enthusiasm. I learned from him more than I can possibly tell you. Then, as in all my later experiences, I found Joe unstinting of his friendship, his praise, his knowledge. And even his failings were endearing. I can still remember how two of us struggled to attach to the shirt of a screaming and protesting Joe the peculiarly intractable collar and collar button the Navy then prescribed. I suppose it gave us pleasure to feel superior to Joe in at least one respect, or perhaps we recognized that his special kind of helplessness was the counterpart of his prodigious intellectual capacity. One could confidently assume that any essay Joe wrote would be brilliant; one could almost as confidently assume that if on some critical occasion somebody forgot his passport, his money, or his lecture notes, it would be Joe.

Fortunately for him in this respect, as in every other, he had Rosemary to help him. I knew Joe and Rosemary from the very beginning of their married life—indeed, I was the best man at their wedding in London—and I saw again and again what great happiness she brought him. Rosemary's loss must be the most painful to bear, and our hearts all go to her and her children.

For the rest of us too the loss is acute. Those of us here have memories, we can still hear his voice; and even people of the future who will never have known him will still be moved by his words. But there can be no substitute for what we have lost, and our consolation must be in our sense of gratitude. So large a gift of warmth, gaiety, and love is rarely bestowed, and our memories of Joe, shadowed now though they are by our grief, will surely remain in the loneliness ahead as our greatest comfort.

REMARKS AT THE MEMORIAL SERVICE IN CAMBRIDGE, APRIL 25, 1969

J. C. Levenson

Even a layman in Chinese history can appreciate the comprehensiveness, the imaginative fertility, and the essential truth-seeking quality of Joseph Levenson's scholarship. But transcending his specialty is what he contributed to humanistic knowledge generally. In all his studies he concerned himself with the problem of how we may be said to possess the past. Most people get along by ignoring the assumptions, often the conflicting assumptions, on which they act; his particular genius was never to stop being curious about the premises of historical inquiry. The problems of historicism and relativism, objectivity and neutrality, value and discrimination were live problems to him, not only when he was in a speculative mood, but when he was pursuing his research and putting together his findings and teaching his classes and talking with his friends.

Relevance, engagement, and commitment are the current terms for themes on which he centered his career. But current questions need more than current answers. He showed how a lifetime of effort in a single direction might yield really nourishing answers. For one thing, he demonstrated that commitment and disinterested inquiry, far from being incompatible, are intellectual necessities each to the other. Secondly, his emphasis on value and discrimination is not only moral, but esthetic. The motive to recover the past and the motive to record the past, these have as their end a human satisfaction and not merely a use. When the humanistic end is served, however, the use may take care of itself. Like many present-day scholars of Chinese history, he began when his subject was generally considered exotic, and he watched it become a crucial subject for the conduct of public life. But it would be discouraging to think that only Mao could affect the relevance of China to American scholarship. Acts of the mind—acts of the mind like *Confucian China and Its Modern Fate*—which consider Chinese in relation to Western experience, make Chinese history a part of our general history. When relevance runs so much deeper than headlines and when China ceases to be a subject merely for *foreign* affairs, we may hope to act more intelligently in a world we better understand.

As a human being, Joe had a sweetness, a wit, and a vital presence that were remarkable to any eye. His colleagues, friends, and students know these qualities in him just as much as a cousin, and I am hard put to think what a cousin may add to these other testimonies. Let me simply stand as witness to the fact of family feeling that was part of his life and that was related, I would suggest, to some of the deepest motives of his scholarship. In an age that is known for its atomism and alienation, he belonged to a family group of the sort that is, we are told, anachronistic. His father and mine were brothers; they were law partners, they lived next door to each other, they enjoyed each other's company all their lives. We grew up, then, next door to each other, but in a large family there were plenty of cousins around who were exact contemporaries. We each tended to play with a so-called peer group, separated by the awful gap of a couple of years. While I was picking out "The Merry Farmer," he was already taking lessons in harmony. The lessons were given by yet another cousin, who lived a few blocks away, and on reflection I take those harmony lessons as a sign that the intellectual life brought together family generations which peer groups could only ineffectually set apart. So for Bud and me, those years of going together from our homes in Roxbury to the Boston Latin School kept us together physically, but it was our great teacher Robert Drummey who first let us see how time and intellectual interest were to make us into contemporaries: he picked us out for two opera tickets he wasn't able to use and sent us together to see a rousing, second-rate, memorable performance of *Rigoletto*. Our adult intimacy I date from the summer when he attended the exciting first session of the Berkshire Institute. At the moment when the world seemed to be opening up for him in all directions, it wonderfully occurred to him to ask his seventeen-year-old younger cousin to come visit him at Tanglewood and share the excitement of new friends, new ideas, new music. It would be easy to make those times sound quaint and idyllic: all the complacent Wilkie buttons strolling about the Tanglewood lawns and a handful of student protesters opposing a "pro-British" benefit concert by withholding their voices from a chorus of three hundred. It would be far easier to make 1940 sound like the very bottom point of modern history. But, for my present context, it is a year I began to understand because Bud shared his understanding of it with me. In the years that followed, here at Harvard, he played a constant and important role in my own coming of age. And in the years after that, as I read his work with delight and did my own writing with him in mind as a central figure of my ideal audience, affection and pride and family feeling have been happily connected with professional aims and academic judgment.

Connected but not confused. Kinship with *him* might suggest my seeing this cousinship as a little theater of social and cultural drama, but it would forbid sentimentality or nostalgia. He invited one to see the family group in relation to the American middle class, and behind that the immigrant Jewish past, and to understand the pressures of modernism that were changing all that. He was able to discriminate the values of family life that ought rationally to be preserved. He also enjoyed his family with a spontaneity which proved the institution to be very much alive —despite the indications of neutral historical analysis. Along with moral and esthetic judgment, joy came easily to him and was one of the ways by which he came into vital relation with the past.

Perhaps in our need to express what we have lost in this man we cherished, we may clarify for each other what survives for us to keep.

AN UNRECONSTRUCTED REVIEW OF LEVENSON'S TRILOGY

Harold L. Kahn

Joseph Levenson does not need revising. The following review, written in 1965 and appearing in the *Bulletin of the School of Oriental and African Studies,* XXIX.1 (1966), pp. 185-187, says something about its author and *the* author then. I could not write the same comments now because both my views and the Trilogy have changed, radically. Which is right. Levenson's work does not need refreshing to remain fresh: no amount of dancing (reverentially: Ch'u's music, for him, while irreverent, was still off-beat) around it will enrich what is rich—though it could I suppose make marks for the dancers.

I sent Levenson a copy of the draft review before it was printed. His response was serious and playful: a flattery for a young dancer, and a lesson in how to tango. It is reproduced here, dated September 9 (1965). I did delete the "exploratory tour of the author's mind and every so often of the mind of modern and pre-modern China," because he was right and I was wrong.

Dear Hal,

Many thanks indeed for sending an advance copy of the review. It's certainly a courteous thing to do, and I'm very glad to have it. It's a careful and eloquent job—no one has ever written anything on anything of mine that shows as much patience, attention, and intelligent concern with the subject matter. Your factual emendations are gratefully received; if I'm ever invited to release this stuff again, I'll make appropriate revisions. In style—well, the outrages are certainly there. I was aware of them as I perpetrated them, and willfully feel I'd leave them in. The basic subject was so serious, the effort to reach conclusions about it and get things into a plausible order, step by step, was so taxing that occasionally I had these overwhelming urges to light a firecracker under my tent and explode the solemnity. It's really in the spirit of flimsy whimsy. I doubt that many readers would have antennae out as sensitive as yours. Perhaps I shouldn't knock the meagre clientele for American-written Asia history, but most of it, I think, will plug through a page looking grimly for peasants and water-control, never knowing that anything like a pun was bouncing off them. "Showmanship", though, I don't care for, and the clause about the "exploratory tour of the author's mind and every so often of the mind of modern and pre-modern China" seems a bit of a low blow, tinged with the suspicion that this is rhetoric not critique.

I'm not entirely persuaded that my "labels" are used too simplistically. I did, after all, worry Confucianism all around the block, including a chapter on "Confucianism and Confucianism: the Basic Confrontation"—trying to explain there and elsewhere that Confucianism could seem to be on all sides of many questions—but maintaining still (as I think one must to avoid interpretive nihilism) that the term Confucianism should not just be banished in some mood of oh-so-knowing skepticism. I saw the problem of using the term *without* settling for a tuppeny definition (for my English readers!) as the real problem of writing Chinese history. And of course, if you use a term, a name, a quiddity (no pun), the nominalists will tell you that you're violating the uniqueness of historical occurrence. If you'll grant that Vol. II was conceived of not as a capsule history of China but as an inquiry into the *modern* decay of a complex tradition, I think that the use of a model of tension, which can then be seen resolved is not a violation of acceptable historical method. I did not use the flashblack capriciously. I know how *types* can be unhistorical. I once reviewed Weber on Protestant and Confucian ethics, with critical attention to that point. But I don't think I was working on those lines, and my "literati-type" does not embarrass me. It comes through, to me, not as a falsification of early dynastic history, but as a valid basis for elucidating a modern historical process, and for showing, incidentally, an early-modern continuum . . . .
Sincerely, Joe L.

ON CONFUCIAN CHINA AND ITS MODERN FATE; VOLUMES II AND III

With the appearance of these brilliant, provocative, often exasperating volumes, Professor Levenson brings to a close his three-part contrapuntal study of the death and transfiguration of

Confucianism. The *leit motif* (to continue one of the author's favorite metaphors), sounded first in volume 1 (*The Problem of Intellectual Continuity,* 1958), is profoundly historical and ultimately tragic: the vulnerability of traditional, universal values in a modern, particularistic world. Time, that is, does not stand still for absolute, hence timeless, values but rather throws up constant alternatives to them. And when those alternatives no longer come from within the tradition and are more compelling than the old absolutes, tradition is in danger of becoming irrelevant. It must either change or die. It is possible that it will change *and* die. This is what happened in nineteenth- and twentieth-century China. As new and alien (though not always foreign) choices pressed in on the old ones, Confucian thought and institutions became drained of real significance. They were vitiated by continuous compromises with modernity until they came to stand for everything they once denied: narrow national pretensions, ethical culture divorced from political responsibility, formal religiosity, a politics of popular rather than heavenly will. Nothing remained of their once confident claim of ecumenical relevance. Their cultural universe, with China at its center, had disappeared and so they became relics—something to point to back in history rather than to act on in the here-and-now. Nothing remained but a memory.

It is this process of decline into irrelevance that concerns Professor Levenson in these volumes. In volume II he treats it in its institutional setting, in volume III in its historiographical setting. In both the technique is the same: to range over most of Chinese and much of Western history in a series of idiosyncratic, largely self-contained and apparently unrelated essays that explore diverse strands of the long tradition that ultimately failed. Anything goes, everything fits, as if the author is challenging history to show him something he cannot use, something that does not fit into the grand design described above. The result is disconcerting though never dull. From a stratospheric discussion of the relativity of ideas (in volume I) to a more earthly treatment of Yuan Shih-k'ai playing the fool in his restorationist's robes, from New Text Han Confucianism to Hassidic folklore, from the courts of K'ang-hsi and Yung-cheng, among others, to those of Versailles and the Hohenzollerns, we are taken on an exploratory tour of the author's mind and of the mind of modern and premodern China. Where the record fails to provide the necessary facts for a needed conclusion, Professor Levenson comes to its rescue with his own supple logic, almost always persuasive but sometimes tinged with the suspicion that rhetoric and history are one.

The suspicion is intensified by the author's highly distinctive style. Professor Levenson is a master of the metaphor, the epigram, the bon mot, the paradox, the pun, and often his history gets hopelessly lost in the verbal thickets. Thus, for his American readers—referring to Yuan Shih-k'ai's fatuity in words that mock Henry Clay's sense of principle: "He would rather the rite than the presidency" (II, 6). Or for his English readers—discussing the *quid pro quo* arrangement of imperial patronage in return for loyal support that marked the relationship between monarchy and bureaucracy: ". . . if the scholar had support to offer, some power to sell for his *quid*, the monarch still fell . . . short of monopoly" (II, 66). Or for his Chinese readers—noting the late Ch'ing obsession with the *t'i* (Chinese "essence") *-yung* (Western "utility") dichotomy: ". . . if the . . . essence could really not be saved, Manchus were endangered, even more than the Chinese *t'i* addicts" (II, 8). And finally, at the end of his study, the worst barbarism of all—a desperate phrase that acts as a stall for time between the last essay and an attempt to pull the whole melange together: "Having concluded roundly, let us conclude squarely, with a concluding conclusion" (III, 110). One wonders whether, in studying the descent of traditional thought into meaninglessness, the author himself does not at times become meaningless.

Yet however crippled by rhetoric, his story still limps along at a pace that other, less courageous history, marching, cannot match. It has many important things to say. It attempts with considerable success to remove Confucianism—sensibly taken as the dominant, though by no means exclusive, mode of Chinese intellectual and socio-political life—from the realm of bland generalization and make of it an organic problem of real and vibrant values—shifting, variable, sensitive to pressures, susceptible of damage, subject to change even within the old order. The tired old myth of a static, unchanging China is thus given a helping hand to oblivion. So is the complacent view that Chinese history is too exclusive and exotic to warrant comparison with Western intellectual and institutional experience. Much of this work is devoted to the difficult task of making sense of comparative intellectual history and as such joins Benjamin Schwartz' important study, *In Search of Wealth and Power: Yen Fu and the West* (Cambridge, Mass.,

1964), as a much-needed corrective to the more usual parochial treatment of the history of ideas.

There is much more here that is good: a strong counter-argument to the historicist view that history is in essence a success story, a debunking of the more egregious assertions of the orientally despotic interpretation of Chinese history, a convincing demonstration of the weakness of what might be called the [C.P.] Fitzgerald syndrome—the need to explain the Chinese revolution as a modern analogue of traditional dynasty-making. Professor Levenson is an historical relativist. He believes that the failure—the hapless character and insignificant event—has a place in the mainstream of history too. Thus, for example, Liao P'ing, the last and by all counts the *least* of the latter-day traditionalists; the other sentimental reactionaries of the May Fourth period; the post-1911 monarchical restoration movement, really only parodies of past reality; and the late and forlorn attempts of K'ang Yu-wei and others to sanctify the dead body of Confucian thought by putting it into the church—were all relevant, all distinctly modern, and, in their way, all important indexes of change. By the same relativist reasoning, the author argues that total terror, the key to oriental despotism's theory of power, is less persuasive as a description of the mechanics of the traditional Chinese state than the concept of tension between monarchy and bureaucracy. In other words, it took two to play the game. Again, and for similar reasons, he rejects the "just-another-dynasty" approach to the present, for it denies the organic complexity of tradition and the radical break with it that made even modern traditionalists strangers to the past.

Of the many problems raised in these volumes I should like to examine just one in greater depth: the nature of the relationship between monarchy and bureaucracy (see all of volume II). Essentially it is understood as a symbiotic tension between two vested interests, each posed against the other yet locked in mutual dependence. Originally, in feudal times, the tension was represented by king and aristocrat, the centripetal claims of monarchy opposing the centrifugal acquisitiveness of aristocracy. As the scholar-bureaucrat intruded on the administrative scene in the long years from the Ch'in to the T'ang, the centralizing emperors began to use him as a counter to the aristocrat. Finally aristocracy was shorn of its independence (though not of all its pretensions): it moved to the side of monarchy, and left the field to civil bureaucracy, now indispensable to the crown yet dangerous too as the new claimant to independent action, wealth, and power. Conversely, bureaucracy needed monarchy to secure its privileges and assure its continuity. And so the two shared the "pie of power" (II, 63-65) in a working tension characterized neither by total terror on the one side nor total divisiveness on the other. As long as it lasted, the dynasty as a viable political form lasted. When the tension was broken after the Taiping rebellion, dynasty was doomed. Bureaucracy abdicated its last claim to independence—intellectual independence of the throne—as it was forced, in order to survive at all, to side with a discredited court against the radical ideology of the rebels and the revolutionary ideas of the West. It came to be looked upon as an extension of the throne rather than as a counterpoise to it, and when the Manchus fell before the new nationalism, Confucianism, embodied in bureaucracy, fell too.

This in broad outline is Professor Levenson's contribution to the theory of the Chinese monarchy. It is not entirely original (see, for example, James T.C. Liu's "An Administrative Cycle in Chinese History: the Case of Northern Sung Emperors," *Journal of Asian Studies*, XXI, 2, 1962, 137-52, where many of these ideas were adumbrated), but it is the fullest statement made so far. How useful is it? The answer is, very. It is the best paradigm of dynastic power that has yet been devised. It substitutes complexity for the monolithic simplicity of other theories that give all initiative in the governance of the state to an unreal, because perfect, tyrant or to an all-wise self-perpetuating Confucian Establishment, or to both in conspiratorial union against the People below. It allows for the growth of imperial despotism, notably after the Sung, without having to make the bureaucrat an abject tool of the throne. In other words, if the emperor got stronger vis-a-vis the bureaucracy, the bureaucracy got stronger vis-a-vis everybody else and retained in the bargain its claim to judge the throne even while being humiliated by it. As a theory of independence and interdependence, it prompts a much more sophisticated and human-centered analysis of Chinese institutions than has heretofore been suggested.

Unfortunately Professor Levenson never really gets beyond a general treatment of the problem. The monographic testing of the theory remains to be made. As it stands it is too perfect, too pat, and leads the author into overstatement and questionable conclusions. The very complicated and critical bureaucratic role of a new breed of aristocrats, the great families, from the third to the seventh centuries A.D. is largely ignored, almost as if this anomaly were an embarrassment to the concept. And since the author insists on retaining aristocracy as an irritant to both monarchy and bureaucracy long after it became politically irrelevant, he has trouble locating his aristocrats in later dynasties. For the Ming, other than the early rusticated princes, they are eunuchs, for the Ch'ing, Manchus. As representatives of special, court-centered privilege, they qualify. As kept men, the *king's* men—attributes he gives to post-T'ang aristocracy—they are more problematical. What of the eunuchs courted by the Tung-lin party at the end of the Ming? Whose side were they on—or did they somehow retain an "aristocratic" independence of their own? What, for that matter, of Wei Chung-hsien, who eventually called the emperor's tune rather than dancing to it? More significantly, what of the great mid-Ch'ing Manchu bureaucrats, men such as Hsu-yuan-meng, O-er-t'ai, and A-kuei, who belonged rightly to both camps, aristocracy and bureaucracy? The clear theoretical lines of tension are in danger here of being blurred by the real complexities of administrative life. One solution, recently suggested in a Yale doctoral thesis by Jonathan Spence, is to replace the Manchu as the eunuch-equivalent in the Ch'ing with the Chinese bondservant, a bannerman of sorts, but not a racial aristocrat. Here was the real king's man, picked for privilege, not born to it. In any case, this problem indicates that the theory will have to be given more precise chronological underpinnings before it can be accepted as valid for any one period or for all.

The weakest link in Professor Levenson's argument, however, is his attempt to pin ideological labels on his participants in tension: Confucian on bureaucracy, Legalist on emperorship, and more neutrally, feudal on aristocracy. By perpetuating these simplistic formulae, he does a disservice to his own commitment to complexity and reduces history to a contest between Good and Bad, Weak and Strong, Realist and Idealist. Monarchy, he says (II, 26-27), patronized at various times nonphilosophical Taoism, secular Buddhism, eunuchs, and trade, and was frequently involved in parricidal and fratricidal family strife, thus offending, respectively, the rationalist, sceptical, civil, aesthetic, and ethical tenets of the Confucian literatus-type. True, perhaps, but not good enough. The trouble lies in the word *type*. Professor Levenson is posing a series of historical realities against a composite ideal. The argument is loaded and unhistorical. Confucianists, as bureaucrats, offended as much against their own ideals as did Chinese emperors. In fact, as local and provincial officials, where in effect they were monarchs in miniature, they operated just as much with the strict code book as with the sacred text. Authoritarianism and *real-politik* were no more monopolies of the throne than idealism was a monopoly of bureaucracy. The emperor, after all, especially after the Sung, was as thoroughly indoctrinated in the ethical curriculum as were his civil servants. They both shared the same intellectual world, one largely circumscribed by set texts and fixed ideas, and if the monarch sometimes only paid lip-service to them, so did the bureaucrat. Neither was a perfect *type*; both were fallible men in an imperfect world.

Without the labels, Professor Levenson's theory of tensions makes sense. With them it does not. Monarch versus bureaucrat suggests a real political issue; Legalist versus Confucian suggests nothing but an airy abstraction.

JOSEPH LEVENSON ON CHINA AND THE WORLD

Franz Schurmann

> This tie, though sometimes hidden, was never lost. But the tradition dies of his alienation, his and so many others.
>
> *Liang Ch'i-ch'ao and the Mind of Modern China,* last lines

When the ping-pong players and then the journalists went to China in the spring of 1971, the old American admiration of China began to be re-legitimized. The stream of articles on what was once reviled as Red China have become uniformly favorable. Some have even suggested that the Chinese are successfully resolving illnesses of modern society such as are now afflicting advanced industrial countries. Others are rediscovering old American values of hard work, discipline, and chastity in the new China. In the late 1950s, we felt we had something to learn from the Russians about technology and technical education. Now China seems to be becoming a kind of model for dealing with human and social problems. It is sad that Joseph Levenson did not live to see these days, for no Western scholar in recent times has written so brilliantly and sensitively in the tradition of explaining the meaning of China for the West as has Levenson.

That tradition is little known in America. American Sinology, like everything else in the country, is a big enterprise. It has its own currents, but they do not encompass the tradition which includes Marco Polo, Guillaume Postel, Montesquieu, and Quesnay. There are American Sinologists who are Chinese by origin or adoption, whose writings are within Chinese traditions of one or another time. There are others who are Sinologists in the classical European sense, explorers of a distant and not yet fully known world. There are those who write as advisers to policy makers. There are those for whom China is a case study for some social science theory or another. There are journalists who report the great events of China. Levenson does not fit into any of these currents. He was a deeply Western man. He was fascinated by the grand outlines of Chinese history, not by its minutiae. He never aspired to any political role concerning China. He was not a professional social scientist, humanist, or even an historian. He had never been to China. His own discovery of China came through beginning study at Cornell and Harvard, wartime service in the Navy, and subsequent graduate study at Harvard. That was the *yung*, the technical attributes of his Sinology. The *t'i*, essence, came from within himself—from an early addiction to culture, art, music, literature; from a lifelong sense of himself as within a religion and among other religions; from a fabulous wealth of spiritual possessions from the entire Western legacy to which he added the legacies of China and Japan. These were the elements out of which the intellectual fibers of his works were fashioned. There were uniquely his own or, in the broadest sense, part of the Western tradition. They were not particularly a segment of American Sinology.

T'i and *yung* and the dialectic of change were the central threads of all his works. *T'i* means body and so conjures up images of bones and flesh and form. *Yung* means use and so implies purposive action toward some goal, like hands fashioning an object. China is obviously an immense *t'i*, by its size, its millennial continuity, the richness of its products. That alone must give it an essence, something that makes it uniquely China, as man is uniquely man and not any other animal. China's *t'i* is so massive that it has seemed to many a constant and immovable essence. Hegel called China the land "of the ever recurring principle." Levenson never agreed with Hegel. He saw traditional China as everchanging. He believed in the reality of the great revolution which turned China upside down, as revolutions do. He wrote of the powerful *yung* which emanated from an expanding Europe since Renaissance times (*European Expansion and the Counter-Example of Asia, 1300-1600*). He knew that this *yung* had finally generated a counter-*yung* in China which has produced the greatest revolution of the twentieth century. He thought little of the popular notion that Mao's China is basically a new Middle Kingdom with a new type of Emperor. Yet if China today is more a land of struggle than of harmony, Levenson was not so deeply interested in its struggles. Nor was he interested in the struggles of the earlier Republican period. Levenson was concerned with *t'i*, not in its static, immanent form but as a changing thing which could die and yet which could live in strange ways. He believed in greatness and believed that what was great must have an essence, must be "value" and not just "history." China is great and must therefore have value. The Western tradition is great and must have value. And both his own Judaic religion and the Christianities which he admired had to have value. But all *t'i* is precarious. It can wither away without being replaced, and what follows will be brittle shell and nasty gesturing. That was pretty much his view of Chiang Kai-shek's China.

The subject of his first book, Liang Ch'i-ch'ao, is conventionally seen as a major figure of "transitional China"—he agitated for reform and then tried to stem revolution. But Levenson portrays him as a man of soul where the struggles of his own conscience and consciousness produced his political actions rather than the reverse. Levenson's Liang Ch'i-ch'ao is first intellectual and then mandarin. Liang was no Hu Shih who began as a blazing reformer and ended as an emissary for a reactionary government. Liang's passions remained quite consistent during his life (only somewhat longer than Levenson's). He always wanted to save something which was essentially China. He hated the obscurantists of the late Ch'ing whose brittle "China" was simply a defense of privilege. He feared the revolutionaries, particularly the fanatic Sun Yat-sen, who wanted to clear everything away so that something new and yet unknowable could arise. Liang Ch'i-ch'ao's position before 1911 was like that of Max Weber in 1918: keep the monarchy but change everything else. Do not abandon the unwobbling pivot no matter how wobbly and rusty it becomes. And when the republic was proclaimed, Liang quickly accepted it as the new pivot and opposed Yuan Shih-k'ai's attempt to make a new monarchy with himself as monarch. Liang's "progressive party" remained a little parliamentary coterie and his own brief governmental service was in the elevated realm of monetary policy. Liang Ch'i-ch'ao, like Max Weber, was fated to remain an intellectual. His *t'i* as an intellectual was more important than any *yung* as a politician.

Levenson was drawn to men like Liang Ch'i-ch'ao, as he was to Weber whom he often cites, not out of sociological faddism but from a real feeling for the soul struggles of that German Liang Ch'i-ch'ao. Levenson believed that in all ages there were men called upon—by God, perhaps—to speak truths which had to be said even if the tides of history swept by them.

Clearly such a view of the intellectual is religious. Liang Ch'i-ch'ao, during the republican years when he abandoned active politics, was drawn to Buddhism. Levenson saw no contradiction between that and Liang's deep-rooted Confucian convictions which outlasted his late nineteenth-century critiques of formal Confucianism. Levenson was always a devoutly religious man, and in his later years drew even closer to religion. In the book *China, An Interpretive History* which we did together but which was guided by his vision, he says of early Han Confucianism: "The sanctions behind these Confucian injunctions were thus hardly moral or philosophical, but openly religious". (p. 90). Had he lived longer, he probably would have extended his religious interpretation of Confucianism. He saw the resemblances between his own religion, Judaism, and Confucianism, and the development of analogic comparison between the two was a major part of his intellectual process. For Levenson as well as Liang, the road led further toward rather than away from religion.

Levenson began his work with "transitional" figures like Liang Ch'i-ch'ao and in his trilogy on *Confucian China and Its Modern Fate,* he went back to traditional China. He loved both those ages, as one could see from the mounds of books in his office and his home. He wrote with sympathy on the Communists and their Marxism in the "transitional" period. He knew that Confucianism was dead, and attested that death by the "museumification" of Confucius by the Communists. But he wrote little on the China that grew up after 1949. There was nothing in his background which instinctively drew him to Marx or Marxism. But neither was there anything which made him reject them, as was the case with so many American liberals of the 1950s. He could as little be an anti-Communist as a pro-Communist. His mind told him that Communism had come to China, that the great sweeping away of the past had to be. But he was never drawn to the People's Republic. He could see that the Communists had finally made China a part of that world history in which he believed. He could see that a Marxism which the entire world shared was the vehicle of the new cosmopolitanism. But he could never get away from the suspicion that Marxism and Marxist China was but a Chinese experience of that gigantic *yung* of science, technology, and economic expansion which made the West and its culture and power supreme in the world. He could see no *t'i* in Marxism, though he would have welcomed it had he seen it. He could not be drawn to anything great which was not somehow nourished by a religious spirituality.

In the mid-1960s, he did an imaginative reader on European expansionism and Asian counter-expansionism. The theme was already well-known: while European nations streamed all over the globe, the Chinese reviled their few expansion-minded statesmen and the Japanese drew a chain around themselves. He probably did it as a contribution to the literature which was trying to combat the then current ideology in Washington about "Chinese expansionism," as in McNamara's labeling of one of Lin Piao's essays as China's "Mein Kampf." In it he notes that both great East Asian nations eschewed expansionism because they were much more concerned with their basic internal stability than with some transient external gains. By contrast, the first great expansionist European country, Portugal, virtually abandoned its own peasant hinterland in search of foreign empire. True, England expanded for mercantilist reasons and France out of a sense of destiny as well as mercantilism. Levenson duly stressed the religious motivation behind European as well as Islamic Expansionism. But for all its grandioseness, he still sees it as an outpouring of Western *yung*. As he says in his conclusions, "The rapid communications which Europeans developed, and their monopoly of communications, gave them an ability to know where to go, what to do, and how to do it, in a way no non-European people could match" (pp. 132-133). His attitude toward European expansionism was that it had to be, just as he felt that Communism in China had to be. But both could be worth it only if they led to the generation of a new *t'i*.

For Levenson, that new *t'i*, whether for Europe in the world or China in the world, had to be cosmopolitan. He believed in something like one world and many times used the word cosmopolitanism with approval. By cosmopolitanism he did not mean universalism where all men would become alike. He liked diversity and indeed saw it as essential to cosmopolitanism. He would have been horrified by a world all Christian, all Marxist, or for that matter, all Judaic. His ideas on cosmopolitanism were undoubtedly formed by his years of concern with Confucianism. Confucianism in its "value" times (before its degradation in late Ch'ing into "history") was a set of standards by which men became civilized and so able to interact with each other over vast spaces and cutting across many diversities. In fact, diversity was essential for Confucianism, for the general could not exist without the particular. Confucianism as value was *t'ien-hsia*—the world. China was always China with its provinces, struggles, landowning, and the myriad manifestations of life lived small and big. There are two traditional words for China: *Chung-hua* and *Chung-kuo*. Only to outsiders and moderns are they identical. In earlier times, *Chung-hua* was what we now call Confucianism, but really that set of standards which men acquire by long education and experience and which enables them to live anywhere in the world and not just in some specific village. *Chung-hua* was China's cosmopolitanism in an earlier day.

As *Chung-hua* became identical with *Chung-kuo*, it had to cease being cosmopolitan. Levenson was no Confucianist in American guise, as one sometimes finds among American Sinologists. But I have no doubt that that *t'i* of *Chung-hua* which once held sway in China was, for Levenson, a model of a *t'i* which some day would arise throughout the world. It is not coincidental that he picks out global communication as the first thing in his conclusions about European expansionism. The Europeans made the world one in physical terms. Like most people in the non-European world and like many in the European world, he did not believe that Europe, the West, was able to create a worldwide *t'i* in the same way. The cultural relativist would respond that no such global *t'i* can or should exist. Economists and *real*politicians would say that the nexus of world interdependence is the real *t'i*. Levenson was not a dualist with respect to *t'i* and *yung*; he did not believe that one came down from heaven and the other grew up out of the mire of earthly doings. But neither did he believe that one grew logically or automatically out of the other. He never agreed with Lenin that soviets plus electrification meant socialism. But he also rejected the notion that right conduct comes out of right beliefs. He did not like the fundamentalism of Mao Tse-tung Thought, and its fanatic appearance in the Cultural Revolution repelled him as much as proselytizing Christianity or Islam. He saw the link between *t'i* and *yung* in the special role of the intellectual. The intellectual was for

Levenson the key figure in the dialectic of change, and the subject of change was what he wrote about in most of his works. If a new *t'i* were to arise to encompass the entire world, it would come from the intellectuals, for whom the ancient scholars of *Chung-hua* could serve as a model.

One of the central concerns in Levenson's work is "the tension between monarchy and bureaucracy." These were the two great institutions of the traditional Chinese state. Except for brief periods, neither was the tool of the other. Neither could exist without the other. Levenson rarely spoke of struggles and he never saw the two struggling against each other, as someone in the Marxist tradition might see them on the analogy of class struggle. Like Max Weber, he preferred the word tension. Struggle implies some tangible goal which many want but only a few can get. While emperors and officials were often involved in such struggles, the issues were less important than the principles. The millennial tension between these two institutions of state arose because they were juxtaposed against each other for principled reasons. For all of his awareness of the nastiness of bureaucrats and his readiness to see the greatness in many monarchs, his predilections were for the best of the bureaucrats—the literati officials. They were the amateurs, the generalists he wrote about—men who administered fairly, who acquired many skills while professional in none, who produced great art and poetry. Politically, their most important function was to temper the absolutism inherent in monarchy. Levenson wrote admiringly of the great voyages of Ch'eng Ho during the Ming, but he never would have excoriated the officials who put Ch'eng Ho down as an ambitious eunuch scheming in the service of tyranny. Those officials, however base and shortsighted they might have been, still did what Tung Chung-shu, the ideologue-official of the early Han, taught them to do. Tung Chung-shu, as Levenson wrote in our *China, An Interpretive History*, wove an ideology moved by religious power (what is now called Confucianism) which was designed to make monarchs do the right thing. Only educated men could say what was right and wrong, because they knew the sacred texts which gave them the ability to interpret correctly all human and natural phenomena.

The early Han bureaucracy was not just an institutional holdover from the Ch'in. Its ancestors were the bureaucracies of the warring states which were modeled on the Chou bureaucracy whose ultimate ancestor was the priestly caste of Shang. Priests are of course concerned with religious essences and are not supposed to meddle in the world. Bureaucrats, as most people see them, are supposed to arrange things without asking questions as to why. But the Chinese bureaucracy, as it developed since early Han, was a repository both of *t'i* and *yung*. It administered but it also interpreted the omens. Others could be found to administer (like Marco Polo), but none could read the omens and the sacred texts except those trained in them. Even a sage emperor versed in all the texts could not equal the bureaucracy, for he was one and they were a corpus.

T'i and *yung* were in a relationship of tension to each other within the individual bureaucrat as they were between monarchy and bureaucracy as institutions. In other societies, Levenson might have said, priests cultivated *t'i* for the benefit of rulers and people, but developed *yung* as a sideline, like acquiring estates and concubines. He did not admire the priesthood of Christian Europe, nor did he like the Reformation. In the former there was no tension because the priests were supposed to be all godly. In the latter there was the tension of revolutionaries who wanted to fit together parts that should always move with each other. Above all others in the world, Levenson felt that the Chinese literati- officials formed a model for that cosmopolitan corpus of acting intellectuals which he hoped would eventually become a force in the world. China, in Levenson's eyes, was the world's most successful society. It preserved a working social and political order on a grand scale longer than any other society in world history. China did not equal Europe in economic dynamism and political conquest, nor, except for the modern interregnum, did it descend periodically to depths of despair and depravity as did all other great societies. All had kings and armies and officials and productive economies and excellent values, but none had a corpus of literati officials like that of China. China never was a sleeping giant drowsing for millennia in unchanging torpor as Napoleon and Hegel thought. Levenson saw it as constantly changing, always full of excitement. The excitement came from the constant drama of everyday life, particularly political life. The literati gentry had to work hard during those long millennia to keep China a living entity. It was the drama of China at all moments through the centuries that made him plan the entire *Interpretive History*, not as another text to fill college classrooms but as a series of volumes going on and on which would show this drama of China in all its kaleidoscopic efforts to make, destroy, and repair the social order.

When that tension between *t'i* and *yung*, between monarchy and bureaucracy ceased, China entered the phase of revolution. Levenson saw that as value turning into history. More concretely, when Chinese became defensively nationalistic about Confucianism, when they said Confucianism is right because it is Chinese and we are Chinese, then it was dead. Liang Ch'i-ch'ao tried hard to keep Confucianism alive, but Hu Shih buried it. Levenson had nothing but disdain for Hu Shih's later nationalism which made him excoriate both Buddhism and Marxism as foreign imports which sooner or later would be swept away by the real "Chineseness." Levenson's cosmopolitanism let him tolerate nationalism only as a temporary expedient to solve some national problems and salve national pride. But as doctrine he regarded it as hollow, serving mainly to entrench in power men like Chiang Kai-shek. Everything about Chiang Kai-shek struck him as phony, and particularly outrageous was his "New Life Movement" which invoked ancient essences to cloak modern scheming for power. Marxism was far superior to nationalism if only because its avowed universalism made it impossible for it to be only a mask for the search for power by ambitious men. Levenson never had any doubt that Marxism, as it came to China in the early 1920s, was the only possible (or visible) successor to a dead Confucianism.

Levenson did not depart from the conventional explanation for the decline of Imperial China—that it crumbled before the impact of Western imperialism. But from his viewpoint of the essentiality of the intellectual in society, he studied it in terms of the crumbling of *t'i*. And here he had no doubt that it crumbled because men like Yen Fu, K'ang Yu-wei, and Liang Ch'i-ch'ao, for all their deep devotion to Confucianism, suspected that the West brought in far more than guns and ships. These intellectuals realized that the universe was much larger than had been sketched out by their own classics, and they had no explanations for it. What happened in China in the realm of ideas in the late nineteenth century was like the Copernican Revolution. The Chinese had known what the physical world was like, but they still believed that their old science could let them figure out all of it, if they wanted to. By the year 1900, they knew this was not so.

Like all revolutions, this one too went on in many parts of China. While K'ang Yu-wei and Liang Ch'i-ch'ao were bending their minds to find solutions, a very young Mao Tse-tung in remote Hunan was reading every Western work in Chinese translation he could lay his hands on. Some of the late Ch'ing reformers had hoped young Chinese would study engineering texts and so had sent students to Europe and Japan. After all, wasn't Europe's superiority due to its fantastic technical skills? But thousands of young men of Mao's age and older were fascinated by this wonderful new wider universe. Chinese finally entered into that age of discovery which Europeans had commenced centuries before. In Europe, the passion of discovery led from the *t'i* of religion to the new *t'i* of science. But Europeans remained in their priestly traditions, and scientists remained scientists, leaving it to technicians and politicians to make use of what they had discovered. China had no priestly tradition, and so the young discoverers wanted to apply what they had discovered. But since what they discovered was of monumental scope, a career as engineer could hardly satisfy them. Let the smart ambitious men of Shanghai and Canton learn skills and make money. The younger ones, with their cries for revolution, soon rapidly outdistanced the Liang Ch'i-ch'ao's. It mattered little that the Chinese word for revolution, *ko-ming*, was an old-fashioned work meaning something like the change of the mandate of Heaven. *Ko-ming* came to mean *revolution* in the Western sense, with all the emotional connotations it still has today. In 1850, poor people from southern China started a vast rebellion which was tantamount to a revolution. But the Taiping Rebellion never gripped the intellectuals of China as a magnificent precursor of their own revolutionary movements. Even the Communists are not that interested in the Taipings. The Taipings introduced a powerful foreign faith, but their image of the new universe was too primitive and magical to appeal to the intellectuals. The intellectuals of China, like the scientists of Copernican Europe, had to discover the new universe by themselves, and when they did all the old paradigms were smashed.

The discovery of this new universe by young Chinese at the turn of the century had to be revolutionary in Levenson's eyes. The old Chinese *t'i* was inextricably bound up with *t'ien-hsia*, universe. It was not merely a set of values, though an anthropologist might describe it as such. It was a cosmology structured like the astral universe with definite principles which explained everything. And since the boundaries between man and nature were fluid, it explained man too. Chinese philosophy is replete with cosmologies. Confucius wrote down and commented on the cosmology transmitted from very ancient times. Tung Chung-shu formulated a cosmology which expounded the principles governing natural and political phenomena. Chu Hsi formulated a cosmology which expounded the human and social order. All were complete and internally consistent as long as there was a known universe. If the universe crumbled, then nothing any longer was knowable and explainable. Man would then die from alienation. Liang Ch'i-ch'ao understood this deep Chinese need for a cosmology and therefore urged that all the material props of the old cosmology not be destroyed at once. If just the monarchy were retained, like the constitutional monarchies of countries such as England and Japan which he admired, then at least the religious skein which holds the human order together would be preserved. And, perhaps, after the country had gone through the traumas of adjustment, a new harmony could reappear. But Liang's hopes in 1911 were already those of an old man, despite his own youth. Young Chinese searched, but only for a brief time. By the early 1920s many of them, far more than just those who formed the Communist Party, had found Marxism. Others found science, like their Western counterparts. A few chose Christianity or rediscovered Buddhism. If China had had a priestly tradition, the Chinese would probably have gone through a long process of discovering the new cosmology. But being the descendants of activist scholars, they wanted a new *t'i* so they could get on with a new *yung*, which was the concrete process of revolution.

There is now but one universe, and China and the West share it alike—so Levenson believed. China's forcible entry into that universe provoked the Chinese Revolution. Since Levenson was what people professionally call an intellectual historian, he left it to others to study the workings of that revolution. He dealt with Communism only when he saw elements of *t'i* coming into play again. Generally he preferred to stand aside and watch, usually with sympathy, as the People's Republic struggled to make a new China. Only once did he react with anger—during the Cultural Revolution. Unlike many, including myself, he believed that the Cultural Revolution was really about culture. As it unfolded, he became more and more disenchanted, not so much by the Red Guard rampages, but by China's growing xenophobia and apparent isolationism. If the Chinese Revolution meant that

China and the West were becoming part of the same universe, the Cultural Revolution appeared to be a step backward, perhaps to the obscurantism of the Boxers. He saw the sprouting of a paranoiac nationalism in China which, in any form, he detested. He could understand the need for finally burying the decayed remnants of the past so that the new could arise. But if Confucian images were to be succeeded by Maoist idols, it meant that China was descending to the base level of any petty "modernizing" power. China was a model, he believed, and thus had a special duty to the world. There could be no worse a betrayal of that duty than xenophobia. Until its time of decay, China had always been hospitable to foreigners, though it found little admirable in them. Only in its worst, if justifiable, moments of desperation had it attacked foreigners and foreign things. There can be no question but that he would have been delighted with the ping-pong breakthrough and what is now evidently a great Chinese return to the world. But the manner and causes of the change would have puzzled him, as much of Chinese Communism did.

In the last years of his life, he became interested in provincialism, a subject not apparent in his earlier writings. I do not know where that work would have taken him, had he lived. At first sight it seems strange that someone like Levenson, who was so concerned with the grander beliefs of men, should become concerned with a subject matter more characteristic of the concerns of anthropologists or, of late, professional historians. I can relate that new concern of his to his continuing puzzlement with Chinese Communism and to his constant search for the evolving cosmopolitanism. I can also relate it to what was a growing conservatism and disenchantment in him. Conservatives, in the old-fashioned and not fascist sense of the word, are supposed to be supportive of diversity, whereas radicals are universalists. So in ancient China, the Confucianists were the conservatives, and the Mohists the radicals. Mohism created the sense of *t'ien-hsia* and Legalism supplied the organizational means, leading to the Ch'in with its *gleichschaltung* of everything. Levenson could not accept Communism's persistent intolerance of diversity, and in particular its hostility to intellectuals, the kind of men he believed essential to any just society. The old Chinese literati, for all their common acceptance of Confucian cosmology, were a diverse lot, as evident in their art and poetry. Levenson could never warm up to Communist cadres, who looked pretty much alike to him. Perhaps, he believed, if the wellsprings of diversity rooted in the various Chinese provinces survived, then it could force upon a Mohist Marxism something of Confucianism's tolerance of diversity. Such a view, if that was indeed what he had in mind, would have been consistent with his notions about the dialectic of change. If Peking is the force for unity, then the regions of China may be the force for diversity bringing about the kind of creative tension that once existed between monarchy and bureaucracy. For Levenson it never was a question of countervailing powers, but rather a tension of opposites which would bring a real *t'i* into being. If Marxism in China indeed was the repository of the new *t'i*, then the tension of diversities rather than monolithic unity would actualize its fullest potential.

Levenson's disenchantment in the last years was apparent to me. Every humane and humanistic impulse in him made him feel revulsion for the Vietnam War. Yet he was horrified by the absurdist character of much of the antiwar movement. While one of the least violent men I have ever known, I do not think it was the occasional violence of the movement—rather paltry now in retrospect—which disenchanted him. Rather it was the antics of some of the early movement leaders, the blind intolerance of their followers, and the open anti-intellectualism of the demonstrations. Neither the Cultural Revolution nor the antiwar student movement in America which occurred at the same time seemed to him to be really revolutionary. He could see what students in China were overthrowing in 1919, but he could not see what they were doing in 1966, except perhaps overthrowing culture itself. He felt the same was happening in America where antiwar sentiments quickly led to nationwide movements aiming at the destruction of the one institution where culture and intellectuals had a legitimate place—the universities. He was not a defender of the university on authoritarian grounds, as were some who violently opposed student radicals. Levenson never sought power, and if he had authority, it came from his knowledge and passion, not his formal position. But he deeply believed that the university in America was the one institution where that cosmopolitan *t'i* which he regarded as so essential could develop. He had his own religion which he felt fed into cosmopolitanism as much as China did, but it was no substitute for the corpus of diverse men in a university who worked to make civilization a thing with essences and not just a particular socio-political order. The American universities were the counterpart of the old Chinese "bureaucracy" in its best sense, the corpus of literati officials. He fully supported all efforts to check the arbitrary power of a regime in Washington waging a foreign war of aggression. He believed intellectuals still had a role to play, that the time for their museumification had not yet come. He felt that too much of the student and antiwar movement masked blind hatred and hunger for power. It was an assault on an American and world *t'i* which was still all too fragile.

His last years seemed similar to those of Liang Ch'i-ch'ao. Like Liang, his early works attested the entrance of China into the new world and he felt a part of that drama. We must remember that the 1950s, once McCarthy had been vanquished, were basically an optimistic period in America. Most China scholars believed that sooner or later China and America would come closer together. Only the benighted few on the far right continued to rail against the spectre of Communism. Levenson was by nature an optimist. Moreover, where intellectuals were earnestly working on matters of *t'i*, as they were doing both in China and America, though in different ways, there was hope for the future. In American universities, learning of all kinds was flourishing. Old obscurantisms were bypassed, and the new ones of the social sciences were unable to impose a totalitarian mold on all thought. Weberism may have become a fad in sociology, but it never obscured the greatness of the man himself. China studies, though they separated into all kinds of currents which were not to his relish, nevertheless retained an indefinable core which could only be called love of China. No matter how hardbitten some of the economists who wrote on China, their attraction to that country and people generally outweighed their predilections for mathematical model-building. Levenson felt good about all this. But disenchantment set in during the mid-1960s, as it did with Liang after the middle of the second decade of the century. Like Liang, Levenson did not withdraw but rather plunged into new kinds of thought, away from the mainstream, but still in accord with his lifelong concern with *t'i*. His death was indeed untimely, because he had just come to a point where he was able to shed the last vestiges of professionalism and let his intellect take him freely where he wanted to go.

Levenson was a great teacher, a role appreciated by himself and his many students. His writings, however, often baffled his readers. Sometimes it seemed a brilliant *tour de mot* was more important to him than a careful laying out of a thought process. He had the habit, both in speech and writing, of saying witticisms when he was actually most serious. There must surely be some Jewish Zen tradition which makes a poet-traveler laugh out loud as he sees God in the mountains. But this was his individuality of style and eccentricity of personality. The substantive passion was always there, and it becomes clearer as his physical presence becomes more remote. Much of the bafflement of his readers comes from the fact that thinking in terms of essences and actions and the dialectic of change is not very common on the American intellectual scene. Look at the way the social sciences have handled the question of "value." Anthropologists in the field and sociologists by reading Weber have discovered that human societies are governed by "values." Since these are social facts, they must be describable as "belief systems" or better still isolated as elements in a logical system. A particularly absurd example of this was the attempt made for years by U.S. military research agencies to formulate the "operational codes" of the Russians and the Chinese, for which they paid much money to well-placed scholars. The voluminous literature in social science on "achievement" which in some Western countries comes from a "Protestant ethic" is another example. Logical positivism is largely an operational extension of a materialism deeply embedded in the American psyche which assumes that man is so atomistically dissectable that ultimately no residue will be left. Obviously that excludes any religious conception of man. But without some sensitivity to religion, Levenson is impossible to understand. On positivist grounds, his contributions can be dismissed as less than a paper on zinc production in Yunnan. There is little in American university training which heightens religious sensitivity. Religion is something you do outside, whether in a church or getting stoned in an apartment. The university is the world of *yung*, while *t'i* is cultivated in the privacy of one's own psyche. Levenson was incapable of such a dichotomy. There had to be the tension between the public *yung* of teaching and studying and the private *t'i* of values, of religion, of human relations.

Some have suggested that Levenson has brought his own Judaic concerns into his study of China, and I suppose that is true. But it is true of all mind workers. Even the cold game theorist brings his predilections into his models. But I doubt that Judaism was on his mind when he thought about China. It is always risky to try to state another man's religious belief, yet I wish to try. Levenson's religion was relevant to his work and so to much of his life and had to do with a sense of the world. Some men in all ages and all times seem called upon to have a consciousness of the great dramas of the world. They feel compelled to work them out in written or plastic form. They have acquired skills which make it possible for them to do this. These are the world's intellectuals. They see the outlines of great landscapes where most men deal only with certain rocks and trees. When they express themselves, as Liang Ch'i-ch'ao did on China, they make clear what the essence of the doings of millions of men is. Levenson never believed that such a sense came about through training in world history or world politics. That might make some mind workers able to construct a pattern of rocks, but never a landscape. A world consciousness had to be formed by something else. He undoubtedly believed that Judaism and the Bible gave him that world consciousness. He knew that the Chinese Classics, when they were yet value and not history, gave the literati of traditional China their world consciousness. Perhaps it is significant that the Chinese amateur literati painters overwhelmingly painted landscapes, each of which constituted a self-enclosed world. Their painting has always been so different from the pettiness of everyday administrative life whereby they fulfilled their bureaucratic functions. I never heard Levenson speak of God, nor do I recollect his ever writing much on that subject. He did not seem to be interested in formal beliefs in God, and when he wrote about the "supreme god" of the ancient Shang dynasty he did not get ecstatic as if the Chinese had independently discovered Jehovah. But he was fascinated by the Chinese Classics, as he was by later Chinese painting. Like the Bible, the Classics laid out a great cosmology which held sway over the Chinese mind for two millennia. That sense of cosmology, of a universe in human terms was, I believe, the major element in his religion, and also an essential part of his work. That his own religion had produced a comparable cosmology for the West was a matter of pride for him, but this did not give it a special preeminence. This sense of cosmology gave him a sense of kinship to all intellectuals, regardless of specific religions or ideologies, who shared with him a similar world consciousness.

This brings me back to Levenson on China. Like De Tocqueville on America for France, Levenson presents China as a model for the world. They both wrote in similar traditions, and in many respects resembled each other in personality. Both approved the inexorable course of revolution and democracy. Both used another country to expound general truths which they felt an intellectual must state. But De Tocqueville's America was a static model (such as models are supposed to be), and he isolated the key elements in that model so that in some way they could be used, at least analogically, in France. De Tocqueville presented America as a country which could be emulated. But Levenson portrays China as a world in process. What makes China unique among all other nations is that, except for recent times, it always was a world, never a nation. Rome created a world for a few centuries, and then others picked up the legacies. But the Chinese created a world which lasted two millennia, the only human society to do so. It was not an abstract world like Christendom or Islam, but a real one where real institutions bound the entire thing together with visible and tangible connections. Since World War II, there has been much talk about "one world." But, practically speaking, if it had come about, it would have been an Imperium Americanum. That Imperium looks rather battered now. Levenson's China conjures up not the word Imperium, but *Chung-hua*, something having to do with culture and institutions impregnated with that culture. The Chinese spread an essence, a *t'i*, over much of the world known to them, and created unity. The institutions and laws and armies followed. Or they grew up in dialectical relationship to that *t'i*.

Levenson was a generalist, an amateur, like the great Chinese literati he wrote about. As such, he had to reject the Marxist notion of intellectuals as mind workers, differing only in terms of a division of labor from the people. He also rejected the current American notion of intellectuals as academics with particular skills or teaching abilities. But if his convictions made him see intellectuals as something special (like artists), he was no mandarin who demanded special privilege and status for them. He liked to live well and enjoyed being a professor, but he never sought the mandarinate in his profession, a style which is rather well developed in the field of Chinese studies in the United States. Like De Tocqueville, he remained on the peripheries rather than seeking the center or the top. But he insisted on remaining in the center of the cosmological drama. His disenchantment came when he felt that fewer and fewer people saw that drama.

If he were alive today, he would ask: is China now, in the aftermath of the ping-pong breakthrough, *Chung-kuo* or *Chung-hua*? If the former alone, he would be saddened; he would be even more saddened by the general trend toward nationalism and protectionism now arising with the weakening of that skein of world relationships America created after World War II. That would mean the world is again moving toward *yung* and away from *t'i*. But he would have been gladdened by the new trend among many young Sinologists to begin looking at China as a model for ourselves. China's moves toward school decentralization would not have been a subject he would have written about, but he would have approved someone studying it, as opposed to another paper on power struggles within the politburo. And if China continued its deep concerns with schools and curricula, he would have seen that as a favorable sign for the return of *Chung-hua*. *Chung-hua* was what all his work was about.

THE HISTORIAN'S QUEST[1]

Angus McDonald, Jr.

Why do Americans study Chinese history?

In the past, most answers to this question have centered around one of two central themes. One asserts that China is far from the real interests of Western civilization and that its study serves as an exotic fillip, a proof that indeed we are capable of mastering any subject, no matter how arcane. Hence Sinology.

A second self-justification, growing in importance after the Second World War and the Liberation of China, asserted that China had a positive importance for the West and should be studied on the principle, "Know thy enemy." Hence Area Studies.

These answers are equally solipsistic in insisting on the centrality of the West, and they suggest important political implications. The Sinologists, by proclaiming the irrelevance of their study of China to any of the problems of the society in which they lived, implicitly gave support to the status quo. Dean Rusk knew more of relevance about China than these China specialists. The Area Studies approach to China helped provide intellectual justification for the American empire in the Pacific. It generally accepted the world view of the cold warriors, an updated "white man's burden" doctrine proclaiming American responsibility for understanding (through "free-value" scholarship) the nature of Asian society, revolution, and Communism so as best to combat these threats.

Editors Note: This is a revised version of an essay which was published in Volume II, No. 3 of *The Bulletin of Concerned Asian Scholars* (1970). We are grateful to the editors of the *Bulletin* for permitting us to include it in this volume.

1. This essay was originally written for Raymond Sontag's seminar on historiography (History 283) at Berkeley, and appeared in the *Bulletin of Concerned Asian Scholars*, II, 3 (1970). For reasons of space parts of the essay that duplicate discussions by other contributors to this collection have been deleted and the seams tucked under by limited revisions. The bulk of the essay is as it originally appeared.

Samuel P. Huntington's well-know justification of the airborne decimation of the Vietnamese countryside as contributing to "urbanization" and hence to "modernization" is but one barbarism of this school.

There is a third, more sophisticated, response to the question that deserves to be taken seriously by scholars interested in both China and the West. As exemplified in the work of many of our mentors and colleagues, it reflects a belief that the Chinese experience, like that of any other people, is an integral part of the human experience and should be understood for what we can learn about the human condition.

One of the foremost spokesmen for this view of China studies was Joseph Levenson, historian of "the mind of modern China," whose work was cut short at the age of forty-eight when the raging Russian River overturned his canoe on Easter Sunday, 1969.

Few men are missed at their passing for more than one or two reasons, but Levenson was mourned by many. He was a warm, humane friend to some, a witty conversationalist, a devoted religious Jew, and a highly respected scholar and teacher. Publicly he aspired to no political influence. What was Levenson doing? Why did he study China?

In the last year of his life he attempted to describe his initial attraction to the field:

> The attraction of Chinese history was its distinctiveness. In studying something about which little was known, there was the promise of no boredom. There was no attraction in becoming involved in a very developed field like American history, where one had to fit himself into an environment of nasty arguments over minor details or over issues of revisionism. . . . Neither history nor my temperament are congenial to such a task. In Chinese history there were big open spaces and the promise of a road that went the long way home. I suppose this involves an appreciation of amateurism.[2]

The modern mixed motivation: on the one hand a professional interest in a new field, new at least to American universities and Western minds, a field yet unencumbered by the mines of past and present battles; and on the other, the "long road home," the mind of China as an approach to the mind of the West. The study of Liang Ch'i-ch'ao highlighted the desperate struggle of Chinese

2. Quoted in Robin Radin, "Joseph R. Levenson: Dimensions of an Historian," manuscript paper for a Berkeley historiography seminar, Fall 1968.

intellectuals to find a means of preserving their great heritage—a source of personal identity as Chinese—while at the same time trying to enter the modern world, to restore to China something approaching its former confidence. The problem of malaise Levenson perceived there was not unique to the Chinese scene:

> The interest in China is an interest in the fact that the questions which confront China are more and more becoming the same questions which confront us. I do not deal with China as an area, but rather as a set of problems, problems which in a cosmopolitan world we all share. . . . On a psychological level there is a comparability between the Chinese and Jewish experience; both are parts outside the main line of Western historical tradition, the European tradition; both are being carried into cosmopolitanism.[3]

Empathizing with the Chinese intellectuals wrenched into a cosmopolitanism whose main roots are European, Levenson felt a special competence to undertake the dual task implied by the twin metaphors of "open spaces" and "the long road home": to impose on the disorder and turmoil of modern Chinese intellectual history an understanding derived from *Western* insights into the nature of man and the historical experience, to create a "paradigm" synthesizing the "facts" of that history—and by doing so, to bring China "into the universal world of discourse," bring it home into the body of knowledge to which we look when we investigate the past of man and consider his future.

Levenson's empathy with the Chinese intellectuals whom he studied was not simply that of a sensitive European or American scholar for whom cosmopolitanism is emotionally assumed. Levenson's empathy was a Jewish one. If malaise is a universal state, it has different roots in different groups. The Jew constantly faces the choice between clinging to the traditions of his ethnic past, thus preserving his cultural identity, or adopting some or all of the history and identity of the country in which he is "in exile," thus going native and easing his sense of exile. For the Jewish intellectual confronted by the march of modernity and rationality, the problem is accentuated by the *traditional* nature of the Jewish culture, preserved and developed over two thousand years by a collective act of will on the part of a people which refuses to

3. Ibid.

disappear. This traditional-ness appears provincial and narrow even to many Jews, but the alternatives imply giving up Jewish history — assimilating.

In the last part of his trilogy, Levenson cited Richard McKeon's essay on Maimonides: "To us today, the sense of tradition is not strong, not so much because we have no tradition, but because we have mixed so many traditions."[4] The problem was to choose an identity with which one could live, as a Jew, an American, and a man. One is reminded of Nietzsche — indeed Levenson the Jew shows strongly the influence of Nietzsche the atheist:

> "I have got lost; I am everything that has got lost," sighs modern man. *This* modernity was our sickness: lazy peace, cowardly compromise, the whole virtuous uncleanliness of the modern Yes and No. This tolerance and languor of the heart, which "forgives" all because it "understands" all is *sirocco* for us. Rather live in the ice than among the modern virtues and other south winds. (*The Anti-Christ*)

The question for the Jew is how to deal with the tension between his intellectual, cosmopolitan world views which make him relevant to the ongoing community in which he lives, on the one hand, and his cultural identity as a Jew descended from Jews for whom *to be* is to *will to be*.

The Chinese are comparable but not analogous to the Jews. Levenson distinguished comparison from analogy. Comparison implies a limited juxtaposition of characteristics, while analogy involves a much wider range of similarity. One of Levenson's most interesting methods throughout *Confucian China and Its Modern Fate,* the trilogy, was to isolate comparable entities, then probe them for failure in analogy, throwing light not only on the Chinese case from the perspective of the West, but by reflection upon the West itself.[5] It is worth adopting this method to investigate the limits of the Jew-Han analogy. To what extent did his synthesis of modern Chinese intellectual history help bring China into a "universal world of discourse"? How far did Levenson travel on the long road home?

4. Joseph R. Levenson, *Confucian China and Its Modern Fate* University of California Press, (Berkeley: 1965), vol. III, p. 123.

5. Joseph R. Levenson, "The Genesis of *Confucian China and Its Modern Fate,*" in *The Historian's Workshop*, ed. Perry Curtis (New York, KMOPG 1970).

INTELLECTUAL HISTORY

Levenson chose the particular thread of intellectual history to follow in his peregrinations through Chinese history, recognizing its limitations.

> Intellectual history, after all, is only a type of history men write, only a method, not an end. Out there, in the history men make, the web is never rent, and intellectual, political, economic, and cultural threads are interwoven. In the specialized approach one tampers with the unity of nature, but the end is to restore the whole in comprehensible form.[6]

He defined his pursuit in dialectic fashion:

> Intellectual history is made by tension between an idea as thought at a particular time and place, by a particular person who derives it from what he can see in the objective world around him, and the idea in a hypothetically abstract, logical state.[7]

The system of thought may appear to be absurd or illogical, but the historian concerned with process and change over time takes *thought* as a secondary phenomenon—a datum—and concerns himself primarily with *thinking*, a psychological act inseparable from context and transformation.

Levenson employed this distinction in his dissertation and first book, *Liang Ch'i-ch'ao and the Mind of Modern China*, but he spoke of it most clearly only later, using Collingwood's terms:

> There is a postulate that states that a body of knowledge consists not only of "propositions," "statements," or "judgments," . . . but of these together with the questions they are meant to answer. . . . A change, then, behind an idea, like a change in the alternatives beside it, imposes change on the persisting positive content of the idea itself.[8]

The ideas of intellectual context, "history" and "value," the search for comparability, and other Levensonian tools were not the product of *Chinese* history, but of a mind trained in Western methods and traditions, a cosmopolitan American Jewish intellectual's way of speaking about Chinese intellectuals. As tools or

6. Ibid. See also Introduction to the 1968 edition of *Confucian China*.
7. Joseph R. Levenson, *Liang Ch'i-ch'ao and the Mind of Modern China* (Cambridge: 1965 edition, Harvard University Press) p. 153.
8. Levenson, *Confucian China,* vol. I, p. xxvii.

categories they mean little to historians of China trained in Chinese historiography, or to Western historians of China trained to the factual, literal narrative.[9] For Levenson the "facts are not the end of study—they are what is left in a good history book (and in good historical minds) as the visible landmarks in a world of discourse."[10] One leaves the documents and begins to ask larger questions. The fundamental question is not how to know history, but again and always, *Why*? What is the significance?

This problem consciousness is central to good historical work. But the carving out of a limited group for discussion, a small elite of intellectuals who share a common problematic, who are asking the same general range of questions, does mean certain problems. Intellectual history becomes a partial, narrow approach to the sweep of Chinese history, and the historical synthesis formulated in intellectual terms leaves out vast stretches of the "open spaces" from consideration. Levenson's approach to understanding the coming of Communism to China is convincing within its context, for it is logical and symmetrical that Chinese intellectuals seeking to make their country relevant to the modern world of the nation-state and rejecting mere recapitulation of Western modernization should take from the West the West's most radical critique of itself. But as an etiology of the Chinese revolution, that is not enough.

Communism's coming cannot be abstracted from the social and political context without distortion. However much it is a *logical* consequence of the search for a resolution of the history/value dilemma, it is not a *necessary* consequence. A raft of variables intervene between the pattern and the practice. The nature of Western imperialism did change between the Opium War in 1840 and the success of the Red Army more than a century later, but Levenson does not fully consider the change. By slighting social problems for emphasis on the rhythm and logic of intellectual change, the synthesis is restricted; but through the use of tools formulated during the writing of *Liang Ch'i-ch'ao* Levenson was able in his trilogy to deal with motivation, anguish, and the

9. Arthur Hummel, a historian trained in the Rankean school for whom the facts speak for themselves or with only minimal annotation or interpretation, roasted *Liang Ch'i-ch'ao* in a *JAS* review that almost cost the young Levenson his Berkeley position: "One cannot penetrate another's thought unless in some measure it becomes one's one thought," he wrote. "The book can hardly be taken as a work of objective historical scholarship."

10. Manuscript notes for Levenson's historiography seminar (History 283) at Berkeley, "History as Art and Science." Professor Frederic Wakeman very graciously allowed me to examine these and certain other manuscripts in his possession.

irrational in modern Chinese history. By posing the problem in terms of the "history/value" dilemma of intellectuals, Levenson supplied a base line, a trail through the uncharted to which others can refer.

His simplified paradigm can become a *lapis philosophicus* for a wide-ranging inquiry into the course of *a* Chinese malaise, making it understandable to Western readers because it excludes so much. It is not merely a case of limited energy or recalcitrant sources: *Confucian China and Its Modern Fate* was possible to write because it is an exercise in discourse, withdrawn somewhat from the sources, with fugue-like variations on the central theme of history and value (e.g., objective/subjective, traditional/modern, rational/emotional, etc.). Despite criticisms of what his accomplishment was not, Levenson's treatment of the dynamics of the irrational may be compared without prejudice to Weber's conjoining of the "Protestant Ethic" and the rise of capitalism in the West, a needed signpost in a complex field.

COSMOPOLITANISM AND "THE LONG ROAD HOME"

In the trilogy that makes up *Confucian China and Its Modern Fate,* Levenson's aim was to trace the way in which older organizations of ideas and concepts were continually revised and reversed as the driving sense of alienation forced continuing innovation. His goal was not to isolate the "essence" of China (illusive sprite), but to discover how the Chinese variant of Communism sits comfortably upon the corpse of Confucius. But the resultant synthesis was only a part of the ambition. Levenson came to China in part to find the long road home, to discover the ties that bound the world of malaise. He had charted a path, established signposts, but with the completion of the first trilogy he envisioned a second that would push the path on toward its beginning: *Provincialism and Cosmopolitanism: Chinese History and the Meaning of "Modern Times."*

The runoff from one of the heaviest Sierra snows in memory drowned that dream, but it was not entirely unrealized, albeit in sketches and articles rather than full-bodied books.[11] These do not

11. "The Province, the Nation and the World: The Problem of Chinese Identity," in *Approaches to Modern Chinese History,* eds. A. Feuerwerker et al. (Berkeley: University of California Press, 1967); "The Past and Future of Nationalism in China," *Survey,* No. 67 (April 1968); "Communist China in Time and Space: Roots and Rootlessness," *The China*

constitute a radical break from the lines laid down in the completed trilogy save in the temporal sense that they are concerned with Nationalist and Communist China rather than with late traditional times. They are a logical extension of Levenson's already established tendency to withdraw ever further from the world of concrete into the world of discourse, his course, the long road home.

It is just this lack of a radical break that is the source of my problems with these essays. His search for the meaning of Chinese identity in the modern world involved an assumption which I think should be examined more closely.

The world is becoming cosmopolitan, and the historian makes a contribution to the cosmopolitanization of the world when he casts wide his toils, making over all lands until, in the mind, they are relevant to one another. This is not objective description, which is "merely bland"; the historian's objectivity is not an escape from the issues of his own culture.[12] The historian's task is, in an important sense, to make over his own epoch, to make history not only as he contemplates the past, but as he communicates with the present and molds the minds that make the future.

But there is a hurdle of no mean measure. Cosmopolitan world culture will not be made through amalgamation, by conscious picking and choosing as though by cultural selection boards taking the best from East and West. Nor will it be made through some universal paradigm, Marxist, Toynbeean, or any other, which would make the cultural destinations of nations essentially the same. This Levenson knows and says.[13] But the historian, making his own history, must make choices and judgments: "this" is part of the coming cosmopolitan world, "that" is not. It was this problem that Levenson was wrestling with in his articles on cosmopolitanism: where must the historian stop being a relativist?

He took his stand this side of the Cultural Revolution, on the side of cultural heroes such as Shaw, Pirandello, and Ibsen. To these men, among others, he thought, China would return after the madness of the Cultural Revolution. He sided with the professionals, the modern men and specialists upon whom the

---

Quarterly, No. 39 (1969); see also the three lectures collected under the title *Revolution and Cosmopolitanism: The Western Stage and the Chinese Stages* (Berkeley: University of California Press, 1971).

12. Manuscript notes for History 283.
13. Levenson, "Genesis."

waves of the Cultural Revolution beat most severely. "Cosmopolitanism, that is, was out. Sophistication, nuance were out. The Cultural Revolution had a provincial cultural spirit."[14] The expert was denied his international community, made to become "red and expert" with emphasis on the red: the nationalist marching in the ranks of the Chinese people. According to Levenson, this showed the desperation of the masters of ideology, their fear that, unless mastered, science would pull important elements away from the authority of Mao and Maoism. He deemed this isolation from the world and its specialized ways a passing thing. Cosmopolitanism is the rising tide, and one way or another China will join the world again.[15]

One of the ambiguities of history writing is that the personal vision is guided by objective parameters: the historian "knows the outcome." He selects from among myriad details the lines and pieces which help develop an understandable pattern "explaining" how a certain end came about. Levenson's dialectical mind provided him with a powerful set of tools for studying the malaise underlying Confucian China's modern fate, but the new dialectic (cosmopolitanism/provincialism) for an epoch the outcome of which is far from certain seems to me unconvincing for several reasons. And these lead us back to the problem of politics and scholarship.

In the first place there is an implicit assumption that, for the West and for the world, the core content of cosmopolitan culture is already determined and that—ultimately—it is a good. Science and art (and the universal history toward which Levenson was contributing), the "best that has been thought and known, broaden and refine the resources of the human spirit."[16] Yet the ultimate in political barbarism grew from the core of Europe. We know that some of the men who devised and administered Auschwitz had been taught to read Shakespeare and Goethe—and that they continued to do so. They listened to Bach and Brahms in the evening shadows, and played Beethoven over the camp loudspeakers. Even more damning, we know that to say that these men did not understand what they read or heard is sheerest cant.

Levenson deprecated the collectivism of the Cultural Revolution as nativist, a backward step on the trail toward universal history.

14. Levenson, "The Past and Future of Nationalism."
15. Levenson, "Communist China in Time."
16. Levenson, *Confucian China*, vol. I, p. 25.

In the work completed just before his death, he failed to consider seriously enough the probability that China is no longer culturally trying to catch up with the West; he overlooked the likelihood that Chinese collectivism is designed in part to insulate the Chinese future from the undeniable horrors of the Western past, a past inseparable from the Western cultural giants who are the core of "cosmopolitanism." He does not take seriously enough Chinese rhetoric about capitalism and imperialism—possibly because the Jewish experience offers little that is comparable.[17]

Moreover, in his search for a transcendent cosmopolitanism, I think we see him working to subsume the controversy in the world he saw about him under an irenic, overarching cultural consensus. By positing the present in the terms he used, he was implicitly denying the centrality of struggle and tension—the very ideas which figure so prominently in his earlier work! He seemed to be making both "history" and "value" intellectual. If both were intellectual, if both were subject to rationality, then mind meeting mind through the medium of the printed page could cope, could resolve the problems of identity and relevance. Politics had no place.

JEW AND EXPERT

It should be clear by this time that I think Levenson's reading of Chinese history in the trilogy (within its limits) is a brilliant and sensitive piece of scholarship, a work of art full of sparks among the difficulties, funny and sad and full. Just as intellectual history may be seen to be propelled by a contradiction between "history" and "value," so art, the best of it in the timeless sense, can be seen as a resolution of the demands of the emotion and the intellect.[18] There is precisely this life in the trilogy, and careful Western readers can find throughout it intimations of the Western problematic—for at summits the "long road home" presents striking vistas of malaise and other conditions of men. It should also be clear that many of those who came close to him, including many of his graduate students, were deeply inspired by the man, by his humanity and grace as a human being and as a guide in

17. See also John G. Gurley, "Capitalist and Maoist Economic Development," in *America's Asia*, eds. Mark Selden and Edward Friedman, (New York, Vintage 1970).

18. See also George Steiner, *Language and Silence: Essays on Literature, Language, and the Inhuman* (New York, Atheneum 1967).

their profession. It is because he was and remains so important, because he bears up so well under searching scrutiny, that it is worthwhile to press on with the argument.

Joseph Levenson was not a teacher of art, nor of humane-ness (save by example). He could not teach the problematic he set for himself in his art. He had to teach the "road," for that was his profession and in the world in which he lived an historian of China either worked for the government or taught in the university. It is significant that the lectures he gave were legendary for their brilliance and wit, but seldom attracted the large audience a major university could afford. Many Chinese students at Berkeley, with an emotional commitment to their past, found his interpretation of Chinese history meaningless. And many American students found it far from their concerns, however enlivened by cross-cultural analogy.

As a professor of Chinese history in an American university, Levenson was obedient to the specialists of the nineteenth century. Wittily he taught his "road"; with insight he explored the labyrinths of Chinese history. Drawn to the generalists of the Enlightenment, still he found himself confined by the dictates of professionalism, by the example of men who leave their emotion home with their half-finished morning coffee. He loved the nonspecialized human contact and tried to reach across the barriers between teacher and student. He disliked the narrow, technical monographs many of his graduate students felt called upon to write (his attempts to encourage wider horizons met with limited success). The role of professional, of professor, means that one must keep one's distance, avoid involvement—or delay it until one's canons of judgement have been satisfied and the student is raised through examination to colleague. He did not take easily to the role. He sought valiantly to bridge the gap by being resolutely responsive to humanness in others, by being a teacher open to his students.

But in the end it was by being a Jew, ethnically drawn to a particular variety of people outside his profession and sharing with them something that neither the nineteenth century nor the twentiety century could entirely eclipse. It was in religious Jewishness that Joseph Levenson the scholar willed the coexistence of his humanity and his profession and found the resources to combat the limitations of the university. He was a Jew and expert—the one informing the other and, I think, making of a scholar an artist, of a professor a man. He was a better Jew for his intellectual interests, and a better teacher and scholar for his emotional commitment to Jewishness.

It was in part the incompleteness of this cross-fertilization that prevented Levenson from seeing the parallel between his views and Mao Tse-tung's notion of Red and Expert. The malaise of the modern world is in part the outgrowth of a split between what is valued professionally and what forms the stuff of one's identity. The bonds of professional community, of specialists engaged in similar work, must not be underestimated. For those of us who are descendants of men who were barbarians in the days of Homer, Plato, and Jesus, extra-ethnic ties may be the only ones which stretch out beyond our immediate neighborhood. But for Jew and Han, whose ethnic heritage is also a cultural heritage, the problem of commitment to that heritage becomes important. Among the forms such commitment can take for the Jew is reformed religiosity. Among those for the Han is study of the thought of Mao Tse-tung.

Here is where the analogy with Han-ness breaks down for the Jew. In China—historically—many members of the intellectual elite reconciled the split between "history" and "value" through a commitment to Communism. But in the West a Jew, if he is to remain a Jew *and* a modern man (if he is to come to terms with both his "history" and his "value"), is irrevocably committed to at least two traditions, two cultures. He cannot simply put his past into a "museum" (at least not outside Israel), where it can be significant for his identity but not threatening to his "relevance." To do so means assimilation. The Jew must have a role in the modern world, but at the same time must hang back from it if he is to maintain his identity intact.

Liang Ch'i-chi'ao's nativism became anachronistic in the 1920s as a younger generation of Chinese intellectuals progressed toward resolving the dichotomy between past and present. But Joseph Levenson's explicit choice of religious Jewishness—comparable with Liang's nativism—is his only alternative to surrendering himself to his academic role and accepting the malaise of the professional twentieth century. By being both a Jew and and teacher he seems to have found some (imperfect) resolution: an eclectic patching job, personally satisfying as long as it is not carefully examined. The synthesis that the Chinese had found in the thought of Mao (if, indeed, such a dynamic and struggle-centered thought can be termed "synthesis") was beyond him as a Jew in exile. He could not redefine his present, nor reshape the community in which he lived.

As I have suggested, Levenson's work at this time can be seen as a denial of politics, subsuming political controversy. For those who have taken to the streets, Vietnam is not merely an intellectual issue, not one that can be resolved outside the political sphere. It is an emotional issue. For scholars who know and value the people of Asia as human beings, the pain is particularly intense, for the intellect informs emotions. Joseph Levenson knew and valued Asian peoples. He did feel pain. He did sign petitions. But because he could find his primary identity in his Jewishness, he did not feel it personally necessary (as so many of his students and friends did) to attempt to rectify an identity-giving American "history" gone mad by public, sustained political action.

If I am correct in my analysis, it should be clear that his reasons for withdrawal cannot be shared by his less religious colleagues and students, men and women who find their "history" and identity not in an organic, ethnic heritage, but as *Americans*. Americans are a heterogeneous race, bound by neither blood nor religion but by an emotional (not rational!) belief in the ultimate goodness of their community and the justness of its laws and institutions. Vietnam and the institutionalized idiocy the war symbolizes rack this belief and strain it beyond existing means of reconciliation.

Joseph Levenson worked hard to reconcile and relate his professional and personal lives. At his best, in the trilogy where emotional empathy and probing intellect pulled together, his scholarship became art, changing the way we see China and our perceptions of ourselves. Even when his work fell short in the later essays, he was as challenging and fascinating for the way he arranged his life as for the way his mind worked. He recognized and coped with the professional dilemma, he made the sacrifices and used the opportunity. If his problematic was different from that many of us have, it was not a narrow task that he undertook nor a constricted ambition that led him on. In his most painstaking and abstruse scholarship he sought signs of the whole and labored to integrate. His students were and continue to be inspired by the man, but their approach to the human condition follows other ways.

PART TWO

Levenson as Historiographer

JOSEPH LEVENSON'S APPROACH TO HISTORY

Lyman P. Van Slyke

Assemble, first, all casual bits and scraps
That may shake down into a world perhaps;
. . . .
Nice contradiction between fact and fact
Will make the whole read human and exact.
Robert Graves

You are not the same people who left that station
Or who will arrive at any terminus.
T.S. Eliot

In the late 1950s, Robert Frost spoke at Berkeley's Greek Theatre. Following a rambling address, interspersed with his poetry, someone asked him to explain the overall pattern of his work. With a sly ingenuousness, Frost disclaimed the existence of any such formal pattern: "I just let things constellate." With a different tone of voice, and different purposes, Joseph Levenson made a similar statement when he described his trilogy, *Confucian China and Its Modern Fate*, as "a 'web' book, not a 'thread' book." He had earlier written of its first volume, "Although its themes may seem separate and miscellaneous at first, and the chronological line irregular, this book deals with one continuous process of change."[1] So also with the rest of his work: the whole was more

1. The first statement will be found in "The Genesis of *Confucian China and Its Modern Fate*, in *The Historian's Workshop*, ed. Perry Curtis (New York: Knopf, 1970), p. 279. For details of this and all subsequent references, see the Bibliography in Appendix B. The second is taken from *Confucian China and Its Modern Fate: A Trilogy* (Berkeley: University of California Press, 1968), vol. I, p. vii.

than the sum of its parts. His writings were the visible nodes of an implicitly patterned sense of history, a pattern in constant process, in process toward (we sense, but cannot fully describe) both a new kind of world history and an intensely personal statement of his relationship to the world of that history.

Joseph Levenson was primarily an essayist, not a writer of narrative history or monographs. One does not go to him to find out about 1911 and all that. Indeed, he took for granted a considerable knowledge of the facts, without which (and sometimes even with which) the reader is quickly in trouble. As essayist, Levenson was prolific but succinct. Few items in his lengthy bibliography run longer than forty pages, while most are very much shorter.[2] He chose those subjects in which he could see historical significance (here the accent can fall on either word); evidence was adduced to illustrate the argument, not amassed to prove it.

The difficulty of commenting on such "separate and miscellaneous" essays is compounded by the extraordinary degree to which Levenson's written style and, in less concentrated form, his spoken style, are essential to his sense of history. His language is close and full of surprises. He compressed to essentials, but essence is complex, not simple, and hence every word is charged—sometimes overcharged—with meaning, nuance, and play. This is why, I think, so many of us feel uncomfortable in trying to explain some thought or idea from his work. Vibrant and rich in his language and in our minds, the paraphrase sounds flaccid and trite. Since we cannot express the thought as he did, we rob it of that fully nuanced tension with which he invested it, and it comes out, "history and value is like mine and true." In trying for high fidelity, we risk sounding like a bad recording. A Levensonian "school" is a contradiction in terms.

A teacher without a school. What lessons, then, that his students can use? Metaphor-as-message doesn't train one to "do" history as he did it. But his use of metaphor, both sustained (the museum, the stage, culture-as-language) and casual, reaffirmed the validity of historical metaphor at a moment when it badly needed help. His example, his examples, might lead one to see that even the most objective and articulated social science model is really also a

2. His first book, on Liang Ch'i-ch'ao, is only a partial exception to this statement. The trilogy, of course, is a collection of essays.

kind of metaphor. Metaphor and model alike are ways of interpreting aspects of reality, but neither is reality itself:

> "Out there," in the history men make, the web is never rent, and intellectual, social, political, economic, cultural threads are interwoven. In the specialized approach, one tampers with the unity of nature; but the end is to restore the whole in comprehensible form.[3]

Levenson's use of context is as tricky a lesson as his use of metaphor. The history of men thinking (rather than the history of ideas per se) immediately suggests context: who is doing the thinking, what are they thinking about, and why? For Levenson, an idea was an answer to a question posed by other men or by an historical situation. Each answer is then a choice among possible answers, so that what is *not* said, what is denied, constitutes part of the meaning of what *is* said, affirmed. When alternatives change, the same idea is no longer the same, just as when the question changes, the same answer takes on a different meaning. There is a double power in this conception. It provides a sure link between the specific and the general, the individual and all those other people, because the latter is part of the significance of the former. Moreover, the conception points to a different way of understanding change through time—a thing transformed as its context changes, even though it appears not to change in itself.

Making use of this conception is the tricky part. If one looks only at what a thing is (e.g., what a thinker said), then the investigation is logically finite. But if the thing is also defined by what it is not, by what lies outside it, then the definition may potentially contain everything else. The problem lies in how to explore what the thing is *relatively* not, what questions elicited this particular answer.

If metaphor and context may be taken, for the moment, to represent Levenson's "methodology," then his most compelling work was less the result of exhaustive, inductive research than of broad reading, heuristic insight, and painstaking exploration of implications. This was not, and could not be, an explicit methodology, communicable in any direct way to his students or his readers. Instead, in the way he worked, Levenson responsibly exemplified what we all too often avoid in the pursuit of our sober craft: to let the mind range and play, to follow the feeling, and to use one's intuition. For Levenson, discipline was necessary, but

3. Levenson, "Genesis," p. 285.

"the discipline" was never sufficient. The result was not the re-creation of the past, but its re-definition on a different level of meaning.

Levenson's intellectual development was in the direction of ever broader themes and concerns. I feel that he was also moving toward increasingly direct and full engagement with the history he was writing. "The history of men thinking" was, in his hands, a marvelously suggestive approach. But his early work, for all its brilliance and genuine insight, comes off the page a little cold and external: Liang Ch'i-ch'ao (surrogate for the mind of modern China) running the intellectual obstacle course Levenson had designed,[4] while the tension between "history" and "value" seemed a problem for Chinese rather than American intellectuals. The history of men feeling did not get independent treatment or equal time. Although Levenson later declared that "thinking was a psychological act,"[5] he eschewed any systematic psychological consideration of his subjects—and we may well be grateful for the absense of facile armchair psychoanalysis, especially of the cross-cultural variety. Yet in the "history/value" formulation, Levenson's early work seems to assume an almost one-to-one correspondence between logical inconsistency and emotional distress. That the two are somehow related is not to be doubted, but if this approach is pushed very rigorously, it can become itself a form of psychological reductionism, from the head down, as it were, rather than from the psyche up. One source (there are others) of reductionism in either direction, I believe, may stem from a less than complete engagement of the scholar's total personality with the subjects he is treating.

Even early, Levenson was less detached than most, and the detachment diminished further with time. Later, he argued beyond the call of his duties as a professional historian for the recognition that the history men write about the past is part of the history they make in the present:

> And Chinese history, then, should be studied because—without making the same designs—it can be seen to make sense in the same

4. In those days, some of Levenson's students facetiously referred to him as an "intellectual determinist."

5. Levenson, "Genesis," p. 285. In his Preface to the 1959 reprint of the Liang book, Levenson wrote: "But this work is not, in its ends, a psychological study of Liang. One should see in it rather a search for news about the 'mind of modern China.'" Yet also, "My effort as historian, after giving the record of what he did, is to find out what wracked him as he did it."

> world of discourse in which we try to make sense of the West. If we can make this kind of sense, perhaps we help to make this kind of world. The act of writing history can be an historic act itself.[6]

Just a little earlier, he had made the case for the moral integrity of relativism:

> In history, relativism is all. But history is not all. . . . The relativism which gives the past its due can really be arrived at only by men who give the present its due. Recognition of the historical relativity of one's own standards is not the same as abdication of standards, nor need it be conducive to that. The aim is to be truthful (to aim at truth), even if the truth cannot be known.
>
> Relativism, then, is essential for historical understanding, but it is a relativism which depends on, not banishes a contemporary acceptance of norms. If it seems merely wilful paradox, a violation of rationality, to suggest that it is proper to be absolutist in order to be properly relativist, that may be because *rationalism is not sufficient for historical knowledge.*[7]

With these two propositions, Levenson is saying much and implying more. The implication depends on the fact that historical observation (like all observation) takes place *at* and *within* the observer; the thing perceived may be out there somewhere, but our perception of it, and our assignment of meaning to it, is always and inevitably internal. "Rationalism is not sufficient for historical knowledge" because the observer is not a wholly rational being, and "this kind of world" is at least as subjective as it is objective. As an ideal, then—perhaps only partially attainable—the exploration of the past and the exploration of oneself are a single continuous, unbroken process. With appropriate substitutions, the former statement, above, might read, "And Liang Ch'i-ch'ao, then, should be studied because—without making the same design—he can be seen to make sense in the same world of discourse in which I try to make sense of myself."

In his earlier work, most of the questions Levenson asked, and most of the metaphors he employed, were energized by a sense of change through time. He pursued this theme through the tension between history and value, through the passage from traditional to traditionalistic and through the halls of museums where the past is enshrined as evidence of its cancelled claim upon the present.

6. Ibid., p. 284.
7. Levenson, *Confucian China*, vol. III, pp. 87-89; emphasis added.

Having begun with questions of time, however, Levenson gradually moved to questions of space. There was no sharp break, no abandonment of earlier concerns, but one nevertheless senses a clear shift in emphasis after the completion of the trilogy.

Beginning with materials published around 1967,[8] Levenson undertook the exploration of space which his own time did not permit him to finish. Provincialism, nationalism, cosmopolitanism, each with a keen sense of time, began to furnish the material on which he focused, not simply as ideas, but as cultural phenomena inevitably rooted to place. Once again, the presence of alternatives, what is included and what is excluded, is crucial. It is this which rendered the Confucian literati, self-sufficient and cosmopolitan within their *t'ien-hsia*, parochial in the Western-dominated modern world. Conversely, Levenson saw that for Chinese intellectuals to become cosmopolitan in Western terms (and, equally, on the West's terms) was to risk estrangement from China, to become men on the margin of cultures, irrelevant to both and truly part of neither.

Dogged insistence on traditional ways simply because they were traditional, and a worldliness which eroded the self-defining particularity of one's own cultural past were equally threatening, in Levenson's view, to the Chinese sense of self-identity. During the height of the Cultural Revolution, however, Levenson saw a double denial, in the name of revolutionary nationalism, of *both* the Chinese past and the non-Chinese world (the drastic narrowing of both time and space). He predicted, perhaps correctly, that it could not last.

Whether, at the start, Levenson's exploration of his own identity as both a Jew and a cosmopolitan intellectual suggested this aspect of his work, or vice versa, the two became fused around the central question of how a Chinese, a Jew, Levenson himself, could reconcile cultural particularity (without a narrow parochialism) with transcultural cosmopolitanism (without rootlessness, or that "spurious universalism" he abhorred).[9]

8. In particular, "The Province, the Nation, and the World: The Problem of Chinese Identity," in *Approaches to Modern Chinese History*, eds. A. Feuerwerker et al. (Berkeley: University of California Press, 1967), and the readings he edited under the title, *European Expansion and the Counter-Example of Asia, 1300-1600* (Englewood Cliffs, N.J.: Prentice-Hall, 1967). In the latter, the readings and his comments form together an extended dialogue between world views with explicitly geographical dimensions.

9. My qualifications for saying anything at all about Judaism and Jewish identity hover between minimal and nonexistent. When Levenson wrote, "To use a word from the K'ai-feng

In the museum metaphor, Levenson had said that in order to make history in the present, the Chinese first had to unmake the presentness of the past, to render it genuinely past so that it had no more claim on the present. Having done that (wondering during the Cultural Revolution how thoroughly they *had* done it), the Chinese could patronize the past in the museums of their land and mind. Thus the extent of Chinese confidence in the present could be measured by the extent of their relativist acceptance of the past.

But for the Jews, for himself, Levenson took the opposite tack. To relativize the Judaic past, into hellenism or into the Judeo-Christian tradition, led not the Jewish emancipation in the present, but to the ultimate annihilation of Jewish identity. In such relativist assimilation, "Jewish identity is watered down so that Jewish survival seems irrelevant."[10]

Levenson asserted that valid Judaism is a religion embodied in a nation and a culture. But with the diaspora, "nation" and "culture" took on symbolic qualities they were not originally meant to have. Nation in the sense of specific ground consecrated as the promised land was denied them, and Jewish culture became Jewish cultures, in many nations, none their own. Indeed, much anti-Semitism derived from the charge—with radical or antinationalist overtones—of Jewish cosmopolitanism and internationalism. Hence, Judaism, lacking both nation and culture in the conventional sense, survived in religion. Only through Judaism-as-religion can Jews survive as Jews:

> There is a *religious* imperative for Jews to live, and the religion has certainly informed "Jewish culture," but the culture is incidental, not the end. The imperative, the Sinai-born *mitzvah*, is the end, and if it [is] just assimilated to "culture" the Jews will be truly assimilated, dissolved, in our version of the final solution (like the classical Greeks)—the culture *as* an end, will come to an end.[11]

Thus Levenson was implying, among other things, that the form of the resolution of the tension between history and value (which,

---

dialect, a title like mine must seem a classic expression of *chutzpah*," my puzzled imagination at first summoned up a group of frightened philosophers. So much for qualifications. "The Humanistic Disciplines: Will Sinology Do?" *Journal of Asian Studies*, XXIII: 4 (August 1964), p. 507.

10. "The Choice of Jewish Identity," p. 98, below.

11. Quoted in Wakeman's Foreword to *Revolution and Cosmopolitanism: The Western Stage and the Chinese Stages* (Berkeley and Los Angeles: University of California Press, 1971), p. xix.

in the history of men thinking, constitutes identity) is different for Jews than for Chinese. However painful and halting their transition from *t'ien-hsia* culturalism to *kuo-chia* nationalism, the Chinese had their own familiar space and a culture rooted with great temporal depth into that soil. But Jews, to whom *t'ien-hsia* conceptions were antithetical, were historically denied *kuo-chia* as well.

Yet Levenson knew he could not rest with the religious imperative for Jews to live unless there was some absolute (not relative) justification in the imperative. Otherwise, so what? Beginning with the argument that the "Judeo-Christian" formulation "dismisses the authenticity of Judaism" by making it a now obsolescent prelude to Christianity, he goes on to assert the intrinsic authenticity of the Judaic message embodied by Jews embodying their religion. He went beyond claiming that this message is simply also true, another truth to be ranged alongside the equally valid truth of Christianity, for this merely shifted the ground of relativism—why choose this truth over that, except for the accident of birth? In asserting Judaism's independence from Christianity, he also asserts (a statement of personal faith, presented in general terms) for it a higher, absolute validity:

> It is the Jewish inference that man cannot identify with God in substance, but can imitate God (within limits) in action. The Christian inference . . . is that the imitation of Christ is not only ultimately impossible, but undesired. Christ is as he is, sinless, not really to inspire men to the same condition, but to compensate for the impossibility of such an inspiration. . . . A strong Judaism, one which does not give way to despair, is proof against the fatal Christian tension between life-denying assumptions (antinomian messianism) and inconsistent institutionalization, which make endemic an apocalyptic frenzy.[12]

The title of the essay is doubly significant. Choice, he argued, lay at the heart of "a strong [i.e., vigorous, vital] Judaism."

> The condition of life, the condition of choice, is not a curse, for the power to choose is the power to break the [Christian] conception of life itself, history after Eden, as an invincible curse for the Fall. To choose well in life is nothing less than to choose life itself. . . . And so Jews unequivocally toast, *l'hayyim.*[13]

12. "The Choice of Jewish Identity," pp. 192-193.
13. Ibid.

But the choice is also Levenson's, a personal, conscious act of both spirit and mind, a full engagement with his own history. He himself must choose to make that choice in order to affirm the particular identity which was for him the liberating necessary condition to an authentic cosmopolitanism. It is as though he needed this place to stand before he could truly make that leap. Thus, again to substitute, it is not "merely wilful paradox, a violation of rationality, to suggest that it is proper to be absolutist [Jewish] in order to be properly relativist [cosmopolitan], because rationalism is not sufficient to historical knowledge [self-knowledge]." Only with this liberating resolution, I think, could Levenson have written at the very end of "Genesis," "I am moving now, with a feeling of continuity of my own, to that cosmopolitan theme, the theme of a cosmopolitanism itself." Levenson's approach to history had become arrival, and he was ready for a new departure.

HISTORY AND CULTURE IN THE THOUGHT OF JOSEPH LEVENSON

Benjamin I. Schwartz

One is reluctant to discuss the thought of Joseph Levenson without the benefit of his scintillating repartee, for the fact is that a monologue on Joseph Levenson will never take the place of a dialogue with him. To me he was a dear friend and a constant source of intellectual inspiration. While my own dialogues with him were too few and far between, they were always a delight in themselves and a constant stimulus to fresh perspectives and new ways of viewing problems.

One would have liked to explore further with him the ultimate bases of his thought on many matters. There are questions on which I found that some of my own perspectives differ from his but there was never any doubt that Levenson related himself to matters of the utmost importance. First of all, in the face of the sterile and philistine behaviorist dogmas which dominate so much of the American academic scene, he remained convinced that what men think and feel about their situations are matters of transcendent importance. One of his grand themes was, of course, the interaction of the modern West with China in particular and with all non-Western cultures by implication. The theme of the growing and increasing interaction of all the cultures of mankind in modern times and the implications of this interaction will, I am certain, remain one of our most compelling and exciting intellectual concerns.

On an even deeper level, he related himself to what Frederic Wakeman in his perceptive Foreword to Levenson's posthumously published essays (*Revolution and Cosmopolitanism*) calls the problem of *meum* and *verum*, or the problem of the relationship of what is mine to what is true. Levenson himslf discussed this problem mainly in terms of the dichotomy of "history" versus "value," but the implications run deeper than the dichotomy. To state the problem crudely, we often cling to values, ideas, and ways of life not only or not even mainly because we find them true but because they are our patrimony, whether from family, nation, culture, or even a certain social background. We find them true because they are ours. Without this sense of a heritage of something larger than ourselves and yet something which is intimately ours, we feel spiritually naked and bereft of a sense of personal worth. Yet in coping with the problems of our own existence, we also desperately need the truth or what appears to be the truth even when the truth runs directly against the grain of what is ours and even when it comes to us from alien outside sources. Those who reject their patrimony outright are not necessarily purer bearers of the disembodied truth than those who cling to their patrimony since their whole outlook may be drastically conditioned and warped by the psychological fact of total rejection. Levenson pursued the agonizing dilemmas which arise from this problem throughout all his writings.

Furthermore, as Wakeman again points out, the profound seriousness of Levenson's intellectual concerns is proven by their existential nature. His interest in the relationship of modern Chinese to their cultural heritage was intimately tied to his undisguised concern with his own Jewish past. It is a concern which I share with him and which made me feel very close to him. Far from impairing his objectivity, it seems to me that it lent an honesty and authenticity to his thought which is not readily found in the writings of many supposedly objective scholars who vainly fancy that they are leaving themselves outside of their work.

The central importance of these Levensonian themes as well as others is beyond question. However, his untimely departure has made it extremely difficult to make any summary commentary on his work, for in the last few years his restless and searching mind was moving in new directions. Wakeman informs us in his Foreword that Levenson was contemplating a new trilogy on the subject of cosmopolitanism versus provincialism to which the posthumous essays were to serve as a kind of introduction. A reading of these essays indicates that Levenson was raising new questions which, it seems to me, were moving in a direction which enriched—and I would suggest—even modified some of his earlier formulations.

Running through Levenson's work one finds certain underlying premises concerning the nature of history and the nature of culture which I should like to consider in the following pages. In all of his writings these more abstract assumptions are, however, inextricably interwoven with more immediate concerns. As a practicing historian, Levenson never divorced abstract theory from his more concrete reflections on China's culture and its "modern fate." Thus in his biography of Liang Ch'i-ch'ao as well as in many of his essays one finds a particular preoccupation with what he once called the "breakthrough of modernity." He was convinced that certain developments in the recent history of Western civilization which we tend to place under the rubric of "modernization" would have an irresistible, irreversible, and all-embracing impact on China as well as on the whole non-Western world. The culture of modernity had, in his view, become the first truly universal culture of mankind. Other societies can survive as societies only (and he assumes the will to survive) if they assimilate essential features of modernity such as specialization of function and the "rationalization" of the world.

These essential features could not in his view be separated from the totality of modern Western culture in all its more vital aspects any more than the vital components of traditional Chinese culture could be separated from the integral totality of that culture. Hence the traditional culture, as a whole, would be displaced by modern culture as a whole. To be sure, fragments of the cultural whole of the past might survive but such fragments would be essentially lifeless and insignificant (except, perhaps, in the aesthetic realm).[1]

The mood of the moment is such that it might be tempting for some to score cheap polemical victories against Levenson by accusing him of Western hubris. Yet the fact remains that quite apart from the military, political, and economic impact of the West (good or evil) on the whole non-Western world, the political and intellectual elites of the non-Western world whether "radical" or "conservative" have not, in fact, resisted the enormous power of Western categories of thought. Thus, even if one rejects Levenson's contention that the search for Chinese roots for democracy,

1. Joseph R. Levenson, *Confucian China and Its Modern Fate* (Berkeley: University of California Press, 1965), vol. III, pp. 113-115.

socialism, and other "isms" is necessarily an inauthentic search for native "equivalents," the fact remains that, as of the present, the categories themselves are Western. While I shall myself raise questions concerning Levenson's totalistic view of the "impact of modernity," it is difficult to negate his view of its power and universality.

What is more, Levenson was acutely conscious of the agonizing dilemmas created by this displacement of cultures. To realize that the survival of one's nation-society required a new alien "truth" which would negate the values of the past which were one's own, was to experience an enormous spiritual loss. While Levenson often seemed to deal with this predicament in an ironic vein, his essential pathos was that of compassion.

In much of what he wrote, his attention was directed to that form of "traditionalistic" thought in modern China which sustained national pride by insisting that the Chinese culture of the past still contained value in an entirely new cultural historic epoch. In doing so, it seems to me that he did indeed reveal the "inauthenticity" of much modern Chinese praise of the past. It is quite true that much modern Chinese nationalistic neotraditionalism appeals to "essentially romantic arguments from national essence," and that many of the efforts to find equivalents in the Chinese past of Western ideas and values are not motivated by a spirit of honest inquiry. Yet is this the whole story? Must all claims to find continuities with the past (whether good or bad) in a "modern," "revolutionary" China be dismissed on a priori theoretical grounds? Must all claims by modern Chinese to find present truth and value within the heritage of the past be attributed to motives of national pride? In order to answer these questions we must again turn to Levenson's larger theoretical views of the nature of history and culture, and it is precisely these views that I would have liked to explore further with him.

Was Joseph Levenson an absolute or true historicist? We live in an age in which most men seem committed to the kind of conditional "progressive" historicism which we have inherited from the last century. Many of us tend to think of values and problems as "functions of" a larger "historical process" moving inexorably forward in time. Expressions such as "so-and-so is out of date" or "keeping up with the times" have entered into the very fabric of common everyday speech. What they seem to imply, however, is not simply the proposition that the movement of time determines value but also the notion of drawing ever closer to the full attainment of certain transtemporal value goals such as liberty, equality, material comfort, or other values. To the extent that the values themselves remain constant, they are outside and beyond history. The absolute historicist can have no such directional view. All values, all problems, all institutions, all "mentalities" and patterns of behavior are strictly embedded in their moment of time. How one defines a moment or epoch of time is, of course, one of the murkier aspects of absolute historicism. It may be nothing less than the "Middle Ages" or nothing more than the "decade of the sixties," but however defined, no important social, cultural, or ethical phenomenon can transcend "its day." An absolute historicism is not a whit more favorable to the idea of progress than it is to any suggestion that universal, metahistorical human values have been striven toward or achieved in the past. Not only is the past passé, but values of the present and future will also soon be passé. By the same token, the believer in "progressive" history, whatever pose of historical relativism he may adopt, can never wholly escape the posture of judgment vis-à-vis the past. Thus, if equality is an absolute human good, the ages based on ethical systems which did not particularly value equality are not only past but also inferior. We may understand and forgive their inferiority, but the element of judgment is never absent.

There are many passages in Levenson's writings (particularly in his essay "Theory and History")[2] which suggest an absolute unconditional historicism, as when he speaks of "the confusion one fosters when one judges other times by his own criteria without acknowledging that he himself, not the culminator of history but the latest comer, has only what his subjects have—ideas, aesthetics, morality that may be reasonable, pleasing, commendable in his own day and age but not surely rational, beautiful, or mandatory as transhistorical absolutes. No one has the norm of norms."[3] Thus those who regard their own values as absolutes simply treat their own times as timeless. This would seem to imply that even though the values of modernity may become universal in the sense that they have come to embrace all mankind, they may be just as timebound as the values of the past. Levenson was acutely conscious of the fact that to absolutize the values of the present was

2. Ibid., 85-109.
3. Ibid., p. 87.

to give the category of values itself a transhistorical status. It was to open the door to what he chose to call "Platonic" antihistoricism.

To the extent that Levenson did commit himself to absolute historicism, he was deeply concerned with the ethical implications of this view. In response to Nietzsche's observation that to understand the values of all times and places in a historicist-relativist way is to subvert the possibility of any value commitment for oneself, he maintains that it is only by having convictions of one's own, only by "taking one's own day seriously," that one can understand the convictions and moral commitment of men in the past even though the content of their convictions belongs irrevocably to another age.

One of the implications of historicism is a kind of organicism or holism in treating succeeding "moments" of history. Within a given moment of time, all aspects of culture are organically related to each other. Thus while "medieval" society and "modern" society are assumed to be radically discontinuous, it is tacitly assumed that all aspects of the medieval or modern age "fit together" synchronically. As Karl Mannheim states it, the historical vertical implies the horizontal organic. Thus Levenson tended to treat the "modern West" as a kind of consistent whole. Yet in dealing with an entirely disparate culture, namely China, Levenson was concerned with another kind of holism, namely cultural holism. Once Confucianism had been established as a state philosophy in China, once the basic vital tension and balance had been struck among the monarchic, bureaucratic, and aristocratic elements in Chinese society and culture, we have something like the vital wholeness of a total culture which is able to maintain itself for centuries as a kind of durable entity. Chinese culture was not outside of history, but it was powerful enough to freeze its flow. The inner balance was indeed so powerful that it could be disrupted only from without.

And yet there is also much evidence in the writings of Levenson which suggests that he was neither an absolute historicist nor an absolute cultural-holist. It is first of all quite obvious that as a man of extraordinary aesthetic sensibility he could respond immediately to the values of art from all times and places. He certainly believed that aesthetic values can be both transtemporal and transcultural. However, Levenson was anything but a mere aesthete. He doggedly refused to exalt aesthetic values over ethical and intellectual values.

More importantly, in some of his most insightful pages, Levenson seemed prepared to treat concrete political and social problems in a manner which marked a striking departure from both absolute historicism and a rigid cultural holism. When he compares the relations of monarchy, aristocracy, and bureaucracy in China to aspects of Prussian bureaucracy or to the situation in the France of Louis XIV, he seems to be asserting that these phenomena *are* comparable across the barriers of time and culture. He is not asserting that Chinese monarchy and Chinese bureaucracy are so ineffably Chinese that they are not comparable to monarchy and bureaucracy in other times and places. He finds himself quite prepared to find comparabilities between the feudalism of ancient China and the feudalism of medieval Europe. *Parts* of Chinese culture are after all comparable to *parts* of other cultures. To be sure, he stresses that comparison is not the same as finding analogies, but it does imply a world of common human problems and conditions transcending both history and culture.

It is, of course, possible that Levenson felt that this way of doing cross-cultural history was applicable only to the premodern world and could not apply across the barrier which divides the premodern world from the world of modernity. Would he have believed it possible, for instance, to compare the relationship of monarchy and bureaucracy in a premodern context to the relationship between an American president and his bureaucracy? The dichotomy which he tended to stress most in defining the divide between the modern world and premodern world (at least the Chinese premodern world) was that of all-around amateurism versus specialization. Did he really believe that this dichotomy precluded any comparison of modern to premodern in any other sector of human experience? Whatever the answer to this question, he was certainly prepared at times to deal with the premodern world in a transcultural and metahistorical way.

Finally, it has always seemed to me that Levenson's commitment to Jewish values as he understood them was a case of preserving a national essence. On the contrary, he found universal value in his Judaism. Indeed, one of the values he found was precisely the notion that the universal must always find its embodiment in the particular. The God of Judaism relates to time and to man in history, but nevertheless Judaism is not historicism. History is not God.

To the degree that Levenson's message was that human problems are best treated within the concrete context of historic situations, to the extent that he insists that comparisons between institutions and ideas in China, Prussia, or France are best made by those who have first made a deep and many-sided study of these phenomena within their own historical and cultural contexts, I have always found myself in total sympathy with him. As already stated, my own differences of perspective arise only in connection with the suggestions of absolute historicism and cultural holism. I first of all find myself somewhat unsatisfied with the solution to Nietzsche's dilemma. It is quite true that we can understand the moral and intellectual creativity of the men of the past only if we ourselves have the experience of moral and intellectual *engagement*. Yet to the extent that we regard our commitments and convictions as belonging only to that ill-defined segment of time called "our day," we do not hold convictions in the same way in which men held them who thought that they were concerned with eternal and universal truths. Can we then really understand such men? Is it not true that the consciousness of the strictly timebound nature of our own convictions would inevitably vitiate the strength of these convictions? Would Nietzsche not still be correct in his view that in order to preserve the strength of our conviction we must expunge from our minds the debilitating effects of historicism?

It seems to me that Levenson at times confronts us with choices which are tyrannically stark. The belief that our values and beliefs are not simply timebound may not necessarily involve an absolutization of "our time." We may accept the sad realization that our own feeble light is as partial, fallible, and as lopsided as any of the views held by men in the past without accepting the view that they are simply a function of the "times" or of the "culture." Without going very deeply into the matter, I would not accept the view that the only alternative to absolute historicism is what Levenson called "*Platonic* antihistoricism." Nor am I convinced that he himself fully accepted this dichotomy.

Once one accepts the possibility, however, that ideas, problems, concerns, and values of a given age may have a metahistorical significance, any notion that the historic past is irretrievably dead—for good or ill—cannot be accepted as can a priori truth. It seems to me unfortunate that much of Levenson's more abstract discussion of this matter revolves about the dichotomy of "history" versus "value." This seems to imply that those who maintain that the past may continue to be relevant do so only because they nostalgically yearn for the present validity of the values of the past.

It is, however, possible to believe that not only values but problems and concerns of the past may have a metahistorical and general ongoing human significance. Indeed, one may even believe that the evils of the past—its demons and monsters—are not forever laid away. In *Revolution and Cosmopolitanism,* Levenson does indeed suggest that the Maoist leadership may entertain the view that the past is not safely dead. One recalls Santayana's dictum that those who know nothing of the past are doomed to repeat its errors.

It is from this point of view that one has questions concerning Levenson's metaphor of the museum. The artifacts in a museum can be appreciated, as Levenson would heartily concede, for their present aesthetic value. On the technological side, one can take pride in the technological accomplishments of our predecessors—the chariot and the stagecoach—even if we have no intention of returning to the stagecoach. Technology provides the clearest paradigm of the irretrievable past since we are not likely to revert to the technologies of the past. The nonmaterial side of culture is, it seems to me, not so easily dealt with in terms of this metaphor. I would suggest that a library may furnish a more apt metaphor. Those who write books more often than not ardently hope that putting their books in libraries will not necessarily assure the deadness of their ideas. Vast numbers of volumes may indeed go unread ever after, but one can never guarantee that they will remain mute.

As already indicated, the pastness of the past is very much associated with the notion of the wholeness of culture. The fragments which may survive the past are no longer vital because they must be imbedded in the new whole of a modernity which changes their very nature. "Sophocles," Levenson states, "holds the stage but Hellenic and Hellenistic culture remain fast in history."[4] I would certainly agree that Hellenic culture as a total Gestalt remains fast in history. Yet if Sophocles can have a present meaning for us beyond the purely aesthetic, I would tend to regard this as at least as significant a fact as that Hellenic culture as a whole is gone forever. I would argue that areas of experience of the past may, for good or ill, continue to have an ongoing existence in the present because the wholeness of culture is *not* that of a biological organism, and that "parts" of the culture of the past

4. Ibid., p. 113.

may live on even when the whole dies. In some sense, the parts are more than the whole and may survive the whole. Similarly, if by "modernity" we refer to Western culture since the Enlightenment, this seems to me to be an even more doubtful whole. The cleavages within the "culture of modernity" run so deep that we cannot even find agreement about the essential nature of this culture. Thus in dealing with modern China, Levenson finds that he must treat Western liberalism and Marxist-Leninist revolution as two quite disparate products of modernity with quite different implications. I would draw from this the conclusion that it is possible for significant parts of the Chinese past to survive the collapse of the culture as a totality and that it is equally possible for parts of the culture of modernity to become detached from other parts. The possibilities of new combinations are certainly not infinite. Absolute incompatibilities no doubt do exist. Yet "Chinese past" and "modernity" may not confront each other as impenetrable wholes.

The implications of this perspective are: (1) When a modern Chinese finds value or truth in some part of the Chinese past, one cannot invariably assume that the ultimate source of his attitude is to be sought in the realm of romantic nationalism even when we reject his views. (2) It is possible that some habits of thought and action deriving from the past may survive for good or ill into the present even when they are not acknowledged. This does not—one must hasten to add—justify those who see continuities everywhere. As Levenson insisted, the fact that specialists and experts are suspect to both Confucianists and Communists does not efface the fact that the Communist all-round man is entirely different from the Confucian all-round man. Yet the possibility of significant continuities need not be denied a priori. The question of continuities and discontinuities, it seems to me, can be dealt with only in terms of concrete investigations of various areas of human experience. It seems to me that in *Revolution and Cosmopolitanism* Levenson was himself moving toward new conceptions which modified and enriched his conceptual framework. In these essays, Levenson addressed himself to certain problems which had emerged out of the Cultural Revolution in China. As we know, this revolution was marked by a two-front assault on both the bad heritage of the Chinese past and the bourgeois cosmopolitan culture of the West. It thus marked a radical and abrupt departure from the "museum" image of the past. "The dead were no longer monuments but ghosts and monsters to be slain again."[5] It was, however, simultaneously an attack on those elements of "modern" Marxist cosmopolitanism which China shared with the world Communist movement. The kind of Marxist-Leninist cosmopolitanism which had allowed Chinese Communist intellectuals to introduce the writings of Goldoni and Shakespeare, Lessing, and Victor Hugo (with proper Communist interpretations) was a threat, in Mao's view, to the purity of revolution. The Communist solution to China's cultural predicament had evidently broken down.

In explaining this breakdown, Levenson looks to contingent historic causes lying outside of his conceptual framework. He finds it in the fear of war with the West and the loss of confidence within. The times called for a new militancy against the West, but the "very intensity of the anti-westernism compelled a corresponding antagonism to traditional Chinese forms."[6] All of this resulted in a new kind of provincialism which might well be called revolutionary provincialism or modern provincialism. One may, of course, quarrel with Levenson's account of the causes of the Cultural Revolution, but our main concern here is with the concept of a modern provincialism or a provincialism within modernity. In his previous writings, Levenson had linked modernity with the universal trend to cosmopolitanism and provincialism with the Chinese culture of the past. Modernity had reduced the universal claims of Chinese culture to the status of provinciality. "Pastness" and "provincialism" had gone together. It is, of course, my assumption that when he spoke of the Cultural Revolution as "provincial" he did not mean to deny its modernity, since Levenson had always treated radical revolutionism as an essentially modern response.

The conception of provincialism within modernity is, it seems to me, most fruitful. It is applicable not only to the Cultural Revolution in China but to many phenomena in the West as well. That academic intellectuals in the various national subcultures of the West still live largely immersed in the particular variants of modernity peculiar to their own national cultures is a well-attested

5. Joseph R. Levenson, *Revolution and Cosmopolitanism: The Western Stage and The Chinese Stages* (Berkeley: University of California Press, 1971), p. 53.

6. Ibid., p. 48. Whether one fully accepts this account of the causes of the Cultural Revolution is a problem not germane to this discussion.

fact. The philosophy departments of England and America dispense linguistic philosophy, while the philosophy departments of France dispense existentialism, phenomenology, and Marxism, and their respective students have little to say to each other. American behavioral political science remains quintessentially American. If we deal with the larger cultural units of mankind such as India, the Islamic Middle East, China, and Black Africa, one would think that the idea of provincialism within modernity will a fortiori be even more applicable. All of these cultures will no doubt undergo the impact of various forms of modernization. However, in those areas where the culture of modernity is itself marked by deep inner cleavages and lack of resolution, one may well expect a considerable degree of selectivity in the response to various trends from the West. Finally, one may still continue to find an ongoing dynamic interplay with elements of the cultures of the past, because of the nationalistic romanticism vividly described by Levenson, but also because of genuine ongoing belief in the contemporary relevance of values of the past, and because conditions and attitudes of the past may actually survive into the present even when unacknowledged. Although China now seems to be turning back from its cultural revolutionary assault on both the Chinese past and the modern West, it will continue to be involved in its own wrestlings both with modernity and with a Chinese past which, for better or worse, may be by no means entirely passé. The mix which may arise out of such wrestlings would still leave China with its own particular physiognomy—its own "provincialism." Thus, the notion that modernity will in itself create an entirely homogeneous world on the basis of some preestablished Western model is not likely to be fulfilled in any discernible future. Indeed, Levenson himself rejected the prospect of what he called "cosmopolitan-mass abstractions and homogenization."[7]

At the same time, we live in a world in which the various segments of mankind are in constant and unremitting contact with each other and a world where we are discovering that the experiences of all of mankind, both traditional and modern, are becoming more and more available to us. This is leading, it seems to me, to a possible perspective which, while by no means "Platonic," may be in some sense transcultural and metahistoric.

7. Cited in Wakeman's Foreword to *Revolution and Cosmopolitanism*, p. xxiv.

The universal human—complex, mysterious, and perhaps never totally comprehensible—does exist. It does not exist in a Platonic sphere apart from culture and history but "history" and "culture" are themselves completely senseless categories when divorced from universal human concerns. In Mr. Levenson's own words, "Chinese history should be studied because it can be seen to make sense in the same world of discourse in which we try to make sense of the West."

TENSIONS

Jonathan Spence

> They do not understand how that which
> differs with itself is in agreement:
> harmony consists of opposing tension,
> like that of the bow and the lyre.[1]

The fragment of Heraclitus survives without context and we do not know where the argument was leading. We know neither target nor tune. We have only the images and their linkage to a sharpened eye and ear; we must guess how shoulder, forearm and fingertips felt after the release of strings stretched to attain their differing goals.

In the earliest Chinese versions of the pictogram that became *kung* 弓, a bow, we see the strings still vibrating |{{; in the *chung* 中 of China and the *Doctrine of the Mean*, the arrow pierces the center of the target. In *yin-yang* cosmological theory, as in the developments of Western unitary *and* dialectic thought, the idea of tension reconciled in creative harmony is central.

Intellectually, Joseph Levenson was both archer and musician, releasing his arrows with force toward a perceived target, or lingering over the notes while themes developed their own impetus and chased their own echoes. But sometimes, too, he fired an arrow straight up in the sky to see where it would fall, or struck a random chord to taste its dissonance. Nowhere in his writings, I

1. Kathleen Freeman, trans., *Ancilla to the Pre-Socratic Philosophers* (Oxford, 1956), p. 28, no. 51.

think, did the disciplined and the casual meet and blur so often as around the core themes of tension and harmony.

Looking over and at Chinese history of the last few centuries (at the time of his death, the range had switched to the world and millennia), Levenson was intrigued by certain paradoxes, among them the Taiping challenge and defeat and the imperial bureaucracy's triumph and collapse. This chronological sequence of challenge, defeat/triumph, collapse, had two long-term sequels: first, traditional learning turned defensive, then self-conscious, then hollow; second, the nationalist radicalism that emerged was searching backward for lost roots even as it ran forward into the future.

These sequences were elaborated with erudition, skill and wit in Levenson's work *Confucian China and its Modern Fate.* But in trying to pin down an immediate Ch'ing background—as opposed to the wider-ranging context of Chinese imperial history in general—Levenson arrived at certain conclusions which were intellectually consistent but historically vulnerable.

What the Taipings destroyed, he wrote, was not the Confucian bureaucracy, nor the Emperor, but rather the dynamic tension that had given life to the relationship between the two. "Confucianism ceased to tense against monarchy because the Taiping stabbed it at the point ('Heaven') where the tension expressed itself."[2] Thus Confucianism "lost its standing as the creative intelligence of Chinese society."[3] This life without tension could be seen in the too-strong literati loyalties of the T'ung-chih Restoration, and played itself out through the internal incoherence of traditionalism and the nonsense of Restorationism —concluding with the final scenarios of Liao P'ing as Confucian "manikin" and Yuan Shih-k'ai as "farceur, a period piece come to life."[4]

To highlight the significance of this loss of tension, it was intellectually necessary to point to a time in which tension had been creatively present—to point to the high days of what Levenson called "the old tension between essentially Legalist,

2. Joseph R. Levenson, *Confucian China and Its Modern Fate* (Berkeley: University of California Press, 1964), vol. II, *The Problem of Monarchical Decay*, p. 111.

3. Ibid., p. 112.

4. Strong early statements of these last two scenarios can be found in essays by Levenson in *Confucian Personalities*, eds. Arthur F. Wright and Denis Twitchett (Stanford: Stanford University Press, 1962), p. 317; and in *Confucianism in Action*, eds. David Nivison and Arthur F. Wright (Stanford: Stanford University Press, 1959), p. 260.

anti-traditionalist dynastic monarchy, whether Chinese or foreign in ethnic and cultural origin, and literati-Confucian traditionalism."[5] The rather cumbersome insertion of the words "or foreign in ethnic and cultural origin" showed that a difficulty had been noted by Levenson: the Ch'ing were the rulers of nineteenth-century China and the Ch'ing were Manchus, ethnically foreign conquerors of Han China. Elements that were important to the Emperor-Bureaucracy tension must exist in Ch'ing as they had in Ming, if the Taiping force was to be felt in its fullness. So Levenson argued that "foreign dynasties may well have been nothing peculiar, only native dynasties to a higher power"; and, swinging the argument around to reinforce the same thought, "perhaps the real issue is not the degree to which alien dynasties proved acceptable to Chinese literati, but the degree to which native dynasties proved alien to them."[6]

This gave a sense of continuity, a coherent field in which the Imperial-Bureaucratic tensions could operate. But this tension was two-way, and if the continuity was pushed back too extensively in time, the tension would be confused by the presence of the aristocracy. To solve this dilemma, Levenson fired an arrow straight upwards:

> Yung-cheng, however, and the Ch'ing dynasty were on the far side of the great divide, the Sung. In that earlier period, though 'outside lords' were already effectively extinguished and the weight was shifting definitively toward bureaucracy and autocracy, the emperor could still seem poised (and sometimes paralysed) between his aristocratic near relations and his bureaucratic aides. But by early Ch'ing there could be no question of the emperor in the middle. He was at one of the poles, and though Yung-cheng had an aristocracy around him, he owned it. Confucian bureaucracy, the guarantor of the harmlessness of nobles, had long since been the status group whose solidarity autocrats had to melt. And formal aristocracy, gratifyingly choked off by bureaucracy as a major threat to the monarch, was fanned into life as part of the flame to be turned against its stifler.[7]

The point was made, but a century of Ch'ing history disappeared. Let us reinsert it.

5. Levenson, *Confucianism in Action,* p. 260.
6. Levenson, *Confucian China*, vol. II, p. 32.
7. Ibid., p. 44.

Nurhaci (1559-1626), for all that he united the Jurched, built the Banner system and named himself Emperor T'ien-ming of Chin, was a great lord among great lords. His attempts to name one heir-apparent as his successor ended in disillusion and disaster.[8] Though Abahai (1592-1643) became Nurhaci's successor, it was only with the consent of the rest of the eight hereditary lords (*beile*); and when Abahai's ninth son Fu-lin was named Emperor in 1643, the nomination was born not of power but of compromise—for Dorgon, Haoge, and Jirgalang had all been in the running.[9] As Shun-chih Emperor, Fu-lin was most decisively an "emperor in the middle." Until Dorgon's death in 1650 he was between Manchu baronial factions; after 1650 he did draw on truly Chinese resources to choke off his aristocratic rivals, but these Chinese were eunuchs and Buddhist monks, not the scions of traditional bureaucracy. Shun-chih was however willing to take daughters from that bureaucracy to his bed, adding ethnically pure Chinese to his Manchu and Chinese banner concubines and allowing them to retain their traditional Chinese style of dress—their feet, presumably, being bound.[10]

On Shun-chih's death, Manchu lords once again took the power, killing or ousting the eunuchs; the Regency run by varying members of the quartet Oboi, Soni, Suksaha, and Ebilun between 1661 and 1669 was forcefully independent of both the young K'ang-hsi emperor and the Chinese bureaucracy.[11] K'ang-hsi brought his regents down by using not Confucian bureaucrats but trusted Manchu and Mongol bodyguards (his grandmother's and his own), and only at the cost of letting Songgotu and Mingju and the Tunggiya clan hold sway. K'ang-hsi then gradually chose from his Chinese bureaucrats those whom he trusted most, but he remained a mediator between Manchu and Chinese political forces, not poised at one pole against the other two. His troubles with his

8. Cf. Nurhaci's killing of his brother Surgaci, his heir Cuyeng, and Erdeni Baksi, discussed by Li Hsueh-chih in "An Analysis of the Problem in the Selection of an Heir During the Reign of Nurhaci. . .," *Proceedings of the Third East Asian Altaistic Conference*, ed. Ch'en Chieh-hsien and Jagchid Sechin (Taipei, 1969), pp. 174-181.

9. Arthur Hummel, ed., *Eminent Chinese of the Ch'ing Period* (Washington, U.S. Government Printing Office, 1943), p. 255

10. T'ang Pang-chih, ed., *Ch'ing Huang-shih ssu-p'u* [Records of the Ch'ing Ruling Family] (Taipei 1966 reprint), p. 50, with references to Shen Shih, a Chihli native and *chin-shih* of Shun-chih 3/3/156.

11. The regents are studied by Robert Oxnam in "Policies and Factionalism in the Oboi Regency, 1661-1669" (Yale Ph. D., 1969). The following remarks on the K'ang-hsi reign are drawn from my ongoing research in the *Veritable Records*, and in *Ku-kung wen-hsien*, cited below.

own heir-apparent mirrored Nurhaci's, and show how the power of great Manchu clans continued into the eighteenth century.

K'ang-hsi did boost Chinese bureaucrats, but the ways in which he did so do not help Levenson's argument. K'ang-hsi sometimes chose those with skills in scholarship to be his ministers and provincial governors and publicly congratulated himself and them as he did so—witness Chang Ying, Chang P'eng-ko, Ch'en Yuan-lung, Chang Po-hsing, Wang Tu-chao. Yet many of those most steeped in traditional *wen*, whom K'ang-hsi used in key positions, were tied to him in a relationship that suggests more the bonds of a captive than the vibrant strings of bow or lyre. Reporting to K'ang-hsi directly in the newly developed palace memorial system, watching others as ordered, and watched by others whose presence they could only guess, these Confucian literati at the pinnacle of their "power" were often used like bondservants.[12] When traditional bureaucrats were flattered by the chance to circumvent the normal bureaucratic channels, what force did "traditional" have?

In handling the decadent later Manchu aristocracy, Levenson sought for "functional equivalence" in ways that would maintain historical continuity. He found this equivalence in late-Ming eunuchs. Manchus, he wrote, like eunuchs, stood over and against the bureaucracy as "auxiliaries," as "a third force"; they were "newer recruits to the monarch's loyal coterie," "centralizer's tools," "private bureaucratic agents" and "a set of instruments."[13] Yet such terms compress too much history and blur too many distinctions—for some Manchus were great lords and some were powerful generals with hereditary troops, and some were common soldiers, and some were opium addicts and some were bondservants. And some Manchu bondservants were menial while others could grow rich and powerful as Manchu "lords" slid to insolvency. Yung-cheng, it is true, broke the Banner lords' powers, and made their troops his own; but there is much evidence to show that he broke the bureaucrats too, and made of the coordinated palace memorial system the perfect centralizer's tool.[14] We enter the world of value judgments here; was the intense deference of

12. Vast amounts of new material on these K'ang-hsi memorialists are now appearing in the quarterly *Ku-kung wen-hsien* [Ch'ing Documents at [the] national Palace Museum] (Taipei, 1969, et seq.).

13. Levenson, *Confucian China*, vol. II, pp. 45-46.

14. CF. Silas Hsiu-liang Wu, *Communication and Imperial Control in China, Evolution of the Palace Memorial System, 1693-1735* (Cambridge: Harvard University Press, 1970).

Yung-cheng's hardworking Chinese bureaucrats toward their master born of pride or fear, was the harmony sprung from tension or from that drained vitality which Levenson found everywhere a century and a half later?[15]

If the vitality was already draining by the 1730s, if there were already at that early time no lifegiving tensions to provide the truest harmonies, then we might have an explanation (not for the Taiping impact and the fall of the Ch'ing) but for the cultural and artistic aridity of the period 1720-1880. After Tao-chi and Pa-ta Shan-jen, Wang Hui and Wang Yuan-chi, Huang Tsung-hsi and Wang Fu-chih—who all died in K'ang-hsi's reign—and after the deaths of the members of the wide artistic and literary circles they inspired and sustained, there is little cultural richness or energy in Ch'ing life, except in the novel; and the novel had never been regarded as "culture" by literati. It was a period of dull painting and poetry, elaborate but stale, of flamboyant jades and porcelains, of conventional philosophy and history. Hellmut Wilhelm has argued that new breakthroughs in human psychology were in the philosophical air[16] and Arthur Waley has shown Yuan Mei to be an amusing and able poet. Silks were still beautiful. But the cultural fruits in general seem too meager to have nourished much life—and the big rise in pure opium smoking begins around 1770.[17]

The Western coming in the late eighteenth century led through opium and treaties and humiliations into the Taiping world; and Westernizing Chinese inevitably formalized their own cultural past and undermined the institutions they thought they were shoring up. The global cultural gleanings became richer, and the Chinese involvement more intense and more difficult. These are splendid themes, and Levenson was moving to confront them as he died; we see this clearly from the three lectures in *Revolution and Cosmopolitanism.*[18] The old preoccupations were still in Levenson's mind, but pushed now in new directions, as can be shown by his last look at the Taipings:

15. Levenson, *Confucian China,* vol. II, pp. 113-114.

16. Hellmut Wilhelm, "Chinese Confucianism on the Eve of the Great Encounter," in *Changing Japanese Attitudes Toward Modernization,* ed. Marius Jansen (Princeton: Princeton University Press, 1965), pp. 283-310.

17. Cf. Jonathan Spence, "Opium Smoking in the Ch'ing Dynasty" (A paper for the conference on local control and social protest during the Ch'ing period, held in Honolulu June 27-July 2, 1971).

18. Joseph R. Levenson, *Revolution and Cosmopolitanism: The Western Stage and the Chinese Stages* (Berkeley: University of California Press, 1971).

> They flouted Confucianism with a garbled Christianity, part of the Western intellectual penetration. And they were pushed over the edge of rebellion by Western economic penetration, which aggravated endemic social bitterness to a new intensity. Intellectual apostasy underscored this bitterness.[19]

And this:

> Confucian literati, the (often literally) official bearers of "high culture," had had a cosmopolitan aura (and provincials to condescend to) in the world that they defined . . . . And although they did not will it, they yielded title to cosmopolitanism to a new youth in a new China, which was now a part of the general world, instead of being world enough itself.[20]

These passages show how Levenson was shifting into world intellectual history, making China a part of something else. From the mood of *Revolution and Cosmopolitanism,* we can guess that he found this a difficult undertaking: so much seemed to have been done wrong, in China, and so much of what had been done right seemed without purpose. Why Pirandello and Schnitzler in 1930s Shanghai? Why seek, for the benefit of would-be Chinese sophisticates, to illuminate the differences between the Viennese and the Berlin spirit?[21] Levenson saw a danger of losing the track of "significance" and "value" that had illumined his earlier writing; the Cultural Revolutionaries had turned things around, true, but advanced nowhere: the China that they dominated was "sitting solitary, her ties back to the Chinese past attenuated, her bridges across to the alien present barred."[22]

The last few lines of *Revolution and Cosmopolitanism* are crammed with images, and the images are somber.[23] There is no lifegiving tension in sight, only juxtapositions of unclear purport, or paradoxes without resolution. The Chinese intellectuals of the 1930s and their controllers of the 1960s—"Cultural intermediaries, Cultural Revolutionaries"—are respectively minnows and whales, stranded on some unknown beach. We do not have to be hyper-imaginative to catch the rasp of dying breath. "They try to speak to the world . . . . Some people are listening.

19. Ibid., p. 22.
20. Ibid., pp. 2-3.
21. Ibid., p. 31.
22. Ibid., p. 55.
23. Ibid., p.a 55 for this and the following quotes.

Maybe some peoples are listening." The pun is friendly, but the echoes of the language are again suffocating—we are sent back to Lu Hsun as a young man, and his visions of the Chinese people shut inside their windowless house of iron. Lu Hsun concluded that we must try to arouse those trapped, who were capable of listening, however much it increased their pain, just on the frailest chance that they might somehow escape; we must "encourage those fighters who are galloping on in loneliness, so that they do not lose heart."[24] Levenson picks up the echo here too: the forgotten translators are "almost solitaries"; the provincialism of China in the late 1960s is "a mark of loneliness."

But it is when Levenson, near the end of this same last paragraph, calls these Chinese foes "semblables" and "frères" that his argument reaches its final allusive complexity. If we pursue this allusion a moment further, it is not to calcify Levenson by footnoting minutiae; nor is it to suggest that we know exactly what he intended by the allusion; nor even to claim that he had an allusion with specific intellectual context and content in mind, as opposed to some cliche that would wrap a sentence up. The purpose, rather, is to pay homage to the richness with which Levenson was opening up this new field, and to hint at the levels of meaning he might have disclosed had he lived to apply to global cosmopolitanism the tools he had developed in tackling Confucian traditionalism.

"Mon semblable,—mon frère!" is no simple fraternal call. It is Baudelaire's salutation to a hypocritical reader who joins him temporarily, not from freedom or affection, but from a shared loneliness in vice, and for a shared assault on the greatest vice of all—boredom:

> C'est l'Ennui!—l'oeil chargé d'un pleur involontaire,
> Il rêve d'échafauds en fumant son houka.
> Tu le connais, lecteur, ce monstre délicat,
> —Hypocrite lecteur,—mon semblable,mon frère![25]

And, as a salutation by Baudelaire, it is not embedded only in aesthetes' heads; it is an international echo that has entered the English world-language via T.S. Eliot's *The Waste Land*—a

24. *Selected Stories of Lu Hsun* (Peking: Foreign Languages Press, 1960 ed.), p. 26.

25. Charles Baudelaire, *The Flowers of Evil* (New York: New Directions, 1963 ed.), pp. 2, 4, 234. For Levenson's interest in Baudelaire, cf. Frederic Wakeman's Foreword to *Revolution and Cosmopolitanism*, pp. xxvi-xxvii.

mocking call, directed to Stetson at nine o'clock on a foggy London morning.[26]

Whether Levenson meant it or not, what we have here is a serious and absorbing cosmopolitan point: Chinese moderns (proletarian iconoclasts) are linked to China's previous moderns (bourgeois adapters, but modern nevertheless in contrast to Confucian traditionalists) by language from the most eclectic of modern Western poems, itself written by an American steeped in European history and "tradition", and edited by another American who loved Chinese poetry.

Eliot's cultural gleanings were scholarly and deliberate; they were also desperate, as he searched for some order in a disintegrating cultural universe:

> What are the roots that clutch, what branches grow
> Out of this stony rubbish? Son of man,
> You cannot say, or guess, for you know only
> A heap of broken images . . .[27]

They offered a little hope ("These fragments I have shored against my ruins"[28]) though not enough, when the alternative to death from the beating rays of the sun was often death by drowning.

From the way that Eliot handled these remnants of his fractured culture in *The Waste Land,* we can catch a glimpse of the path that Levenson might have chosen in developing his own themes of cosmopolitanism. The challenge would have lain in stretching the things that history normally did, in comparing chronologically, culturally, geographically, occupationally, and all at the same time. In the circles of Eliot's poem, we find "Mr. Eugenides, the Smyrna merchant/Unshaven, with a pocket full of currants/c.i.f. London" and "Phlebas the Phoenician, a fortnight dead" as well as Stetson, "You who were with me in the ships at Mylae."[29] Each of these men is an evocation and a symbol, as well as being historically and geographically placed; each can be linked to the other by pun and memory: Phlebas "Forgot the cry of gulls, and the deep sea swell/And the profit and loss./A current under sea/Picked his bones in whispers."[30] And as the language is rich

26. T.S. Eliot, "The Waste Land," lines 76 and 69.
27. Ibid., lines 19-22.
28. Ibid., lines 431.
29. Cf., in order, ibid., lines 209-210, 312, 70.
30. Ibid., lines 313-316.

in evocations, so is it rich in opportunities that only our descendants will be able to seize.

China, the world, language, intellectual passion; sorrow and inheritance; the living, the dead, the unborn, time, memory, work, mirth—that was what Levenson sought to grasp.

> "Gentile or Jew
> O you who turn the wheel and look to windward,
> Consider Phlebas, who was once handsome and tall as you."[31]

31. Ibid., lines 319-321.

A NOTE ON THE DEVELOPMENT OF THE THEME OF BUREAUCRATIC-MONARCHIC TENSION IN JOSEPH R. LEVENSON'S WORK

Frederic Wakeman, Jr.

Levenson's great trilogy, *Confucian China and Its Modern Fate*, asked again and again, "why, during so much of Chinese history, have new ideas had to face tests of compatibility with received tradition, while in more recent times tradition has had to face tests of compatibility with independently persuasive new ideas?"[1] His second volume, *The Problem of Monarchical Decay*, posed the problem in institutional terms: "why have monarchy and bureaucracy been so intimately involved in the Confucian view of culture that abolition of the first, and transformation of the second, have rendered partisans of the third more *traditionalistic* than *traditional*?"[2] He answered that question with a Nietzschean insight ("Almost every party understands how it is in the interest of its own self-preservation that the opposition should not lose all strength")[3] and proceeded to define the Chinese imperial system paradoxically: a Confucian monarchy founded on anti-Confucian Legalist principles. The paradox was institutionally expressed as a vital tension between bureaucracy and monarchy. When this ambivalence, "this Confucian-monarchical attraction-repulsion," was lost, the Chinese state expired.

The Problem of Monarchical Decay opens with the symbol of that attrition: Yuan Shih-k'ai's "imperial masquerade" on January

1. Joseph R. Levenson, *Confucian China and Its Modern Fate*, 3 vols. (Berkeley: University of California Press, 1958-1965), vol. II, *The Problem of Monarchical Decay*, p. vi.
2. Ibid.
3. Nietzsche, *The Twilight of the Idols*, cited in Levenson, *Confucian China*, vol. II, p. 23.

1, 1916, when he inaugurated the shortlived Hung-hsien reign. This inauthentic imperial restoration offered Levenson sure proof of "the draining of the monarchical mystique." And because Yuan Shih-k'ai had coupled his plans for a restoration with an elevation of Confucianism, this also signified the "untraditional" identification of Chinese monarchism with "intellectual traditionalism pure and simple." In "live imperial days" monarchy was far from purely Confucian, and certainly not committed to conservatism in the modern sense. Indeed, monarchy at its height was sometimes pitted against the Confucian conservatism of the bureaucratic intelligentsia.[4]

Levenson was not the first to emphasize the competitive relationship between a ruler and his ministers. Max Weber had pointed out in *The Religion of China* that the "free and mobile stratum of literati" of the Warring States period, courted by the various princely regimes, had become affixed prebendaries after the Han unification, struggling among themselves for existing offices. Weber mainly stressed this social change to explain the rise of Confucian orthodoxy. "As Chinese prebendalism grew, the originally free mental mobility of the literati came to a halt."[5] But he also emphasized the way in which the examination system kept candidates "from joining together into a feudal office nobility,"[6] while allying with their monarch against the great families of the "feudal period." After the Sung, when these feudal adversaries no longer existed, the literati's main opponent was "sultanism and the eunuch-system."[7] The literati "submitted to the ruler if the ruler in turn submitted to their ritualist and ceremonial demands."[8] For Weber, then, the bureaucratic-monarchic relationship was a fairly static balance—a stable buttress of the traditional order, conservatively resisting economic changes that might otherwise have taken effect. Levenson, on the other hand, viewed the relationship as a vital tension flexing over historical time—a condition of cultural vigor rather than just a compromise between political competitors.

Yet the culture it invigorated was by certain standards only stylistically alive. Volume One of *Confucian China and Its Modern*

4. Levenson, *Confucian China*, vol. II, p. 10.
5. Max Weber, *The Religion of China* (Glencoe: The Free Press, 1952), p. 112.
6. Ibid., p. 119.
7. Ibid., p. 138.
8. Ibid., p. 141.

Fate, while warning against a "presumptuous western question of 'failure' in Chinese civilization,"[9] nevertheless described "the abortiveness of empiricism in early Ch'ing thought," and thereby implied a substantial lack of intellectual vitality behind the high Ch'ing's political vigor. From that point of view, Levenson appeared to belong to what has been called the Harvard School of Chinese historiography. He did, of course, join the extraordinary cohort of Far Eastern historians who gathered after the Second World War under John K. Fairbank's intellectual influence. Although it would be tendentious to define so rich a set of minds in conclusively general terms, most did share an interest in assessing China's response to the impact of the West, basically supposing that China resisted immediate adaptation to the challenge of imperialism because the old order was so successfully integrated by Confucianism. And because the old order did shortsightedly defend itself so well, its fall in the end was all the greater. For Levenson, that fall began with the onslaught of the Taiping rebels—a common enemy which created joint interests between the bureaucracy and the monarchy, erasing the mutual tension so essential to Chinese political culture. Complete integration was thus necessarily followed by complete disintegration.

Because there is a circularity to this argument, Levenson almost seems to have discovered that vital tension as an afterthought. Volume Two begins, after all, with the Hung-hsien restoration: a mock Confucian coronation of a king by his henchmen rather than a genuine recognition of an emperor's right to the mandate by his ministers. Was Levenson's discovery of the once-vital tension between the latter then just a corollary to his perception of the romantic compromise of Confucianism in the twentieth century? Or did his awareness of that tension in earlier periods emerge independently and as a forethought based upon other intellectual constructs?

To answer that question I would like to show precisely how the concept of a bureaucratic-monarchic tension developed in Levenson's own thinking before *The Problem of Monarchical Decay* was actually written. The published work itself does not permit such a reconstruction, but Mrs. Joseph Levenson has allowed me to study the original working notes for *Confucian China*, which were

9. Levenson, *Confucian China*, vol. I, *The Problem of Intellectual Continuity*, p. 13.

found among her husband's papers after his death. It is from these that I have traced the development of that concept.[10]

Levenson made his first tentative connection between bureaucratic-monarchic tension and the vitality of the imperial system in his early study of Liang Ch'i-ch'ao's works. Noting that these "twin centers of traditional China" were engaged in a situation "of endemic tension," Levenson sensed even then that a "sign of [the] *modern*" might be a "decadent fusion of the two."[11] But before he could pursue that idea to its conclusion, which was of course the relaxing of the tension itself, he had to define the system in its vitality. Max Weber's *Politics as a Vocation* suggested the next step. Weber had written:

> The prince, coming more and more into the position of dilettante, sought to extricate himself from the unavoidably increasing weight of the expertly trained officials through the collegial system and the cabinet. He sought to retain the highest leadership in his own hands. This latent struggle between expert officialdom and autocratic rule existed everywhere.[12]

Ruler and bureaucrat might be just as opposed to each other in China, but Levenson immediately noticed that Confucian officials did not appear to protect themselves by acquiring professional expertise. Rather, "in China the struggle was between *amateur* officialdom and monarch—[so that there existed an] officialdom which sees its independence of possession by [the] monarch [as] bound up in its amateur standing." Thus it was by way of negative analogy that Levenson first conceived of the "amateur ideal," which was to become such an important theme in the first volume

10. These notes are now filed in the Bancroft Library of the University of California, Berkeley. References which hereafter lack footnotes come from these notes.

11. Tracing the origins of Liang Ch'i-ch'ao's nationalism—the transformation from *t'ien-hsia* to *kuo-chia*—Levenson pondered Liang's claim in 1900 that China lacked nationalism because the court, not the country, was the focal point of allegiance. See Liang Ch'i-ch'ao, "Chung-kuo chi jo su-yuan lun" [On searching for the origins of China's accumulated weaknesses], YPSWC 15, 23b-25, written in 1900. Liang's claim inspired the following rough note:

> This modern double critique of traditional Confucian and monarchical assumptions—definition of nationalism as negative of either one or other of twin centers of traditional China—their attraction thus perceived. Their "repulsion" also implied (but not by Liang—perhaps sign of *modern*, i.e. decadent fusion of the two) in that both bureaucracy and emperor ultimately identified "nation" (*kung*) with self against the other, seen as *ssu*, i.e. imperial centralization. Strong man and central office militated vs. private (i.e. gentry-bureaucratic) aggrandizement.

12. Max Weber, "Politics as a Vocation," in *From Max Weber*, eds. Hans Gerth and C. Wright Mills (New York: Oxford University Press, 1958), p. 89.

of his trilogy. Three other studies helped refine the theme. First was an article by Alexander Soper on Northern Sung painting which suggested to Levenson that Confucian bureaucrats resisted the monarch's academic painting styles by adopting a *wen-jen* (literatus) style of their own.[13] Second was the example of literati arrogance during the late Roman Empire, when high culture was so dramatically wielded as a weapon against aristocratic landowners.[14] Finally, there was an article by Jen Chi-yu on the traditional status of professional Chinese medical studies which reinforced Levenson's conviction that the Confucian gentleman was a self-conscious amateur for reasons of self-protection, since the state "*ideally* would professionalize its bureaucracy."[15]

By 1956, therefore, Levenson had succeeded in connecting amateurism and bureaucratic self-interest. That is, contrary to the Weberian model where bureaucrats defended themselves by becoming technocrats, Levenson's Confucian scholar-official resisted both the Legalist despot and the military aristocracy by exploiting civil culture.[16] Beyond the "amateur ideal," however, remained the problem of institutional forces. These Levenson explored in terms of a triangular struggle between monarchy, aristocracy, and bureaucracy. The conceptual dimensions of that struggle were expanded by his readings in European history during 1957-1959. For instance, the later Roman empire showed how the throne could fail to use the bureaucracy as an ally against the great senatorial landowners, whereas in China "organization [was] possible on the basis of emperor + bureaucracy" against the aristocracy. But precisely because the latter was "so submerged" by

13. Alexander Soper, "Standards of Quality in Northern Sung Painting," *Archives of the Chinese Art Society of America* 11:8-15 (1957). Soper's comparison of the Northern Sung Imperial Academy to Louis XIV's in France caused Levenson to note: "Louis analogy points up despot's use of tools; criticism points up Confucian literati's resistance—and *effective* resistance—[in that] bureaucracy sets styles, not the monarchy, for values of Chinese world."

14. Levenson got this impression from Andrew Alfoldi, *A Conflict of Ideas in the Late Roman Empire: A Clash between the Senate and Valentinian I* (Oxford: Oxford University Press, 1952), pp. 107-111.

15. The article which Levenson commented on was Jen Chi-yu, "Chung-kuo ku-tai i-hsueh ho che-hsueh te kuan-hsi" [The relation between medical studies and philosophical studies in ancient China], in *Li-shih yen-chiu* 5:59-74 (1956).

16. In some ways, his concern for the aristocracy grew out of cultural problems. Reading Shimizu Morimitsu ("Kyu Shina ni okeru sensei kenryoku no kiso" [The basis of autocratic power in pre-revolutionary China], *Mantetsu Chosa Geppo*, 17.2:1-60 [February, 1937]), Levenson noted how the term *shih* (gentleman] persisted long after feudalism in a new moralized and "civilized" sense of the literatus. As the "civil" (*wen*) was "enshrined" at the expense of the "martial" (*wu*), the civil-military (*wen-wu*) antithesis was a counterpoint to the bureaucratic-aristocratic struggle.

Sung times, the "emperor + bureaucracy alliance [was] not perfectly forged. [Therefore] strains and tensions [were at] work."[17] Even more instructive was the Prussian case, as viewed through Hans Rosenberg's scholarship.[18] Levenson was able to see clearly how the military-bureaucratic power apparatus of the Hohenzollerns first existed side by side, and later effected a compromise, with the landed nobility. It was now possible to conceive of a situation in which a bureaucracy established relative autonomy by conceding enough to the landed aristocracy to maintain it as a counterbalance against autocracy. Not only that; a particular style of culture, a *Bildung*, could overcome the traditional separation of classes and enable a Prussian sharing of *wen* (civil) and *wu* (military), unthinkable in Confucian China.

From Prussia Levenson moved to France. Rereading Tocqueville's *Ancien Régime*, he at first assumed bureaucratic-monarchic centralization to have been completely effective against the nobility. But Douglas Dakin's study of Turgot[19] persuaded him that Tocqueville had imagined the bureaucracy to be stronger than it actually was. Since the aristocracy was neither entirely reduced to impotence (as in China) nor so favored to check the throne (as in Prussia), the nobility retained enough power to obstruct government and appear parasitic.

As his notes at the time put it: "Such a bureaucracy [as existed in France] (like Confucian [bureaucracy] in non-expertise) [was] not calculated to make the monarch effectively despotic (and in fact, did not, in France). But in France, unlike China, [there was a] revolution—because [there was] an aristocracy (parasites) in being." Perhaps when revolution finally did occur in China, monarchy and bureaucracy fell together because there was no such parasitic aristocracy to divert the attack, but that was less significant to Levenson than the functioning pattern itself. In fact, he struggled hardest to account for a vital tension continuing between bureaucracy and monarchy long after the aristocracy had ceased to exist in China. He both assumed the Naito thesis[20] to

17. Levenson had read William G. Sinnigen, *The Officium of the Urban Prefecture during the Later Roman Empire* (Rome: American Academy in Rome, 1957).

18. Hans Rosenberg, *Bureaucracy, Aristocracy, Autocracy: The Prussian Experience* (Cambridge, Mass.: Harvard University Press, 1968).

19. Douglas Dakin, *Turgot and the Ancien Régime in France* (New York: Octagon Books, 1965).

20. First in *Shina ron* (Essays on China, 1914), and then later in a famous article entitled "Gaikatsuteki To-So jidai kan" [A general view of the T'ang and Sung periods, 1922], Naito Torajiro (1866-1934) argued that China's modern history began in the late T'ang period, when the aristocracy was destroyed and the emperor began to develop absolute powers.

be correct and knew of all the evidence pointing to an actual increase in despotic authority during the late imperial period. In either event the bureaucracy stood to suffer, since the "amateur ideal" could only serve individual scholar-officials. However, Levenson found it easier to take the absence of an aristocracy into account than to reconcile the growing power of the throne after 1200 with the idea of a bureaucracy independent enough to generate the tension so necessary to Confucian vitality. If Frederick Mote was right about the great increase in Ming imperial power after 1381, then might not bureaucrats have lost their independence altogether?[21] No, answered Levenson, noting that Mote's description was consistent with his own "interpretation of [the] *parallel* rise of monarchical and bureaucratic power, [and] not at [the] expense of each other." This was (again from his notes)

> because only then does *bureaucracy* become so influential (aristocracy defeated, etc.) that it at least shares in the domination of the state, i.e. [the] emphasis (by Mote and others) on [the] enhancement of *monarchical* power in Sung should not be taken to imply despotic mastery of [the] bureaucracy, but [a] parallel enhancement of [the] position of bureaucracy.

Moreover, emperors continued to defer to—even canonize—officials who morally criticized the throne. One reason was simply that

> [the] very Confucian insistence that [the] emperor's virtue [was] involved and possibly impugned by conditions in [the] arena of *official* power does not elevate him to the empyrean where *officials* alone have a responsibility.

In other words, Chinese monarchs avoided becoming divine but helpless rulers, like Japanese emperors, by respecting a Confucian moral judgment which made their own personal political intervention necessary.

But it was still easier to find powerful emperors rather than autonomous bureaucrats in the late imperial period of Chinese history.[22] How, in fact, could one explain away such symbols of

21. Frederick W. Mote, "Terror in Chinese Despotism with Special Reference to the Early Ming Period," *Oriens Extremus* (September 1959).

22. For Levenson the best example of this was the Yung-cheng emperor about whom he read in Miyazaki Ichisada, *Yo-sei-tei, Chugoku no dokusai kunshu* [The Yung-cheng emperor, China's autocratic ruler] (Tokyo, 1950). He was also specifically interested in the more administrative side of the late Ch'ing which he absorbed from the *Chia-ch'ing hui-tien*. This he read in a version translated into Japanese: "Rinji Taiwan kyukan chosakai dai-ichi-bu

bureaucratic servility as court floggings or the demeaning kowtow? Perhaps here, too, "real" interests were expressed in psychologically contradictory ways so that the minister's deference to his monarch actually masked bureaucratic power. Levenson developed this thought as he read over a paper by Mark Mancall on China's first mission to Russia.[23] Noting that the Chinese envoys' kowtow before Czarina Anna Iovanova was not mentioned in the *Veritable Records,* Mancall suggested that the Yung-cheng Emperor was concealing the need for a Russian alliance from his own court. Levenson disagreed.

> My conjecture (unlike Mancall . . .), [is] rather literati interest, because it (the kowtow to Russians) countered their conception of throne—[the] literati making more extreme claims for [the] emperor—*as [a] means of restraint*—than [the] emperor made [for] himself. . . . In China, insistence on [the] kowtow flattered both dynastic and bureaucratic preferences—but *for different reasons* . . . . For Confucianists, he [the emperor] is the son of Heaven; . . . the literati interpretation of the act was such as to derogate, really, from the purity of his despotic power.

Orthodox Confucian evidence for this was to be found in the words of Ch'eng Hao that the proper course for an emperor was "to distinguish between those who are loyal and those who are disloyal." Thus, remarked Levenson to himself,

> the onus is on the emperor. He may not define loyalty as unquestioning obedience to his wishes. Rather [the] true Confucianist defines [the] content of loyalty by his advice, and [the] emperor must recognize that those who agree with such sage advice are the loyal ones.

Furthermore, because subservience as such reflected the intensity of one's loyalty, it was a sign of personal—and therefore independent—morality which ultimately legitimized bureaucratic dissent. Reading Charles Hucker's study of the Tung-lin struggle,[24] Levenson considered the famous example of Tso

hokoku" [Temporary commission of the Taiwan government-general for the study of old Chinese customs, report of the First Section], *Shinkoku gyoseiho* [Administrative laws of the Ch'ing dynasty], *kan* 1 (Tokyo, 1914); *kan* 4 (Tokyo, 1911); *kan* 5 (Tokyo, 1911).

23. Mark Mancall, "China's First Missions to Russia, 1729-1731," *Papers on China* 9:75-110 (August 1955).

24. Charles O. Hucker, "The Tung-lin Movement of the late Ming Period," in *Chinese Thought and Institutions*, ed. John K. Fairbank (Chicago: University of Chicago Press, 1957), pp. 163-203.

Kuang-tou, tortured at the emperor's orders, who died with the words, "my body belongs to my ruler-father," on his lips. Hucker described this as "legalist sycophancy," but Levenson thought instead that the act emphasized

> the *personal relationship* [between minister and ruler]—cf. Mote on despotism: This kind of evidence for despotism . . . is actually [a] confirmation of [a] Confucian kind of freedom—[in which the official is a] person, not [a] cog.

Therefore, even the most dramatic cases of imperial tyranny demonstrated the bureaucrat's moral commitment, and were so used by Levenson to verify the survival of that vital tension between literatus and emperor well into the nineteenth century. For he was more than ever convinced that "tension equals power."

> [A] good society is [a] "tense society" which has mastered its tensions. The *weak* society—recent China—is [a] society which has let its tensions go. If it is to have power, its basis is *new* tensions and controls.[25]

But how did recent China get so weak? How did those former tensions let go? France again provided the most suggestive analogy:

> In France, [the] monarch made his aristocracy parasitic and simultaneously kept his bureaucracy unhonored. In China, post-Ch'in monarchy [was] unable to separate honor from bureaucratic authority . . . . [The] ruthlessness of Ch'in both ended aristocracy and repelled potential bureaucracy, which enforced on Han its Confucian "amateur" detachment from unbounded despotic control . . . . [That is] tantamount to saying that China had its revolution with Ch'in, [its] feudal class overthrown, [and] hence [its] potential for revolution stifled. France had no [early] revolution, but [rather an] evolution of monarchical power to absolutism; [the] aristocracy [was] changed but not overthrown, hence [the] potential for revolution [was] preserved.

Thus, the Ch'in "revolution" of the third century B.C. precluded a revolution of the classic French sort two millennia later.

The absence of a feudal class was certainly one cause for the endurance of Confucian China, but Levenson still had to find a

25. At this time, Levenson was deeply influenced by Walter Kaufmann's study of Nietzsche, which quoted the philosopher as arguing that "one should measure the health of a society and of individuals according to how many parasites they can stand" (pp. 243-244). This suggested that a man who was strong enough to continually master strong and vehement passions was more powerful than someone who ascetically suppressed those impulses.

consistent explanation for the internal dynamics of 1911 when monarchy and bureaucracy finally did fall. He therefore enlarged the metaphors which his notes had already employed. If tension were power or vitality, then the bureaucracy's health depended upon Confucianism maintaining the inner tension between its various schools of thought. Tseng Kuo-fan's relaxed eclecticism thus invited the breakdown of Confucianism. For, wrote Levenson:

> [There is a] difference between a Confucianism with inner tensions (i.e. vitality) and holistic Confucianism in which the parts [are] still there but [the] tension [is] gone. It is when Confucianism loses its own "inner tension" that it loses its "outer tension" with monarchy.

And if a revolution like France's depended upon a portion of the ruling class becoming parasitic, then Confucian bureaucrats must also have been viewed as parasites before 1911—a corollary of the metaphor which alerted Levenson to the importance of Taiping charges against the gentry.[26] Those attacks, when combined with the Taiping Heavenly Kingdom's claims for transcendental monarchy, forced both the Confucian gentry and the imperial throne into such a tight defensive alliance as to erase the tensions between them. "When Confucianism [was] drained"—Levenson's notes concluded—"and Confucianists [were] helplessly monarchical, [a] revolutionary situation [was finally] established."

The final version of Levenson's theme of bureaucratic-monarchic tension did not appear in precisely the form described above. By the time he had written *The Problem of Monarchical Decay*, his own research in the primary sources had altered and refined the original perception. But the major motifs persisted much as they appeared in process—even though some of the heuristic analogies between China and the West were dropped along the way. Levenson's belief that there had once existed a politically crucial and culturally necessary tension between ruler and minister was therefore not just a theory inspired by Yuan Shih-k'ai's tragicomic restoration. The general idea had occurred to Levenson while he was writing his dissertation on Liang

26. "When revolution does come, it is with detachment of intellectuals from literati-bureaucrats (Taipings proto-rev. precisely in sense that they have ideology quite alien to Confucian world). This detachment is (a) that of non-bureaucratic types (peasant, compradore) who for first time can articulate selves outside Confucian society—i.e. rise of class feeling; (b) that of heirs of literati who feel petrifaction of Confucian thought and become 'western' intellectuals, hence separated from Confucian bureaucratic element which is now converted to French aristocratic model—purely parasitic."

Ch'i-ch'ao, and was then developed through his later study of Chinese history "in the same world of discourse in which we try to make sense of the West."[27] The relative autonomy of this complex concept thus lends it greater historical validity. Naturally, Levenson's description of the bureaucratic-monarchic relationship has been, and will be, modified by later Chinese historians. However, the Nietzschean hint that men may impose their own chains to serve their power will endure as the heart of his argument. And, like so many of Levenson's insights, this concept will continue to remind those who have learned from him that paradox is intended to reveal an unrecognized element of truth.

27. Levenson, *Confucian China*, vol. II, p. ix.

PART THREE

The Levenson Legacy

STYLE AS IDEA IN MING-CH'ING PAINTING

James Cahill

The paradoxical thing about paradoxes is that they can seem just as true upside down (i.e., rightside up) as they do rightside up (i.e., upside down). Once the paradox has made its point, revealing some unexpected truth that seemed untrue only a moment before, one is perfectly free to overturn it and see once again as the truth what had looked true all the time. This is because a paradox can only be a construction of the mind—in being other-than-what-is-expected, that is, it requires someone to do the expecting—and so is always susceptible to a different construction by a different mind.

The argument of Joseph Levenson's "Paradox of an Academic Anti-Academicism," the central and crucial section of his essay, "The Amateur Ideal in Ming and Early Ch'ing Society: Evidence from Painting," is of this kind, viewable either topsy or turvy.[1] On its own ground, it seems convincing enough, and in following it through all its implications, as Levenson develops them, one is presented with important insights about Ming-Ch'ing painting and Ming-Ch'ing society. But one can also, by bringing to bear other evidence—whether written (from among those few books and articles that Levenson seems somehow not to have read, or chose not to cite), or just as important, pictorial—and by seeing the problem from another viewpoint, overturn the paradox and recognize the contradiction to be more apparent than real. The criticism that is implicit in my attempting to do so is not directed primarily outward at Levenson's essay, the value of which depends

1. Joseph R. Levenson, *Confucian China and Its Modern Fate,* vol. I, *The Problem of Intellectual Continuity* (Berkeley: University of California Press, pp. 15-43.

not upon rightness in every detail but upon its having employed a new mode of attack on Chinese painting, and having formulated the problems in new ways, offering a wealth of unique and stimulating perceptions (a rereading still recalls the excitement of first reading it, in 1955, as an unpublished conference paper). My criticism is rather directed inward: a consideration of the points where his argument is weakest, and the reasons for the weakness, will expose the ways in which we specialist historians of Chinese art have failed to provide the kind of understanding of our subject that can serve the needs of those who, like Levenson, want to include it as one element in a broader treatment of Chinese cultural history.

THE NON-PARADOX OF A SOMEWHAT ACADEMIC SEMI-ACADEMICISM

Levenson's paradox is in two parts, the first of which is headed "The Confucianist Choice of a Buddhist Aesthetic." He puts it in the form of a question: ". . . how could Ming Confucian intellectuals, the most academic of men in their literary practice, . . . reject a theory of painting which they associated with learning, and prize instead an anti-intellectual theory of mystical abstraction from civilized concerns?"[2] The reference is, of course, to the theory of the Northern and Southern Schools of painting propounded by Tung Ch'i-ch'ang (1555-1636), the greatest painter and most influential writer on the history and theory of painting in the late Ming. Just as there are Northern and Southern Schools of Ch'an Buddhism, Tung said, which advocate respectively the gradual and sudden means of achieving enlightenment (*wu* or *satori*), so are there Northern and Southern Schools in the history of painting. The Northern, in Tung's system, is made up chiefly of professional artists who attained their technical mastery gradually, through formal training and practice. The Southern School is roughly identified, at least for the later periods, with the tradition of the amateur artists, known as *wen-jen hua* or "literati painting." Southern School painting, the approach that the intellectuals "prized," thus corresponded, in Tung's symmetrical formulation, with Sudden Enlightenment ("subitist") Ch'an.

From that correspondence to the characterization of the amateur artists' system of beliefs as "an anti-intellectual theory of mystical

2. Ibid., p. 24.

abstraction from civilized concerns," however, is still a long and risky leap. I have suggested elsewhere that Tung's analogy is to be understood as just that, an analogy, and not as an argument for any such close dependence of Southern School painting theory on Ch'an as "The Confucianist choice of a Buddhist aesthetic" suggests.[3] It is true that some of Tung's ideas about painting, and those of his predecessors, have a distinct Ch'an flavor, and that Tung, who was passionately attached to Ch'an, liked to refer to "the Ch'an of painting" or even to see painting as a form of Ch'an.[4] But the basic tenets of *wen-jen hua* theory, established centuries before Tung's time, have closer ties to Confucian or Neo-Confucian thought than to Ch'an, while Tung Ch'i-ch'ang's particular conception of how the images of perceptual experience are transmuted in the mind (and with the brush) into the forms and structures of painting also seems to have its closest parallel, as recent studies (to be cited below) have persuasively shown, in Neo-Confucian thought. As Ch'an elements in the theory of literati painting, Levenson cites its advocacy of a spontaneous manner of working and an intuitive (rather than analytical) grasp of reality. But such creative approaches were by no means peculiar to Ch'an. The idea of an intuitive communion between the painter and his subject is at least as old in China as the (pre-Ch'an) theoretical writings on art and literature of the Six Dynasties, although of course the idea is not worked out there with the same elaboration as in the late Ming. The intuitive communion that Tung and the others speak of is in any case not identical with the direct and immediate kind that Ch'an fosters. On the contrary, the suggestion has been made, and convincingly, that the literati painters' way of transforming raw sensory data into artistic form, and particularly into reusable schemata (the "type forms" for trees, rocks, etc., that were later codified in such manuals as the *Mustard Seed Garden Manual of Painting*) is best paralleled in the operation of *liang-chih*, "clear intelligence," in Wang Yang-ming's Doctrine of the Mind, by which objects of the world, while they exist always in a latent state, come into full existence and acquire meaning in the mind only when they are roused from latency in the act of

3. James Cahill, "Confucian Elements in the Theory of Painting," *The Confucian Persuasion*, ed. Arthur F. Wright (Stanford: Stanford University Press, 1960), p. 116.

4. See Nelson Wu, "Tung Ch'i-ch'ang: Apathy in Government and Fervor in Art," in *Confucian Personalities*, eds. Arthur F. Wright and Denis Twitchett (Stanford: Stanford University Press, 1962), p. 289 and n. 116.

perception.[5] An epistemological mode that in effect imposes a human-set system of meaning and value on the outside world, and thereby brings it into a condition of intelligible order, does seem to be paralleled in a kind of painting in which a similarly human-set order and value is imposed on the forms of nature. All this is not incompatible with Ch'an, since it posits an intuitive or empathic apprehension by the mind that is expressed as an identity of subject and object, but it tends in a different direction. In addition to these objections, the kind of correspondence that Levenson and others have tried to draw between Southern School painting and Southern Ch'an Buddhism, through an overreading of Tung's analogy, would seem to require the same correspondence between Northern School painting and Northern or Gradual Enlightenment Ch'an; and except for Tung, whose statement of it seems somewhat forced, Chinese writers avoid suggesting any such correspondence.[6] To have done so would have shaken the whole structure of ideas, preferences, and prejudices with which the literati painters had surrounded themselves. The painting of the "northern" professionals was no gradual path to *satori*; it was no *satori* at all. Northern School painting was not another kind of Ch'an, but anti-Ch'an, a pictorial exemplification of the very analytical and rational approach to knowledge that Ch'an devotees were in flight from, by whichever path.

The answer to the question of why Confucian intellectuals chose a Buddhist aesthetic, then, is that they didn't, really; or rather that they did so to the same degree that Wang Yang-ming and his followers chose a Buddhist metaphysic. The presence of Ch'an ideas in late Ming painting theory is not essentially different from the presence of Ch'an in other areas of late Ming thought and

5. Victoria Contag, "The Unique Characteristics of Chinese Landscape Pictures," *Archives of the Chinese Art Society of America*, VI (1952), pp. 45-63. She renders *liang-chih*, rather freely, as "aesthetic judgment." See also Ho Wai-kam, "Tung Ch'i-ch'ang's New Orthodoxy and the Southern School Theory," mimeographed paper for "Artists and Traditions: A Colloquium on Chinese Art" (Princeton: Princeton University Press, 1969), pp. 13-15; and Ju-hsi Chou, *In Quest of the Primordial Line: the Genesis and Content of Tao-chi's Hua-yu-lu* (doctoral thesis, Princeton University, 1970; published by University Microfilms, Ann Arbor, 1971), pp. 23-27.

6. Tung compared the Northern School painter with the adept who "became a Bodhisattva only after a long and meritorious record of hardship" (*Jung-t'ai pieh-chi*, VI, 48a; quoted by Wen Fong, "Tung Ch'i-ch'ang and the Orthodox Theory of Painting," *National Palace Museum Quarterly*, Taipei, II: 3 (January 1968), p. 1. See also Chou, *In Quest of the Primordial Line*, p. 73 and n. 40.

culture; it is not a separate phenomenon in need of special explanation.

Very well, one might respond, but this is quibbling; Levenson's main point and paradox is that an anti-academic theory of artistic creation, whether Ch'an-inspired or not, stressing spontaneity and originality, was preached by people whose practice of painting was academic and derivative. The artists seem to acknowledge this themselves, stating in their inscriptions that they are imitating this or that ancient master, and the critics say it of them, not in disparagement but in praise. Levenson gives examples:

> There was no getting around it. The free, natural southern souls of literati-amateurs were pervaded with traditionalism. It was said of Tung Ch'i-ch'ang . . . that he copied the works of the old masters—especially those of his Sung namesake, the Ch'an artist Tung Yuan—with such a zeal that he forgot to eat and sleep. A late Ming source reported that a wonderful scroll by Shen Shih-t'ien had been executed, in the true amateur spirit, as a gift for a friend on his travels; that the scroll was modelled completely after Tung Yuan; and that it later became the outstanding treasure of a most famous connoisseur. Obviously, with the anti-academic Ming and Ch'ing critics, no painting failed of an accolade just for its being patently derivative. It was right and proper to imitate the ancients—because the ancients were spontaneous.[7]

How could one quarrel with this? The examples cited—and hundreds more could be added—appear to lead inexorably to the conclusion reached. And yet the passage exemplifies one of the classical pitfalls that open before anyone writing about art: taking at face value what the artist, or someone else, says about the work of art, without checking this judgment or characterization against the work itself. On the evidence of his own inscriptions, or the eulogies of contemporaries and later critics, Tung Ch'i-ch'ang must indeed be seen as a derivative artist: he recapitulates the achievements of the Four Great Masters of the late Yuan; he "imitates" Tung Yuan (who was not, by the way, a Ch'an artist); he imbues his paintings with an antique flavor. But the appraisal of his work to which these writings would lead holds only until we look at his paintings, and their position in the history of Ming and Ch'ing painting. When we do, Tung stands forth as a brilliantly

7. Levenson, *Confucian China,* vol. I, pp. 26-27.

innovative master, who more or less singlehandedly accomplished a major revolution in landscape painting.[8] It is not that his inscriptions and the critics' comments are deliberately deceptive; they wrote what they felt was true about the paintings, and what they wrote *is* true in that, rightly understood, it is part of what can properly be said about them. What they did not pause to point out on each occasion when they made such a statement, no doubt because it had been said so often, is that the kind of "imitation" Tung practiced was in no way incompatible with originality, and sometimes can scarcely be said to have affected the painting significantly at all: one of the little games of Chinese painting studies is trying to figure out, at times, what the artist can have meant in inscribing his pictures as "in the style of" some earlier master. If we were to place the scroll by Shen Shih-t'ien (i.e., Shen Chou, 1427-1509) that Levenson cites, quoting at second hand a "late Ming source," as "modelled completely after Tung Yuan,"[9] beside any of the scrolls ascribed to Tung Yuan himself, and ask someone sensitive to artistic style but unfamiliar with Chinese painting to comment on their relationship, he would probably decide that the differences far outweigh any similarities; he might have difficulty detecting the features of "Tung Yuan style" in Shen Chou's scroll at all. They are there; they take the form of rather remote references to conventions that were associated with the older master and his following, but they occur within a stylistic complex that is essentially of the fifteenth century, and Shen

8. See my catalog *Fantastics and Eccentrics in Chinese Painting* (New York: Asia Society 1967), pp. 16-20, The assessment of Tung Ch'i-ch'ang's position in the history of painting put forth there has recently been stated even more strongly by Max Loehr: "But for Tung Ch'i-ch'ang's 'radically new style' . . . representing a really new position, there was no such thing as a development in Ming painting." ["Phases and Content in Chinese Painting," paper for International Conference on Chinese Painting (Taipei, 1970), p. 6.] Against this view is, among others, Ju-hsi Chou, who can "detect no sign whatever that [Tung] was an iconoclast" and who feels that "It would indeed be more plausible to view him as the culmination of Ming painting, rather than the moment in which the latter underwent another phase of radical departure." (Chou, *In Quest of the Primordial Line*, p. 54, n. 48.) There is no point in arguing here against this view, although it seems to me quite untenable, considering the nature of landscape painting before and after Tung's time; such contradictory assessments cannot be profitably discussed, or even persuasively put forth, without continual reference to actual paintings, or at least to specific elements of style: of what aspects of Ming painting are Tung's works the culmination? How to account, if not by seeing Tung as having contributed much that is radically new, for certain important features that appear in early Ch'ing painting and cannot be traced further back than his works?

9. Levenson, *Confucian China*, vol. I, p. 27 and n. 50. The painting is in the Kadokawa Collection, Tokyo; a section of it is reproduced in the reprint of Levenson's book, *Modern China and Its Confucian Past: the Problem of Intellectual Continuity* (Garden City, New York: Anchor Books, p. 1. For a reproduction of the whole scroll, see *Kokka*, no. 545 (April 1936).

Chou's own. One can only dismiss these paintings as "patently derivative" on the basis of what has been *written about them*; in themselves, they allow no such judgment. A Chinese critic's designation of a painting as "completely after Tung Yuan" might mean no more than we mean when we say that Cezanne belongs (very loosely) in the stylistic lineage of Poussin, or Renoir in that of Boucher. The dependence indicated is usually far less than, for instance, Van Dyck's on Rubens (i.e., that of any true master-pupil relationship), and the erosion of originality less. Painting of the late Ming and early Ch'ing period exhibits, in fact, a burst of inventiveness and creativity such as occurs at only a few points in the centuries-long development of the art.

The creativity was confined, as always, to the major masters (by which we mean to designate those who were truly creative—the statement is circular); there were of course hundreds and thousands of painters in the Ming and Ch'ing to whom Levenson's charge of derivativeness applies very well. The Su-chou School after the time of Shen Chou and Wen Cheng-ming was staffed largely by minor men woefully short on new ideas, and the Orthodox School of the Four Wangs and their associates, whose claim to the legitimate Southern School succession in the post-Tung Ch'i-ch'ang era was upheld by all, included artists in whose works an adherence to rules and conventions did indeed stifle creativity. Even such an illustrious figure as Wang Shih-min (1592-1680), oldest of the Four Wangs and probably (somewhat paradoxically) the one most responsible for creating their collective style, lapsed into stereotypes in much of his production, especially in his later years. But his fault was not an adherence to ancient modes; it was rather in an easy repetition of his own earlier creative achievements, a common enough way for an esteemed master to come to a bad end. His grandson Wang Yuan-ch'i (1642-1715), by contrast, using a vocabulary of forms quite as narrow as that of any of the others, built brilliantly, inexhaustibly varied landscape pictures on a few compositional types. The sameness that some viewers profess to find in his *oeuvre* is the same sameness that the beginning listener is likely to find in the music of Mozart: the work follows a fixed form, and its substance is in large part familiar and unexciting. But it is just this controlled context that allows the individualizing traits of the particular work to register most distinctly on the consciousness; again, a charge of stereotype misses the mark.

Such distinctions are not peculiar to Ming-Ching literati painting, and if we could somehow quantify originality and imitativeness, we would probably find them there in roughly the same proportions as in, say, painting of the Southern Sung period. Moreover, the imitative works would be observed to be over-dependent, not so much on the distant past, but (again as always) on the recent past and present: an unoriginal painter was not that because he "worked in old styles," but because he did so in the same ways that the painters around him did.

What we are left with, then, is the commonplace phenomenon of a somewhat anti-academic theory of art held by painters in whose works the incidence of academicism is about what it is elsewhere—scarcely the stuff of paradox.

THE PROBLEM OF FANG (IMITATION)

Where the later scholar-artists differ significantly from their predecessors, with respect to imitativeness, is not in their practice of it but in their critical and theoretical tolerance of it, their insistent advocacy of "imitating the old masters," which has misled so many into supposing that their painting must be uninspired pastiche. Herein lies the basis for the considerable residue of validity that remains in Levenson's conclusions even after his central paradox has been overturned (into an upright position, that is): while the conflict between anti-academic theory and academic practice proves to have been more contrived than real, since the equation of their kind of "imitation" with academicism will not hold, a certain contradiction does exist, within the theoretical writings, between an insistence on spontaneity and originality, in one direction, and on conformity with old traditions in the other. This contradiction can be resolved, or accounted for, in various ways. Levenson, typically, does not resolve it at all, but turns it to use: in the formulation toward which his whole argument has been tending, it is a conflict between the ideal of "spontaneous creativity," to which the Ming-Ch'ing literati were committed through their theoretical positions and critical judgments of value as connoisseurs of earlier painting, and the conservatism and backward-looking stance dictated by their status as members of "a dominant social class, traditionalistic, humanistic, and essentially opposed to specialization."[10] This situation he is

10. Levenson, *Confucian China*, vol. I, p. 31.

able to see as symptomatic of the tensions and contradictions of late Confucian society, the conflict between the amateur ideal and the need for specialist expertise in the modern world, that led to its decline and eventual breakdown. Chinese writers, by contrast, from the time of Tung Ch'i-ch'ang to the present, have attempted internal resolutions, defining the kind of free imitation called *fang* (not, as Levenson has it, *lin-mo*, literally "copying and tracing," which refers to a more faithful replication) so as to reconcile it theoretically with originality and individual creativity. Tung Ch'i-ch'ang provides the classical reconciliation, distinguishing direct copying (*lin-mo*) as practiced by the "common painter," from the more difficult and desirable attainment of a "spiritual communion" (*shen-hui*) with the earlier work and its author.[11] The product of the latter need not—should not—resemble its model closely at all; Tung goes so far as to say that such a close resemblance in fact removes the work *further* from the model.[12]

It is possible also to argue that there *was* no contradiction between imitating nature and imitating the old masters. Thus Wai-kam Ho interprets Tung Ch'i-ch'ang's statement ("A painter who models after the ancient masters is on the right track. But to advance himself he must model after the heaven and earth") in the light of the metaphysics of the T'ai-chou School and Wang Yang-ming's Doctrine of the Mind:

> According to this school of Neo-Confucianism, "the universe exists only in one's mind"; and since there is no reality outside the mind, to learn from nature therefore means to learn from one's own mind. Similarly, "all truth in the classics exists only in one's mind," and . . . "to return to the past is therefore to return to one's own mind."[13]

Another recent treatment of the problem by Ju-hsi Chou similarly relates *fang* to the Doctrine of the Mind, which "alone could have provided a conceptual basis for *fang*: for, in spite of its imitative overtone, *fang*, ironically is an expression of the subjectivism of *hsin-hsueh* under which the two poles of originality and imitation can find their subsumption in what may rightly be considered as a

11. Tung Ch'i-ch'ang, *Jung-t'ai pieh-chi*, VI, 6a.
12. Ibid., 19b. See Mae Anna Quan Pang's essay "Late Ming Painting Theory," in the catalog *The Restless Landscape: Chinese Painting of the Late Ming Period* (Berkeley: University of California Press, 1971), p. 23.
13. Ho, "Tung Ch'i-ch'ang", p. 13.

cerebral sublimation of man's intuitive faculty."[14] However, in a subsequent discussion of the individualist painter Tao-chi's opposition to the practice of *fang*, Chou himself points out that "even though the Doctrine of the Mind is fundamental, the connection is not a reversible one"; the same Doctrine of the Mind could "lead to a contrary solution where a direct application of the *liang-chi* ('clear intelligence') over external phenomena was the case."[15] That is, the Doctrine of the Mind could serve as the basis for *fang*, but equally for an opposed, anti-*fang* stand. This interchangeability of relationships, which is present elsewhere as here, reveals the limitations and nonexclusive nature of such formulations. The acceptance of any one of these "internal" resolutions of the problem of imitation vs. originality not only as true but as *the* truth, excluding others, would clearly obviate explications such as Levenson's which introduce extrinsic historical factors; no need to account for a contradition that does not exist. But in fact these resolutions do no more than attempt to show that A can be reconciled with B; they do not, and cannot, show that A and B can be reconciled *only* in this way. The tension between the two elements that occasioned the attempt is not thereby dissipated, and is still susceptible to such an analysis as Levenson's.

ARTLESS STUDIES OF ART

What I have here termed internal resolutions and external explanations are all, in another sense, external; they move between theories of art and ideas operating outside art, or between theories and historical situations, never touching more than glancingly, if at all, on the works of art themselves. Their authors seem unaware that their field of discourse is so removed from their supposed subject; often they seem to be assuming that in manipulating concepts from art theory and criticism, and relating these to currents of thought and historical circumstances, as though art and statements about it were equivalent or identical, they are effectively integrating art into its intellectual-historical context. But that integration, while it may to be sure have its own interest and validity, takes place outside art proper. The Chinese literature on painting, in its volume and richness, offers unusual

14. Chou, *In Quest of the Primordial Line*, pp. 14-15.
15. Ibid., p. 85.

opportunities for studies of this kind; but it offers also the temptation to stop within it, and not go beyond the written sources to relate them convincingly to the works of art themselves, by demonstrating how theoretical positions were (or failed to be) put into practice. To assume that the beliefs of Ming-Ch'ing artists and critics sometimes affected Ming-Ch'ing painting is safe enough (although ordinarily the theories come later, to rationalize or justify an existing practice); but to assume this does not absolve us from trying to move past the theories and show *how* they affected, or were exemplified in, painting. A discussion of the *fang* mode of imitation in Chinese painting, for instance, that does not deal with how it is manifested in actual works can obviously provide only a limited understanding of the phenomenon. One might similarly write an analysis of metaphor in English poetry without quoting any uses of it in particular poems or even referring to them; but such an analysis would be condemned from the start to maneuver on the periphery of its subject without ever quite penetrating it.

It is obvious also that such an analysis of an artistic phenomenon cannot, in turn, serve as an adequate basis for moving further outward, as Levenson sought to do. From his position as an intellectual historian, he made what use he could of the information and interpretations available to him; his conclusions were in part faulty, not so much because of faults in his method, but because the art historians, at the time he wrote, had not done their job properly. No one had described, clearly and accurately, how the practice of *fang* worked in Ming-Ch'ing painting, or what kind of painter Tun Ch'i-ch'ang really was, or in what relationship his works stand to those of the Yuan dynasty and earlier masters he professed to follow.[16]

When we suggest that theoretical and critical concepts can serve as intermediaries through which art can, so to speak, be approached from outside, we should recognize the danger that is involved in doing so—the danger, that is, of assuming (as writers on art so often seem to do) that the connection between theory and practice was necessarily always close, and that the artist simply

16. An exception should be made here of Victoria Contag's article of 1952 (see note 5), illustrated with paintings by Tung Ch'i-ch'ang and others; while it does not deal with questions of style, it could have provided Levenson with a better understanding of the literati artists' use of type forms and old styles than any of the writings he cites (although these include three others by the same author). Nelson Wu's major work on Tung Ch'i-ch'ang was finished by then, but was (and still is) in the form of an unpublished doctoral thesis.

exemplified in pictures what he wrote in words. We have too many examples in our own time of painfully obvious disparity between profound utterances and banal paintings, or statements and works that seem otherwise irreconcilable, to assume anything of the kind. Suppose, for example, we were able to establish firmly that Tung Ch'i-ch'ang in his writings, and presumably in the thought behind them, held a certain theory of the nature of perceptual experience and cognition, and the relationship between them—a theory that seems to derive, let us grant, from Neo-Confucian ideas. Having established this, we read Tung's own statement that the artist, while he should study the old masters, must in the end learn from nature in order to achieve greatness. We might then seem justified in going on to assume that Tung meant by "learning from nature" this Neo-Confucian mode of acquiring knowledge, and that this kind of knowledge of the world, embodied in his paintings, is the source of their particular artistic qualities. We would appear thus to have established a firm, although once-removed, relationship between works of art and a system of thought. But is the basic assumption really sound? One might equally argue (and I do not mean here to take either position, but only to present them as alternatives) that Tung's activity as a painter, whatever he may (as a theorist) say about the importance of learning from nature, was in fact more analagous to the creative activity of the composer, the qualities of whose music are not ordinarily attributed to any special manner in which he experiences the sounds of everyday life (notions of musical creation according to which Chopin hears the rain dripping from the eaves and composes the "Raindrop Prelude" are no longer taken seriously) but rather to his ability to create, largely independently of everyday auditory experience, abstract structures of sound that possess aesthetically satisfying form, and somehow embody, or evoke through formal similarities and congruences, human thought and feeling. Might not the fundamental nature of Tung's paintings, that is, be that they present structures of visual form as the composer presents structures of sound? That these paintings are also more or less recognizable as pictures of landscapes does not by any means rule out this possibility, since their status as images of nature need not be crucial to their qualities as works of art. Which view of Tung's paintings is the true one is a question that can be decided (to the extent that it can be decided at all) only through a study of his paintings, and not through his theories, since the often-assumed correspondence between theories and paintings may or may not be present, and always remains to be established. The paintings are the ultimate reality, to which all outside factors stand in relationships that are more or less tenuous and in which simple causality, in either direction, can never automatically be assumed.

To say this is not to deny the *possibility* of such causality; ideas current in philosophy can, of course, affect painting, either directly through attitudes held by the artist, or indirectly through theories of art by which he is influenced. Similarly, events of history can affect paintings by way of their impact on the lives of artists, or on the circumstances in which the works are created. It would be foolish to see art as so self-contained a phenomenon as to deny, for example, that the destruction of the Hangchow court in the thirteenth century, and the dispersal of the artists in its Painting Academy, was a causal factor in the sudden decline from central importance of the Academy styles. But when we move from simple quantitative effects of that kind to the qualitative, in which it is the nature of the work that is affected, we are again on unfirm ground. Such suggestions can of course be convincing without being provable. Werner Speiser, for instance, points out that the great Individualist artists of the early Ch'ing period were mostly born in the period 1610 to 1630, so that they experienced the fall of the Ming and the coming to power of the Manchus during their formative years. He characterizes those born in these two decades as a "hard-pressed, storm-racked generation," whose paintings express their sense of anguish and outrage in somber landscapes and tortured forms. The paintings by artists born after 1630, who generally accepted Manchu rule as a fact of their lives, tend to be more stable and unimpassioned.[17] Taken as an hypothesis to be tested and modified by further evidence—research done since Speiser wrote, for example, indicates that the greatest of the Individualists, Tao-chi, was probably born around 1641, later than was previously supposed[18]—this observation is stimulating and worthy of serious consideration. For the mood and temperament of the painter to be in some part set by the historical circumstances of his time, as well as by the events of his personal life, and for these in turn to set in some part the expressive content of his paintings, is a perfectly plausible sequence. But here again

17. In his section "Painting" in vol. III of *Chinese Art* (London, 1963), pp. 33-34.

18. Wen Fong, "A Letter from Shih-t'ao to Pa-ta Shan-jen and the Problems of Shih-t'ao's Chronology," *Archives of the Chinese Art Society of America*, XIII (1959), pp. 22-53. Speiser gave 1620 as Tao-chi's birthdate, without identifying his source of information.

we must beware of stopping on the periphery of art, and supposing that a presentation of the painter's biography with the appropriate references to these circumstances and events, and conjectures about his response to them, will suffice to "explain" his paintings. To suppose so would be to fail to recognize the complexity and unpredictability of his mind, which is not to be regarded as a simple machine for transforming stimuli from outside into pictorial expressions. We might say, if we wish, that the fall of the Ming dynasty made Ch'en Hung-shou (1599-1652) an embittered man, but we cannot say that it made his paintings what they are; no such simple causal relationship can exist between an event and a style. We should in fact mistrust *any* formulation that states or implies simple causality in seeking to link the style of a work of art with factors outside it. (Other features of the work than style can of course be so linked; an artist may for instance depict a certain subject because he is commissioned to do so.)

PAINTINGS IN HISTORY

My own beliefs about the kinds of relationships that can validly be drawn between art and other elements of human history are based on those of Max Loehr—understandably, since his pronouncements on this subject in seminars still ring in the heads of his students. He said, if I may paraphrase him from memory, that the art historian is evading his responsibility whenever he accedes with the common notion that art is to be seen against an historical and intellectual *background*, like a picture against a wall, and that it is illuminated by that background, and best understood in relation to it. His proper task is not merely to accept what others supply, and bring it to bear to explain his subject; he must see art and the rest of human cultue in a more dynamic and organic relationship than that, one in which art is an active force, not just a passive recipient of influences from outside.[19] Loehr, and those who follow his way of thinking, are thus suspicious of the usual formulations

19. "If, as in ordinary parlance, it is said that a work is expressive of its time, we must keep in mind that the expressive element, its style, corresponds to no objective reality supplied by its time or its character or spirit, the *Zeitgeist*; on the contrary, this work is a constitutive feature in a pattern which comes to be accepted as representative of a time. The *Zeitgeist* is nothing but a hypostasis of the pattern engendered by a group of works." Max Loehr, "Some Fundamental Issues in the History of Chinese Painting," *Journal of Asian Studies*, XXIII: 2 (February 1964), p. 190.

in which developments in style are somehow occasioned by (or "reflect," a more evasive word which we frequently use) historical developments, or intellectual currents, or shifts in social values. In these formulations, art is given the status of a kind of decoration to history, taking its character from events in other spheres, the ones that are held to be really determinative. It is like a flower which, somehow lacking any latent characteristics in its seed, takes its form and color from the soil in which it grows, and is thereby reduced to the status of a useful indicator of the composition of the soil. Art should be more. If, on the other hand, the art historian refuses to accept this view and works first to reach an understanding of his proper subject in all its complexity—to chart its broad development and see individual contributions against this, to find out what the artistic issues were and what they meant in their time—he will then and only then be in a position to make his contribution to our understanding of, for instance, late Ming society and culture. Whether he himself attempts to draw wider implications from the patterns he perceives and to relate them to others outside his field of study, or whether he leaves this to be done by specialists in other disciplines who use his conclusions, matters less than that the segment of the history of art he constructs be in itself sound and true to the works of art he is treating.

Why, it will be asked, cannot the social historian, the intellectual historian, or anyone else deal directly with the works of art, without this intervention of the art historian? Art is after all a universal language, and the interpretation of it should require no special expertise. The best way to answer that question, without digressing into a consideration of the flaws in the notion of art as a universal language or a general defense of specialization, is to point out that the historical significance of a work of art (as distinct from its inherent meaning and value) is a function of its relationship with other works of art, its position and import in a sequence or some other kind of context made up of related works; and the defining of such historical context and significance is an important part of what the art historian does, as another kind of historian finds meaning in historical events through understanding how they relate to the circumstances that surround them. All the aspects of painting that are at issue in the foregoing discussion, and in Levenson's, are of this nature, aspects that paintings possess only in relation to other paintings, and to the history of painting.

A painting is not in itself, that is, either orthodox or individualist, innovative or derivative, embodying allusions to the past or free from them; and none of these aspects can be derived from the individual work. These are the aspects of painting that figure in the arguments of the theorists, along with questions of tradition, school, lineage—all matters of interrelationship—and these are the aspects through which painting can most effectively be brought into a larger historical complex. Art enters history through the history of art.

To say this is not to diminish the importance of the individual work, but to enhance it; it is to recognize that the choices the artist made in creating it were made in a context, an art-historical situation, in which certain possibilities were open to him, and in which certain values were attached to those possibilities, so that his choices take on significance in relation to that context. In this sense, the creation of a work of art has the character of an existential act, its meaning defined by its relation to the circumstances under which it is undertaken. Attention to this aspect of the work of art must not divert us from full consideration of its individual qualities; but it allows us to ascribe additional meaning, and in particular historical meaning, to those qualities, as we cannot do so long as the work is considered in isolation. We must see it as both object and event.

The medium through which significant interrelationships between works of art manifest themselves, and the main matter of the art historian's study, is style. The word is used in a number of senses, which have been admirably defined in a famous essay by Meyer Shapiro;[20] we need not attempt such full definition here, but will say only that we will use it, not in the very broad sense that Levenson intends, for instance, when he writes "The Ming style was the amateur style,"[21] but in more limited meaning, to comprise those elements and features of the works of art that determine not only their expressive content but also their individuality (or lack of it) with respect to other works. Used thus, style can be regarded as an indicator of the special qualities of the art of a particular person, group, locale, or time. It is by operating in the realm of style that the art historian can move between art and the surrounding culture.

20. Meyer Schapiro, "Style," reprinted from *Anthropology Today*, ed. A.L. Kroeber (Chicago: University of Chicago Press 1953) in *Aesthetics Today*, ed. Morris Philipson (Cleveland: World Publishing Co., 1961), pp. 81-113.

21. Levenson, *Confucian China*, vol. I, p. 16.

> By considering the succession of works in time and space and by matching the variations of style with historical events and with the varying features of other fields of culture, the historian of art attempts, with the help of common-sense psychology and social theory, to account for the changes of style or specific traits.[22]

Thus Shapiro; and I would demur, for reasons indicated above, only at the "account for" at the end.

Two special conditions give to the treatment of style in Ming-Ch'ing painting a special importance, and a special complexity. One is that the artists' intense concentration on style leads them to lose interest in subject matter, which is so diminished in variety and significance that it would be only a small exaggeration to say that most of later Chinese painting, and much of the best of it, has no subject. The same river scenes, along with a few other standard landscape types varying only in style (compositional variations on an established type being of course elements of style), make up the bulk of it; and we are forced to conclude that the status of the painting as a picture cannot account for any essential part of its raison d'être. Behind most scholarly studies of European art is the assumption—usually safe for that material—that different ways of representing a subject can be taken as indications of different attitudes toward that subject, or conceptions of it or feelings about it, held by the artist and also, to some degree, by others in his society. No such assumption can be made about the later Chinese painting; otherwise, we would have such patent absurdities as studies of "Eighteenth Century Attitudes Toward Blossoming Plum Branches," or "The Early Ch'ing View of River Scenery." Moreover, where historians of European art can analyze meaning of other kinds—iconography, mythological allusions, symbolism—and find another level of historical relevance there, the historian of Chinese painting has little besides style on which to base his distinctions and his conclusions.

The other special condition is the presence in much of the painting of an additional element, an added dimension, which is perhaps not to be found so pervasively in any other body of art: the element of stylistic allusion, references to the styles of masters of the past. This second condition partly compensates for the first, since the earlier style functions, in a sense, as the subject of the painting,

22. Schapiro, "Style," p. 81. Cf. Max Loehr: ". . . representing as it were the datable outcome of a dialogue between an individual and the sum of tradition, style remains tied to its period, remains an historical aspect." ["The Question of Individualism in Chinese Art," *Journal of the History of Ideas*, XXII: 2 (April-June 1961), p. 149.]

or in place of the subject. A painting can be about the landscape style of some old master, that is, more than it is about natural landscape. We have come back to *fang*, discussed above as a kind of imitation. We can now see it in still another light, as a means through which the artist, besides achieving the old Confucian aim of demonstrating cultural continuity,[23] takes a part in establishing, to a degree, his own art-historical position by choosing the referents by which his work is to be understood and judged. His control is not absolute: a work by a late Ming painter imitating Ni Tsan of the Yuan dynasty must always be, in some fundamental features, a painting in a late Ming style; but it is not so in as simple as sense as, for instance, that in which a painting by a mid-fifteenth century artist working in Florence must be in a mid-fifteenth century Florentine style. We might clarify our discussion by using a different term for the derivative element, and saying that his painting is in the *manner* of Ni Tsan; but we would still be left with a more complex concept of style, since the use of a particular pre-existing *manner* will inevitably affect the *style* of the work, however we define it, and the two are in any case not easy to separate.

Regarded in this way, the adoption of old landscape manners by so many Ming-Ch'ing artists can be seen as the outcome of their deep involvement with earlier phases of their art, with stylistic schools and lineages, with their particular form of art history. In choosing to disengage himself partially from the history of art, by declining to settle meekly into a temporally and geographically assigned place in it, the style-conscious artist engages himself with the whole of it. Ming-Ch'ing painting, as a late stage in a very long tradition, exemplifies ideally the general truth that the course of development of any art can be seen in terms of a gradual growth of consciousness of its own means and processes. Moreover, when styles are consciously chosen, the choice can take on an added significance in that particular values were attached to styles, values involving local pride, or social status, or even intellectual or political commitments. Styles come to have implications that go

23. This desire was one of the constants of Confucian society; cf. David Nivison: "It is normal to find a Chinese philosopher 'deriving' his thought from some ancient writer, book, or phrase; this is, however, a cultural compulsion, not a truly derivative process. What actually happens is something much more like reading ink-blots—or interpreting the hexagrams." *The Life and Thought of Chang Hsueh-cheng (1738-1801)* (Stanford: Stanford University Press, 1966), p. 66.

beyond the confines of art. Traditionalism, for example, is not an issue so long as a tradition is strong and authoritative, and an artist can take his place in it unquestioningly, unconsciously. This was still possible in the middle Ming period, when an artist working in Su-chou would normally paint in a recognizable Wu School style, and a Hang-chou artist in a Che School style, and when amateurism and professionalism were still relatively distinct stylistic determinants. When traditions no longer exercise this kind of compulsion, or not so strongly, and the artist can *choose* to align himself with one or another, his position there has a new meaning. By the late Ming, everything was in question; dogmatism of the kind that Tung Ch'i-ch'ang and others display can grow only when nothing is naturally accepted. A painter in Su-chou might turn against his local tradition and choose to follow the rival school of Tung and his friends in nearby Hua-t'ing; a scholar-official in Nanking might choose to work in a landscape manner derived from a professional tradition of the Sung dynasty, in clear and stated opposition to the prevailing amateur trends. Issues are drawn more clearly and explicitly than ever before, and the range of choice widened through the opening of new areas of the past to be mined for stylistic ore.

The relevance of all this to the question of how art can best be correlated with history is obvious: when it reaches such a condition, the history of painting begins in important respects to resemble intellectual history, social history, political history, and the issues to interlock. Styles function as ideas: they originate, evolve, conflict, develop tensions that may be resolved; they are asserted or denied, often with vehemence; they can be combined or opposed to one another; they may comment on or criticize other styles; they have implications that go far beyond their actual expressive content. The patterns they form in their interaction can be recognized as congruent with patterns in other spheres of culture and society, in part through the presence of common issues.

The period and the body of art that Levenson was concerned with, then, offers unusually fertile ground on which to carry out the kind of synthesizing study for which his works will remain as models. Before painting can be brought into such studies as an integral element of Ming-Ch'ing culture, however—painting itself rather than ideas and statements about it—it must be better understood in itself: what the major currents were and what the minor, how they interacted, how local schools are to be distinguished in terms of style, what the collective achievements were and what the principal innovations, what patterns the stylistic development of individual masters followed and what were their particular contributions, what were the crucial issues and what meanings were attached to them. We must map out the complex network of interrelationships within which the individual works take their places; we must know and be able to interpret, for these works, what is the ultimate concern of the historian of art: the humane significance of style.

CHINA'S WORLDS: COSMOPOLITANISM, NATIONALISM, AND THE "PROBLEM OF CHINESE IDENTITY"

Ralph C. Croizier

> China dies at the latest with the fall of the last dynasty; and what presents itself to our eyes today under the name Chinese is only one of the quasi-European and interchangeable civilizations which characterize our time. In fifty years one will have great difficulties in distinguishing China from any country in Europe, Africa, or America. Then the universal harmony of the Celestial Empire will have been replaced by the global ennui to which modern man is tending. Perhaps this future China will offer important aspects to the sociologists. Alas! It will be divested of interest for the historians of culture.
>
> *Willy Hartner*, "Classicisme et declin culturel dans la civilization chinoise"[1]

We start with one of Levenson's own paradoxes: ". . . the technological revolution, making nations more and more alike . . while passions rise for national independence."[2] Not one of his more novel or challenging observations, when every contemporary

1. Willy Hartner, "Classicisme et declin culturel dans la civilisation chinoise," *Classicisme et declin culturel dans l'histoire de l'Islam* (Paris: Editions Bessons-Chantenerle 1957), pp. 367-374. Quote used as Final Exam question in Levenson's proseminar on Modern Chinese Intellectual History, Spring 1962.

2. Joseph R. Levenson, "The Province, the Nation, and the World: The Problem of Chinese Identity," in *Approaches to Modern Chinese History*, eds. Albert Feuerwerker et al. (Berkeley: University of California Press, 1967), p. 273.

world civilization textbook notes, and often laments, the same phenomenon. Then why start an essay on so original a thinker as Joseph Levenson with so unoriginal a remark?

Again, paradoxically, it is appropriate. Many of Levenson's most brilliant insights started with a re-examination of the trivial or commonplace. This ability to put the familiar in a startlingly new perspective, to shake more meaning out of what had been taken for granted—to make a minor figure like Liao P'ing historically significant or a hoary cliché like "Confucian China" vibrantly meaningful—was one of the most striking features of his work. Moreover, he was especially fond of the paradoxical as a stimulus for probing beneath the surface of historical phenomena. Probably this was because paradox entails tension between an unlikely juxtaposition of forces and such dichotomies, or "creative tensions," were central to Levenson's method. There was also the delight he took in the ambiguities and shifting meaning of words and ideas.[3] Labeling, the fetish for precise and limiting definition, was one of his bêtes noires: "To resist the taxonomical zeal for precision, the literalist's restriction of one phrase to one concept is both an intellectual and moral requirement for the historian."[4] In any event, such paradoxes as an anti-academic academicism in literati painting, formerly iconoclastic Communist revolutionaries' patronage of traditional Chinese culture, or assertive national identity in a cosmopolitan world, often formed his starting point. And resolving the paradox by showing how the logically incongruous were compatible (necessarily compatible) historically was often his method. Let us then take his last great unresolved paradox and unfinished theme—cosmopolitanism and nationalism—as our point of departure.

It is not surprising that he was challenged by, and in turn challenged, this paradox. In retrospect, it seems inevitable that his work and his own inner concerns would lead him to systematic exploration of the question of particular identity (national, cultural) and universal (cosmopolitan) values. Although he explicitly took up this theme only late, it is foreshadowed in that fountainhead of many themes and questions, *Liang Ch'i-ch'ao and*

3. This is not an essay on Levenson's "methodology," which in any event is too hard, dry, and social scientific a term to describe the way he worked, but I cannot resist noting his sensitivity to language, and especially semantic shifts, as an indicator of historical change.

4. Joseph R. Levenson, *Confucian China and Its Modern Fate* (Berkeley: University of California Press, 1965), vol. III, 85.

the Mind of Modern China, and runs close beneath the surface throughout the *Confucian China* trilogy. The "quest for equivalence" with the West which he identified as the major continuity and preoccupation in Liang's thinking was in response to a threatened loss of cultural identity as the pillars of China's traditional world collapsed and she was pulled into a new and larger world of aggressively competitive nation-states. The same theme—loss of tradition and the need to find a new but still distinctively Chinese identity—was further developed in the "history and value" dichotomy of *Confucian China and Its Modern Fate: The Problem of Intellectual Continuity*, while the second volume of the trilogy, *The Problem of Monarchical Decay*, orchestrated the transition from culturalism to nationalism in terms of institutional change. Then with the final volume, *The Problem of Historical Significance*, Levenson turned to history itself (modern Chinese reinterpretations of their own history) as his last rendition of the death and transfiguration of Confucian China.

It ended with the Chinese Communists, as inheritors of China's history, "museumifying" the past that their own sense of Chineseness would not comfortably let them denounce in total. Museumification soon proved to be a less stable basis for new China's relationship with her past than he had thought and it also did not locate modern China in the new larger-than-Chinese world around her. The problem of identity, for modern Chinese and for modern man everywhere, still worried Levenson as he saw technological unification and cultural homogenization creating "a cosmopolitan world of interchangeable exhibits."[5]

> In a true world history, when all past achievements are in the museum without walls, everyone's past would be everyone else's; which implies that quite un-Confucian thing the loss of a sense of tradition. To us today the sense of tradition is not strong, not so much because we have no tradition but because we have mixed so many traditions.[6]

Thus, Confucian China's modern fate becomes *pari passu* that of everyone and of every tradition. It was not a conclusion he was comfortable with and he had to return to it.

5. Joseph R. Levenson, *Revolution and Cosmopolitanism: The Western Stage and the Chinese Stages* (Berkeley: University of California Press, 1971), p. x.
6. Levenson, *Confucian China*, vol. III, 85.

Examination of its implications began with his essay, "The Province, the Nation, and the World," in the *Festschrift* for John Fairbank published in 1967. It was just a beginning, for as explained in the only footnote to it, "what follows is an essay, not an article—an essay in the sense of first attempt, some theses thrown at the paper, a suggestion of a larger work in progress."[7] The larger work was to be his second trilogy, tentatively titled, *Provincialism and Cosmopolitanism: Chinese History and the Meaning of "Modern Times."*[8] The subtitle was indicative of the broader than Chinese history concerns that motivated him, just as the subtitle for the *Festschrift* essay, "The Problem of Chinese Identity," expressed what had long been an important theme in all his work on modern China.

As a preliminary sketch, this essay did not fully work out all the ideas Levenson had on this question, but it did clarify much of what was only alluded to before. Put simply (at the risk of oversimplification), he saw Confucian China as being a world in itself with a perpetual, but vital, tension between the transprovincial cosmopolitanism of the high Confucian culture of the imperial bureaucracy and the local provincial identity of peasants and of scholars as local gentry. When the West intruded into this Confucian world and new intellectuals were attracted to external ideas, the old cosmopolitan world of Confucian high culture was made to seem both anachronistic and "provincial" in the context of this larger world. Thus, emerging nationalism forced erstwhile cosmopolitan culturalism into a provincial guise. "In short, the Ch'ing's, the Empire's 'cosmopolitans' became the Republic's, the nations's, provincials."[9] But what of the real provincials in the Chinese provinces—Hunan, Kwangtung, Chekiang, etc.? Nationalism also demanded that such local or regional loyalties, which had been the symbiotic correlative to Confucian cosmopolitanism, also be transcended by loyalty to the Chinese nation: "Chinese nationalism involved a scaling up from a congeries of provinces, a scaling down from a world."[10]

But, of course, it was not that simple. There was the new nationalism's "romantic" (provincial) attachment to Chinese cul-

7. Levenson, "The Province, the Nation, and the World," p. 268.

8. Joseph R. Levenson, "The Genesis of Confucian China and Its Modern Fate," in *The Historian's Workshop*, ed. Perry Curtis (New York: Knopf, 1970), p. 285.

9. Levenson, "The Province, the Nation, and the World," p. 287.

10. Ibid., p. 287.

ture. There was the wounded pride in seeing China relegated to provincial status (just one of the underdeveloped nations) on the world map. There was the peculiarly modern malaise of cosmopolitan rootlessness. And there was the paradox of modern Communist indulgence and patronage of many aspects of provincial identity—provincial theatre, local dialects, folk arts. Most of Levenson's effort did not go into explaining the shift from Confucian to modern cosmopolitanism, for in slightly different terms *Confucian China and Its Modern Fate* had already done much of that. The emphasis now turned to the provincial-cosmopolitan tension in the post-Confucian modern world.

Communist patronage of such provincial characteristics as regional theatre in local dialect was at first glance puzzling. In theory, anyway, earlier nationalists like the Kuomintang had not been nearly so tolerant. Integral nationalism demanded that expressions of local genius be blotted out or subsumed in one national identity; the Communist government, also nationalistic, seemed to celebrate provincial differences. Levenson found two previously used clues for resolving the paradox: first, the Communists' sensitivity to class analysis of culture; second, their waning enmity to once-dangerous forces that seemed to have lost any ability to threaten the new order. Just as time and historical change had made active anti-Confucianism no longer necessary, had allowed them to museumify their old enemy, so once-threatening provincial identities seemed to be no longer dangerous to a firmly unified People's Republic. From the Communists' patronage of provincial theatre, another metaphor was suggested—theatre itself. Once-authentic provincial traditions nurtured in a local setting became acted-out roles for a national audience: Shensi folk dances in Szechwan, Szechwanese opera on tour in Shensi, and both as regular performances in the national theatre in Peking. In the new setting, "As a repertoire of roles, not a congeries of identities, such traditions would no longer be a range of natural styles which divide the nation or abort the nation's birth."[11]

And to class-conscious Marxists the popular association of local culture also served as a redeeming virtue. "Cosmopolitan" Confucian high culture had been a gentry preserve; modern cosmopolitan culture smacked of bourgeois Shanghai and the

11. Joseph R. Levenson, "'Provincialism' and the Place of Chinese Communism in History" (Paper prepared for Center for Chinese Studies Seminar, April 19, 1965), p. 2.

capitalist West. Popular culture had been an answer to the search for a nonliterati Chinese cultural tradition; local or provincial cultures could be part of the answer to a new, but non-Western, Chinese culture. In both cases the real concern was class and nation, not tradition or province. "Chinese Communist 'provincialism' (like Chinese Communist 'Confucianism') means to make the provinces past, by collecting their historical offerings as bequests to the modern synthesizing nation."[12]

Class analysis also had implications for the other side of the provincialism-cosmopolitanism dichotomy. It contained possibilities for linking the revolutionary Chinese nation to the larger world as well as for transcending her own provinces. Levenson demonstrated these possibilities through another of his virtuoso performances in semantic analysis. In the terms *min-tsu* (nationality) and *jen-min* (people) he located a revealing dichotomy. *Min-tsu* had been used by the Kuomintang as an expression of organic national unity transcending class. *Jen-min* was used by the Communists with a specific class meaning as "the people" (i.e., the masses). The class meaning of the latter term gave it a more than national application. The "people" (even more than the proletariat) are everywhere, transcending provincial differences and national boundaries. China, of course, has more than her share of people and as a People's Republic (the only authentic, nonrevisionist one?) has claims for special affinity with "the people" throughout the world.[13]

> As *jen-min*, provincials have supranational not subnational associations. "The people," located first at their most particular in the local earth of the provinces, then move into the abstract as the transnational, transcultural, universal ground of a more-than-Chinese vision of the world.

It looked like a happy ending for the Chinese search for a respectable way back into the world. It was also an ingenious working out of the contradictions inherent in the provincialism-cosmopolitanism dichotomy.

But even as he was arriving at this solution, events in China were making it inadequate as a final resolution of China's new place in the world, for with the outbreak of the Great Proletarian Cultural

12. Levenson, "'Provincialism' and the Place of Chinese Communism," p. 3.
13. Levenson, "The Province, the Nation, and the World," p. 28.

Revolution, a new and harsher wind blew across China's relations with the rest of the world and with her own past. From Rangoon to London diplomatic relations and people's diplomacy alike broke down in the ideological gale emanating from Peking. China seemed more isolated than at any time since the nineteenth century, while internally neither museum nor theatre withstood the storm. Museums harbored "the four olds" which evidently were not so safely out of the way after all; theatre, by dictate of Madame Mao, was to be devoted solely to glorifying the revolutionary present. For this revolutionized national theatre, Peking opera was the chosen medium, not the regional variants.

Levenson trimmed his sails, and his interpretation of Communist China, to meet this new storm with much more finesse than most of his colleagues. His last essays, including the small posthumously published volume *Revolution and Cosmopolitanism*, rather convincingly explained the latest unforeseen developments in the same categories used in earlier analysis. The "provincial cultural spirit" of the Cultural Revolution was seen as manifestation of a crisis of confidence in the course of the revolution, the fear that traditional and revisionist forces might yet pervert its goals. In this context, the cultural tolerance of museumification was over. Revolutionaries were "back at action stations" against a not-so-dead past.

They were also on guard against dangerous influences from without. Earlier in *Revolution and Cosmopolitanism* Levenson had discussed twentieth-century China's liberal cosmopolitans and their efforts to bring modern world culture (specifically in drama) to China. They had been disowned and denounced in the People's republic for their emphasis on "Art for art's sake" and on a classless "universal human nature."[14] But "progressive" world literature and drama, especially but not exclusively that from fellow socialist countries, had been approved in the first decade after the revolution. It was only with the coming of the Cultural Revolution by the mid-sixties that the door was slammed on these contacts, that a "provincial spirit" seemed to animate the Chinese cultural world.

One way of explaining this was to link the anticosmopolitan tone of the Cultural Revolution to its anti-urban policies. With cities, home of the "urban overlords," seen as centers of privilege and

14. Levenson, *Revolution and Cosmopolitanism*, p. 31.

revisionism, once again emphasis had to be placed on the rural areas. So in education, medicine, and industry the Cultural Revolution attempted a massive shift of emphasis from city to countryside. Cities everywhere, especially ports, are the natural foci for cosmopolitanism, and the countryside the natural home of provincialism. From that alone, one might expect that the campaign against urban privilege would be anticosmopolitan in tone.

But Levenson saw more than simple anti-urban provincialism behind the new cultural policies. He also picked up his old theme of amateurism and professionalism to show the social and ideological motives behind this new provincialism. The professionals—technical specialists, or "experts" in Maoist parlance—were necessarily linked by their specialization to specialists elsewhere. Physicists everywhere must read the latest international journals if they are to keep up with their field. At least in their own specialty, they must share a kind of cosmopolitanism. To the more zealous defenders of ideological purity there was the fear that this "expertness" would come before "redness," would separate the professionals from the masses and pervert the goal of the egalitarian society. Communist industrializers could not disdain technical expertise the way their Confucian forebears had in the old agricultural society, for experts or professionals were needed to build the new China. But they were suspect for their separation from the people and, since the people were the nation, from the nation as well.[15]

> . . . the sophisticates, detached from the *jen-min* by their culture, were detached from the *min-tsu* by their worldwide affinities with fellow cosmopolitans. Specialties, expertise, know no national boundaries.

Rootless cosmpolitans were advised (and more than just advised) to seek roots among the village masses. Scientists, because they were so vital to defense and industry, probably suffered less, but violinists and English professors were prime targets for the people's nationalistic (and provincialistic) wrath.

The spirit of 1966 recalled to some with a historical bent the Boxer summer in Peking seven decades before or Ch'ien Lung's

15. Ibid., p. 47.

supposed disdain for foreigners and things foreign. Levenson adamantly resisted the analogy, as he did all analogies between past and present that suggested there was an eternal Chinese essence beyond the reach of historical process. He insisted that China had become part of a larger world even when it was at odds with most of it: "Chinese may see the world as China-centered again, but China can never be self-centered again, as the only world that matters."[16] Similarly, when Chinese Communists had more confidently assessed their relation to the people of the world and the advancing revolutionary tide, the view was not traditionally Sinocentric.[17]

> To the culturalistic Confucian spirit (Ch'ien-lung's) Chinese history was the only history that mattered. To the nationalistic Communist (Mao), the satisfaction comes in having Chinese history matter to the world.

Levenson hardly found the spirit of the Cultural Revolution appealing. Its anti-intellectualism, its cultural vulgarity, its crude anticosmopolitanism, all offended the cosmopolitan side of his own personality. But his analysis of the Cultural Revolution located China firmly in her contemporary world, not in any return to the past. And he was convinced that the crisis-induced new provincialism would not last. In the closing words of his last work, ". . . China will join the world again on the cosmopolitan tide. Cultural intermediaries, cultural revolutionaries—neither will look like stranded minows or stranded whales forever."[18]

Perhaps our cosmopolitan-provincialism theme could close here with Levenson's last published words on the subject providing what seems to be a nice polite cosmopolitan call for world unity. But this would end on a false note, for Levenson was not a straightforward one-worlder or admirer of homogenized cultures. Up to now this has mainly been a summary of Levenson's thoughts about cosmopolitanism, provincialism, and nationalism, admittedly with a strong interpretive thrust in trying to connect them all to his underlying concern with the modern problem of identity. Now we

16. Joseph R. Levenson, "Marxism and the Middle Kingdom," *Diplomat*, XVII, No. 196 (September 1966), p. 50.
17. Levenson, *Revolution and Cosmopolitanism*, p. 26.
18. Ibid., p. 55.

should try more "objectively"[19] to test how well his brilliantly-argued theses fit Chinese history (more specifically, the development of Chinese nationalism), and what they might say to us about nationalism elsewhere in Asia, or about cosmopolitanism everywhere.

One of the peculiar aspects of Levenson's work on Chinese history is how he was able to establish communication with Western historians outside of the China field, but not with Chinese historians. I do not refer here to the Mainland, with the obvious political barriers, but rather to Chinese scholars in Taiwan, Hong Kong, or even in the United States. With a few exceptions among Western-educated Chinese historians in the latter group, his interpretation of modern Chinese history seems to have had little impact on Chinese thinking about their own history.[20] There could be several explanations for this. His prose style at times drew complaints from native English users for its complexity and literary effects. It could not have been easy for someone to whom English was a second language. Moreover, intellectual history of another culture—telling another people what they really thought and why—perhaps contains more potential for arousing resentment than any other kind of history. If, as Levenson argued, a deep desire "to own their own ground" was basic to all modern Chinese intellectuals, it is not surprising that they should resist this foreigner's version of the meaning of their modern history.

But do nationalistic pride and difficulties of communication explain it all? Or is there the possibility (nagging doubt for all Westerners who study China) that Levenson was projecting alien concerns onto Chinese history? Was the cosmopolitanism-provincialism dichotomy, and the burning concern for cultural and national identity we have seen behind it, just the creation of a rootless Western cosmopolitan, or rather of one trying valiantly to maintain roots in a synthesizing cosmopolitan Western culture? When Chinese historians for the most part seemed to find their national identity flowing out of the Chinese past or in a Marxist

19. I am painfully aware not just of the problem of objectivity in general, but the particular problem of standing back from ideas which, combined with the man who held them, had so powerful an influence on my own view of China, and of history. Of necessity, this must be a rather stilted and subjective exercise in objectivity.

20. This is my personal impression, possibly erroneous, based mainly on contact with historians on Taiwan. I know of no translation of any of his work into Chinese. None of his books had the honor of being pirated on Taiwan, although the political sensitivity of his subject matter may be adequate explanation for that.

view of the future, could all these fancy theories be just so many castles in the air?

We will compound the charge from a very different quarter, before attempting to reply. Lucian Pye in his highly controversial "psychocultural study," *The Spirit of Chinese Politics,* explicitly denied the existence of any "identity crisis" in modern China.[21] According to Pye, Chinese culture has been highly malleable and even discardable in modern times. Instead of culture, a profound sense of "biological history" has sustained "their identity and their feeling of association with greatness." Unlike most other developing countries, the Chinese know who and why they are with no *weltschmertz* about joining the modern world or leaving their ancient one. Pye's overall interpretation of modern China is probably even more unpalatable to Chinese tastes than Levenson's, but it shares with Chinese views the denial of any significant "problem of Chinese identity."

It is difficult to reply to these kinds of charges and probably the best answer lies in each reader judging for himself from Levenson's own books. My personal reaction to Pye's opinion was to recall the quotation from Alfred North Whitehead with which Levenson opened volume one of *Confucian China:*

> A traveller, who has lost his way, should not ask, "Where am I?" What he really wants to know is, Where are the other places? He has got his own body, but he has lost them.[22]

In Pye's terms, China had its own body (the biological continuity), but beyond that we can see her still confronted with a real problem in redefining China's relations with the world, not just in political terms, though that has been problem enough, but also culturally and psychologically. After all, nationalism and national identity are always defined in terms of relations with something or someone external. To know where, and who he was, the modern Chinese nationalist had to locate himself both in time (relation to the national past) and space (relation to the modern world). Strong sense of corporate identity or not, it has not been that easy.

21. "It will be the theme of this book that the critical difference between the Chinese and most of the other developing countries begins with the fact that the Chinese have been generally spared the crises of identity common to most other transitional systems." Lucian W. Pye, *The Spirit of Chinese Politics: A Psychocultural Study of the Authority Crisis in Political Development* (Cambridge, Mass.: MIT Press, 1967), p. 5.

22. Levenson, *Confucian China,* I, p. xiii.

Moreover, if culture and cultural identity have not been problems, why have they been so frequently discussed by modern Chinese intellectuals from Liang Ch'i-ch'ao on? Why the cultural polemics of the May Fourth period? Why a controversy over "*Cultural* Construction on a Chinese Basis" in the mid-thirties?[23] And why should Maoists launch a *Cultural* Revolution to remake Chinese politics or their enemies on Taiwan reply with a *Cultural* Renaissance movement? Trying to stay away from Levensonian categories—history and value, culturalism and nationalism, provincialism and cosmopolitanism—we still seem to see cultural concerns and cultural identity all over the map of modern Chinese intellectual history. Unless all this, and all intellectual history, is mere froth on the surface of deeper biological ties or social processes, we have to take it seriously for understanding modern Chinese history and modern Chinese nationalism.

Of course Levenson had an outsider's, and a highly individualistic outsider's, view of Chinese history. He would have been the last to deny that a historian's own values and viewpoint enter into the history he studies. But this outsider's perspective—we will not call it objectivity for he, too, must have his subjective concerns—can catch facets of historical process hidden to the insider. Levenson certainly was highly interpretive, but compilation and documentation are not the end task of any good historian. One can even acknowledge that he uncovered very little really new material, but through his mind, through his projection of universal concerns into the particular problems of Chinese history, he made that history meaningful in a new way.[24] Starting from individual and universal concerns of his own, locating Chinese nationalism in the web of contradictions between provincialism and cosmopolitanism, Levenson made China part of a universal history and Chinese nationalism something more intelligible to a larger world.

The question then arises: are these insights into the dynamics of Chinese nationalism transferable to the growth of nationalism in

23. The original manifesto by ten university professors appeared in *Wen-hua chien-she* [Cultural Construction], vol. 1, No. 4 (January 1935), pp. 3-5. Subsequent issues carried extensive discussion by many of China's leading intellectuals. The manifesto and Hu Shih's reply is translated in *Sources of Chinese Tradition*, ed. Wm. Theodore DeBary et al., vol. II (New York: Columbia University Press, 1964), pp. 192-195.

24. I am reminded of Nietzsche, ". . . the fine historian must have the power of coining the known into a thing never heard before and proclaiming the universal so simply and so profoundly that the simple is lost in the profound, and the profound in the simple." *The Use and Abuse of History*, trans. Adrian Collins (New York: Liberal Arts Press, 1957), p. 40.

other Asian countries that have shared roughly the same experience of Western domination and forced cultural change? Essays elsewhere in this volume indicate that many of his individual insights from modern Chinese history might illuminate certain aspects of modern Asian history elsewhere, but it might not be possible to apply the history-value or provincialism-cosmopolitanism framework intact. For one thing, few of the traditional Asian societies were so cosmopolitanly self-contained culturally as China. Japan had a peripheral, "provincial," identity with regard to the Chinese cosmopolis. All the Buddhist societies of South East Asia were located between two great radiators of cultural influence, China and India. The Arab Middle East was never isolated from Europe. Only India is really comparable to the cultural cosmos of traditional China, although open to much more serious cultural as well as political inroads from Western Asia. In my own work on modern revivalist movements in traditional medicine and their nationalist implications, it was only in India that I found anything comparable to the controversy over traditional medicine in China.[25] The point is that most Asian societies, even in pre-Western prenationalist times, were accustomed to defining their own identity in terms of a larger world and to drawing on external sources of high culture. Resentment at European intrusion might be Asianwide, but the agonies of changing culturalism for nationalism need not be so intense where the basis for any traditional culturalism seems much more problematical. Similarly, relocation in a modern world might be easier where traditional society had not been conceived of as the whole world.

Levenson himself never claimed to be setting forth any model for Asian nationalism in general and his comparative thrusts were more often with Europe than other Asian countries. Only in his very last unfinished writings, what would have been the second volume of the cosmopolitanism trilogy, did he put China in a really comparative context with other Asian countries, and then the motive was more to relate Asian cultures to the cosmopolitanizing modern world than to compare them with each other.[26]

25. Ralph C. Croizier, "Medicine, Modernization, and Cultural Crisis in China and India," *Comparative Studies in Society and History*, XII, 3 (July 1970).

26. Only forty-two typed pages, chapters on India, China, and the beginning of one on Japan, exist of this manuscript titled, "History and Cosmopolitanism: East Asia and the Meaning of 'World Classics.'"

But this unfinished fragment is important to our understanding of Levenson and his work. In the first place, it underscores the continuing concern for cultural identity which we have taken as the key to all his work, including the cosmopolitanism theme. Moreover, it is here that he develops earlier hints about deculturization and loss of tradition through the modern cosmopolitan mixing of traditions. The title he chose for this volume, *History and Cosmopolitanism*, was revealing of his intent, for, like the title for the entire trilogy, *Provincialism and Cosmopolitanism*, it suggested a tension between the two terms. He saw the modern cosmopolitan trend to create "world classics" by taking works out of their particular historical and cultural tradition to make a world cultural amalgam as both unhistorical and corrosive of any continuing cultural autonomy or cultural vitality. The museumification process he saw in modern China becomes a universal phenomenon in our global "museum without walls"; loss of particular cultural identity, the universal malaise of rootlessness, becomes "the meaning of 'modern times'" to which his title for the trilogy refers. Levenson again alluded to Richard McKeon on the loss of one's own roots, "mixing so many traditions that one has no sense of tradition."[27]

In reading this I was reminded of my own surprise years earlier at a remark Levenson made about the gastronomical variety available in a cosmopolitan city like San Francisco. To me, fresh from the provinces of Western Canada, such variety, the possibility of choosing between Basque, Szechwanese, Indonesian restaurants, was a delight and a revelation. But Joe, although his own palate was attuned to all those tastes, pointed out that the creation of all these local cuisines had been in specific places and within specific cultural traditions. Lifted out of those places, roots uptorn, they were in some way no longer authentic (no matter how genuine the ingredients or how good the cook), no longer part of living traditions. It seemed a peculiar remark to me then, although I grasped something of its metaphorical significance. Only gradually did I realize that the creation of a cosmopolitan cuisine may begin the end of the provincial cuisines which made it possible in the first place. Only gradually did I appreciate the significance of the metaphor for cultural diversity and vitality in a technologically unified world.

27. "History and Cosmopolitanism," p. 8; see above, page 169, for fuller version of this quote.

Thus, his discussion of Indian and Chinese classics (mainly the *Bhagavad Gita* and the Confucian *Analects*) in their new translated role as "world classics" sounded a note already familiar to me. Lifted out of their own traditions, "as though by cultural selection boards, taking the best from East and West for a nice synthetic balance,"[28] these classics are denatured, drained of their cultural particularity and instead become mere examples of some supposedly universal cultural essence. For instance, the *Gita* as "living, contemporary message"[29] became a plea for peace—quite appropriate for a bound-together world where that commodity is so desperately needed. Or, in Ezra Pound's version, the Confucian *Analects* become a general, timeless (but very timely) call for order and stability.[30] Other versions might find other contemporary messages—democracy, social justice, or humanism. The point was that all these versions shuffled off the historically particular to find the "timeless messages" that were demanded by our own times. "*Gita* and *Analects,* together, stand for Asia, where they once stood, respectively, for two traditions very far apart."[31] And what had made them stand together? The increasing technological unification of the "global village" plus distinctively modern feelings generated by the process of that unification—"a sense of assertiveness (for old worlds lost) in Asia and a sense of guilt (for old worlds destroyed) in the West."[32]

The impulse toward unity, and recognition of everybody's potential contribution to that unity, was laudable in itself. But, apart from his awareness of the costs in terms of cultural variety, Levenson did not believe that world history, world unity, or world culture could be made in that way—by a "mystic leap to oneness, out of history."[33] He did not jump from his distrust of artificially mixing so many traditions to the conclusion that each culture should cultivate only its own garden and fence out everything else. He did not advocate bringing back compulsory Greek and Latin while relegating Asian cultures to a few learned Orientalists. That would have been "provincial" in a modern world that is now larger than the West, even if it was the West that originally made it one world.

28. Levenson, "Genesis of Confucian China and Its Modern Fate," p. 283.
29. Levenson, "History and Cosmopolitanism," p. 15.
30. Ibid., p. 33.
31. Ibid., p. 37.
32. Ibid., p. 23.
33. Ibid., p. 22.

Instead, Levenson looked for another road to a cosmopolitanism that would not seek noumenal essence behind phenomenal reality—"placelessness and timelessness"—but rather one built on a mutual understanding of different histories and traditions.[34]

> Working in history still has much to commend it—the hope of moving out *in time* towards making the phenomenal world one, instead of lunging towards the noumenal.

And working in history meant work for historians. It meant that they had to construct a world history intelligible without resort to universal paradigms or artificial lifting of "selected values from particular histories." This required eschewing the search for unhistorical noumenon (the timeless, archetypal meaning behind each concrete historical phenomenon) and concentrating on what is mutually understandable in the historically particular, understandable to those from different cultures and histories because of the universality of certain key human concerns. "Pain is universal. Everyone has a heart. But the tones of the heart's expression of pain are infinitely various."[35] The historian must respect the infinite variety of tones while catching the expression of a universal human feeling. Establishing this "universal world of discourse," not blanching all cultures of their individuality, was his hope for unifying "the world on more than a technological level."

Personally, I think Levenson came very close to the heart of "modern times" and much of its malaise in his analysis of what cosmopolitanism and change meant in terms of identity. The pace of change can be frightening, and in the accelerating and mindless thrust of the technological dynamic, frightening not just to the timid or conservative. Part of the fear stems from the possibility of unchecked technology physically destroying man and/or his environment. But part of it is over the consequences for values, for culture, for the psychic well-being of men. Involved in the latter is the bleaching effect technological determinism seems to have on cultures everywhere. Modern architecture, modern art, and modern dress are basically global styles, not static but so transitory as to give no sense of continuity. And behind this, modern man (also technologically determined?) becomes culturally homogenized and culturally uprooted.

34. Ibid., p. 22.
35. Ibid., p. 32.

It is a price that the toughminded, especially among social scientists, might willingly pay for abolishing the threats of disunity. Thus, B.F. Skinner dismisses the problem:[36]

> The process of cultural evolution would not come to an end, of course, if there were only one culture, as biological evolution would not come to an end if there were only one major species—presumably man.

But just as naturalists are unhappy with the latter prospect, humanists generally find the former unattractive. To Hartner, the world "will be divested of interest for the historians of culture."[37] Behaviorists might not find that such a tragedy, but there is more to it. The loss of any tradition by mixing and blurring all traditions in the accelerator of modern change may also have, and be having, serious adverse consequences on the individual and society. Another currently fashionable modernist (or futurist), Alvin Toffler, finds the loss of a sense of tradition, and of an identity based on it, at the heart of the social neurosis he labels "future shock."

Back to paradox once more. A rapidly changing and increasingly unified world may need the sense of tradition and particular identity for its own sanity, i.e., for modern man's ability to function competently and comfortably in his changing environment. But it will be impossible to use tradition as a preservative of the status quo, or cultural identity as a barrier to cosmopolitan contacts. There is a paradox and a contradiction here, but perhaps not an irreconcilable one. It may be true, as Levenson wrote, "A Jewish style of life, for example, may be more endangered when everyone eats bagels than when Jews eat hot cross buns."[38] But I doubt that he would have wanted to deny the rest of us our bagels. He did not deny himself *pao-tzu*. The only answer would seem to be a special taste for one's own, while knowing and appreciating the alternatives. Tradition then had (in Levenson's own terms) become traditionalism. It is a "romantic attachment," something not taken for granted, but consciously worked at. Yet, if the malaise of rootlessness is to be eased, it may be necessary to work at it.

36. B.F. Skinner, *Beyond Freedom and Dignity* (New York: Knopf, 1971), p. 138.
37. See above, p. 157, fn. 1.
38. Levenson, "The Province, the Nation, and the World," p. 278.

In any event, these concerns were central to Levenson as a person and as a historian. In the introduction to *Liang Ch'i-ch'ao and the Mind of Modern China*, he borrowed from Whitehead the concept of a "personal identity or personal unity, which pervades our life-thread of occasions."[39] For Liang he located this in a "need for conviction of China's equivalence to the West." What we have isolated as a personal unity in Levenson's works from *Liang Ch'i-ch'ao* to "History and Cosmopolitanism" is the need for identity. It informed his sensitivity to Liang's dilemma; it runs through *Confucian China and Its Modern Fate*; it is even more evident in the cosmopolitanism writings. As he once wrote of Liang, "In his Beginning was his end."[40] There is an extraordinary wholeness to the man's work.

Yet, in another respect he differed fundamentally from Liang, for the inner need, the question behind Liang's personal unity, was one that, in his own lifetime, time passed by. His ideas, then, as responses to that question ended up in anachronism. But Levenson's question, the need for identity, seems just as relevant at the beginning of the 1970s as it did at the beginning of the 1950s: a still living question, and ideas that still speak to us in living terms. We can expect that each will hear them in somewhat different tones. But for all of us who were exposed to the man and his ideas, he and they continue to speak to us about history and the historian's worlds.

39. Joseph R. Levenson, *Liang Ch'i-ch'ao and the Mind of Modern China* (Cambridge: Harvard University Press, 1953), p. 4.

40. Ibid., p. 10.

PART FOUR

The Choice of Jewish Identity

NOTES ON "THE CHOICE OF JEWISH IDENTITY"

Rosemary Levenson

The inclusion of so personal a piece as "The Choice of Jewish Identity" in a memorial volume to Joseph Levenson has aroused controversy. I am glad that it is being included since I feel that it widens and enriches understanding of his published works and offers a glimpse of a specialized and fully professional historian whose life and thought, religious convictions, and academic loyalties were not kept in separate compartments.

The essay was discovered in a shabby manila folder on Judaism which I did not find until three months after his death. It was tucked away under a stack of carbon paper in his desk at home. In it was the draft of the manuscript which follows, clippings of book reviews, scribbled outlines for talks, and odd IBM cards.

Had Joe lived, the piece would never have been published in its present form. The manuscript was a rough first draft of the first chapter of a book—untitled—which Joe used to call his "retirement book" on Judaism. (There was to be another—jottings only—on historiography.) As far as I am aware, he discussed this book with no one but myself, except for a brief mention to a Berkeley colleague. He was very conscious of the audaciousness of the undertaking and took a deep and somewhat surreptitious delight in the writing of it. Some of the gusto would probably have been edited out in the numerous revisions which he made in all his work.

He was preparing the Judaism book much the same way as he had the first trilogy, *Confucian China and Its Modern Fate*, and the finished portion of the second trilogy, tentatively titled "Provincialism, Nationalism, and Cosmopolitanism." He lectured on the topic at Hillel Foundation, and presented some of the themes less formally at a Jewish luncheon club which met for many years at Berkeley to encourage speakers to talk about subjects of concern to Jews on which they were *not* specialists. On one occasion, he also filled the slot normally taken by the Rabbi's sermon at the orthodox synagogue to which we belong. His books on Chinese history, with the exception of *Liang Ch'i-chao and the Mind of Modern China* which was an elaboration of his Ph. D. thesis, were prepared in the same way. The ideas were worked out in lecture courses, seminars, colloquia, and professional meetings of various sorts, refined, clarified, and improved by the criticisms and suggestions of students and colleagues. And, just as a tale from the Baal Shem concluded the third volume of *Confucian China*, so Chinese metaphors have been interwoven in the structure of his work on Judaism.

Many of the concerns which informed Joe's first trilogy, and inspired what was to have been his second, are also visible in this essay. The tensions between history and value, particularism and universalism, separation and assimilation, characterized all his historiography. His alertness to these questions for the Chinese in China or in the Nanyang may have been partly awakened by his perception of the dilemmas of Jews in Israel and in the Diaspora.

The title "*The* Choice of Jewish Identity" has been left. I think it would have been changed had Joe lived. We worked together on the editing of his books and articles, and he accepted about 85 percent of my suggestions for revision or change. (The revisions were usually in the direction of expanding his dense sentence structure and allowing hints of discursiveness.) *The* choice of Jewish identity can be taken to imply a moral imperative of a brutal nature that would have been completely foreign to Joe's intentions. Though disliking the position of Jews who converted to other religions, particularly Christianity, he was always personally kind to them and to those in his immediate family who could not share his beliefs.

Judaism is not a proselytizing religion, even between Jews, and Joe was no Jewish missionary. He thoroughly enjoyed conducting family Seders (the Passover meal and service) but did not care to have the occasion diluted by the anthropological curiosity of either non-Jews or uncommitted Jews.

He liked to go to Synagogue on Saturday mornings, had studied cantillation, and taught the different notations for the Torah and

Haftarah readings to his oldest son, Richard, before his Bar Mitzvah. He enjoyed taking his turn in chanting the weekly passage from the Prophets. The day before he died was the Sabbath which falls in Passover week, and Joe read the passage from Ezekiel, Chapter 37, verses 1-14, the resurrection of the dry bones. "And he said unto me, Son of man can these bones live? And I answered, O Lord God thou knowest. . . . So I prophesied as he commanded me, and the breath came into them, and they lived and stood up upon their feet, an exceeding great army." I asked how he could read that, and believe it; he answered, "It's only poetry, metaphor."

Invasion of the privacy of the dead is, perhaps, the unforgivable insult. But to share some of the joy and creative energy that Joe found in the practice and study of his religion with others seems right to me. In *A la recherche du temps perdu* the times are not altogether lost.

In *Revolution and Cosmopolitanism*, Joe said, "One way or another (the choice of ways is fearful) China will join the world again on the cosmopolitan tide. Cultural intermediaries, Cultural Revolutionaries—neither will look like stranded minnows or stranded whales forever." So he believed of Jewish life and thought. "It is *a* choice of life."

THE CHOICE OF JEWISH IDENTITY

Joseph R. Levenson

I. INTRODUCTION

Almost everybody who is interested in Jews at all sometimes asks the question, "Are the Jews a people or a sect?" Is Judaism an identity masquerading as a religion—a national identity ("the Hebrews") or a cultural identity ("Jewishness")? Valid Judaism invalidates the question. Judaism, a religion, is embodied in nation and culture. These are intrinsic and essential. In the medium is the message. Judaism has an almost Confucian feeling for the "oneness of knowledge and action," and action has its performers and its forms.

Many people call it a religion, all right, but a "lower religion," ethnocentric and tribal. At best they see it as abortively universal, missing out on its own implications, which were yielded to the Church. Ezra Pound, putting it at the worst, gives the Hebrew Bible the same standing as tales of the Choctaw. Many observers, though milder than Pound, agree that Jews may travel but Judaism doesn't: for all the fact of Gentile conversions to Judaism, hellenistic and after, it looks like just a derivative of "the religion of the Semites," a part of a cultural repertoire. The religion is anthropologically interesting, not the other way round—the anthropology, or the community anthropologized, is not religiously interesting. How should it be, if the religion is just a department of a single people's (though a complex people's) life? What is this people's kinship structure, what are its taboos?

If Judaism is just cultural baggage, everyone knows that cultures change, and never so fast as in modern times. Even those who search for roots—as modern a quest as the search for innovation—are traditionalistic, not traditional: (Jews *were* made for Sinai, not Sinai for the Jews). And modern liberal values, at least, say that cultures ought to change. A rationalistic ethic proclaims freedom, release from the authority of tradition. Certain traditions may appeal to modern taste—the very idea of tradition may appeal—but then taste, not tradition, has authority. A credo (runs the liberal imperative) should not be imposed by birth. The liberal imperative is Kant's: so act—and, by implication, so believe—that you conceive your governing principle as a universal principle. This has seemed subversive of Judaism. Kant thought so, and so have many Jews, for Judaism appears to be so hopelessly particular.

The apologetic that stops short at "Jewish spiritual discoveries" (e.g., an equation of Judaism with Kantian reason itself) is no answer. The very example of Kant shows that this idea of reason, considered as a truth, is available to anyone. Truth is universal: a very persuasive tautology. Therefore, a necessarily *Jewish* commitment to a broadly compelling truth would be superfluous.

And so Jews may resent being identified as Jews, identified with a cultic commitment they never made. If they happen to agree, for example, with historically Jewish demurrers about cardinal points of Christian doctrine, shouldn't they make it clear that it is *they* who demur? Unitarianism or Ethical Culture or disaffiliation ("religion: none") would be their proper platform. This, presumably, universalizes their doctrine, making them free and respectable intellectually. Many Jewish parents, not out of sloth or unconcern, but in all conscience, object to any Jewish education for their children. Let them grow up, become intellectually responsible, and then decide. What do these parents imply?—that it is biased, unfair, to foist on children a prerational, a particularistic, association. Must they be children of Israel?

Of course one could make debating points against this point of view. No one reaches maturity with a *tabula rasa* mind, antiseptically rational; and so bias (in this case, anti-Jewish) may be assured, not removed, by an early Jewish default. But it is the ground of the debate, not one of the sides, that has to be challenged. For Judaism as an abstract, intellectual, universal proposition—indeed a subject for modern choice or rejection—subsumes under itself concrete, non-intellectual, particular *existence*, a people, an historical quantity. General truthseekers, Jews among them, ask why Jews have to remain visible. What has this to do with rational acceptance of whatever spiritual quality a religion may possess? The answer—another tautology—which this book means to elucidate is that Jews are a people that has to remain visible. It is not just that history made them visible (and may yet close over them). They are not just a people which is available for anthropologizing, religion and all. They live as a people that has to live and that is their definition. Of course their values are facts, their norms can be described. But the descriptions pertain to prescriptions. To be is not to be, but to will to be—and to be willed. Thou (not "one"), thou (so there are others), thou shalt have (not thou will have) no other god before me.

A Jew always reaffirms that his people, from which he is not separate himself, must stay visible, historically surviving in all its generations. This is a religious position, not a social preference, A taste for "cultural pluralism" has nothing to do with it; nor defeatism about anti-Semitism, nor even a sense of honor in fact of anti-Semitism; nor vicarious thrills in chess championships or the special and general theories of relativity. In spite of the Nazi experience, maybe partly because of it, the assumptions most Jews make today, their hopes or fears, are plausible. One can get lost in America or England, even in Russia, quite easily. Cultural eclecticism, a general modern trend, lets anyone get anyone's "ethnic foods" at the market, anyone (exit Russia here, if not before) hear Israeli folksongs in his favorite *boîte*, anyone read the Bible as "living literature," or even as spiritual refreshment. Brave people in Mississippi can try to do justice and love mercy without reading Micah, or without reading him as Jews, or with only a passing pleasure, but no stab of command, at finding lofty thoughts in a book of Jewish provenance. One can read Confucius and nod one's head (for a number of reasons) at his sage dicta, without being Chinese. Who needs to be a Jew in order to have some Jewish spices in the cosmopolitan recipe?

A Jew needs to be a Jew—Judaism is compelling—for reasons other than "Jewish contributions." That is a futile defense, anyway, against Jewish dissolution; simply as an eclectic modern, he could take these contributions. But more seriously, the trouble is that men who "place" Judaism in this fashion, as just an early contributor to our catholic modern culture, have missed the meaning of Jewish experience. For Judaism is not a drop dissolved in a synthesis, not a spice of life, a motif in history. It is a choice of life. History is a motif in Judaism, and the latter's very particularism—such a scandal to so many open minds with large views, impatient with closed communities and petty selves—does not, in fact, constitute parochialism, but converts it. The Jewish people, by its very existence, and only in its existence, its historical visibility, states a general proposition. Judaism does not fall short of the "truth" of universalism. It stands against that spurious universalism which is so often invoked against it.

II. HISTORY

The Relation of Jewish Particularity to History

Deuteronomy 4, 14-20: "And the Lord commanded me at that time to teach you statutes and judgments, that ye might do them in the land whither ye go over to possess it. Take ye therefore good heed unto yourselves . . . lest thou lift up thine eyes unto heaven, and when thou seest the sun, and the moon, and the stars, even all the host of heaven, shouldest be driven to worship them and serve them, which the Lord thy God hath divided unto all nations under the whole heaven. But the Lord hath taken you, and brought you forth out of the iron furnace, even out of Egypt, to be unto him a people of inheritance, as ye are this day."

Here is the God of nature and the God of history, one God, with two realms of creation. Nature is universal ("divided unto all nations"). It is not to be worshipped. History is the particular. Non-Biblical thinkers like Aristotle (setting poetry as the realm of eternity against history as the realm of ephemera) and anti-Biblical thinkers like Voltaire (setting essentialist, all-pervading deism against the accidental, petty history of Jewish revelation) confirm it. And history is essential to the Jews. It is not that God gave history only to Jews. "Are ye not as the children of the Ethiopians unto Me, O Children of Israel? saith the Lord. Have I not brought up Israel out of the land of Egypt, and the Philistines from Caphtor, and Aram from Kir?" (From *Amos,* in one of the *Haftaroth* or weekly chantings from the Prophets and Writings in the cycle of the Jewish year.) It is, rather, that Jews see man's relation to God—until the days of the Messiah—in history, in particularity. Jewish particularity stems from a positive definition of a vessel of meaningful life. It does not have—as the exclusiveness of the "white race" does have—the spuriousness, the lack of inner self-existence, of mere negation.

The Sabbath, after the sixth day, when "the Heavens and the earth were finished, and all their host," commemorates the creation of universal nature. It also commemorates the creation of particular history—creation of the Jews as a people, a vessel of history, ready to start out from slavery as an inchoate mass in the "iron furnace," on to the commitment at Sinai, and on and on to the brink of the land of promise, where the scroll of the Torah ends. This is The Land, *Eretz*, the small earthy plot that confirms the creation of a people by rooting them in a finite patch of soil. The Sabbath Kiddush, the sanctification on the eve, the ceremony that recalls the creation of the world, also calls the Sabbath "a memorial to the departure from Egypt." Nature and history, the universal and the particular, are brought together.

If God is one, nature and history must be brought together. Nature without history invites cyclical thinking, no sense of process but the cycle, in magical sympathy with the cycle of the seasons, with no "In the beginning." And this means no sense of individuation: one seeks accommodation with nature (involving a mystical loss of self-consciousness), harmony, not creative change. To deny this is the importance of God as creator ("In the beginning," with a straight extension of time), and the importance of the related Jewish injunction to *imitatio Dei.* God starts history. Jews make history.

When Israel hears, or is commanded to hear, that the Lord their God is one, this historical people must accept the combination of nature and history as the issue of one Creator. History is not meant to deny nature, but it must not be denied itself. Cycles figure in Jewish thinking, the cycle of ritual observances and the cycle of reading the Torah, so that the death of Moses and the creation of heaven and earth meet in sequence at Simchath Torah, the festival of rejoicing in the Law. And throughout the year, historical and natural events combine to inform the festivals, such as the Feast of Weeks—Shevuoth—relating to the epiphany at Sinai and the gathering of the sheaves. But in each of the basic holiday seasons, Passover and the High Holy Days (Rosh Hashanah—Yom Kippur), there is a careful disjunction of nature and history. It is not a denial of one or the other, but a singleness of emphasis.

This, Rosh Hashanah, the Jewish "New Year," the special celebration of the creation of the world, is in the seventh month, not on the natural New Year. The transcendental creation of nature (linked with the Jews' reaffirmations of their ethical imperatives, their commitments to act, as the act of creation suggests) is deliberately separated from involvement in the cyclical renewal of nature. For the natural cycle is associated with an immanentist, not a transcendentalist, conception; and immanence, in universal perennial-philosophy fashion, suggests the abstraction of man, in contemplation, from action and history-making. *Nissan*, the first month of the natural year, in the spring, is the month that is marked for Exodus, the historically Jewish, not the natural and universal point of departure. The spring-festival character of Passover is overlaid with history. When it gets down to commemorating the two realms of creation, Jewish practice links them in the Sabbath, but preserves a creative tension by keeping them individual in the year, so that the particular is not just subsumed, swallowed, in the universal. Until history ends, history must be savored and respected, newly fashioned in action, in memory of the Creation.

History in Judaism and Judaism in History

"There shall be neither Jews nor Greeks." How does a Jewish sense of history, a transcendentalist conception, relate to a Greek universalism, with its immanentist character? Usually, in the conventional comparison of "hellenism" and "Hebraism," Christianity is filed under Hebraism, with all the appropriate cliches—somber, brooding, and so on, as against the life-enhancing Greek light. In Merejkovski's novel, *The Death of the Gods*, the black shadows of monks blot the white marble of the Parthenon.

Many scholars, like Moses Hadas in *Hellenistic Culture: Fusion and Diffusion* (New York, 1959), have taken the starkness out of this confrontation. Hellenic light was not dimmed by the dark from the East, in some Manichaean struggle. Rather, a hellenistic fusion, a mingling of colors (powerfully furthered by the conquests of Alexander), created an ecumenical culture which Hadas, in good historically relativist fashion, will not describe as a falling-off; and the hellenistic age gave later Europe the configuration of its culture. Thus, in Hadas' synthesis, the age is vindicated in terms of value (e.g., it is said to have achieved recognition of at least the potential equality of all men and the consequent conception of all humanity as forming a single society), and in terms of historical continuity—its values came down in time. Hadas sees it affirmatively, as making the Europe we know, not negatively, as breaking a classic ideal.

Isocrates emerges as the great spokesman for diffusion of hellenism from the Greek center, and Plato as the thinker most influential in the areas of diffusion, influential in underlying the hellentistic fusions. But it was only Isocrates, not Plato, who defined Greek-ness in terms of education instead of race. Plato's ethnic bias was clear in his dictum that strife among Greek cities was really civil war, to be avoided or carried on humanely, while Greek-barbarian strife was real war, which ought to be fought out ruthlessly. Now, there is a striking identity of views in this matter between Plato and a seventeenth-century anti-Manchu Chinese scholar, Wang Fu-chih, who used precisely the same relation of civil and "real" war to civilized standards and ruthlessness. But Wang was relatively obscure and eccentric, while Isocrates' cultural viewpoint was overwhelmingly characteristic of Confucian civilization. This has its importance here, because it raises a question about Hadas' Isocratic explanation of not only hellenistic diffusion but fusion, too: "If racial barbarians could be honorary (i.e., culturally) Greeks, then their own cultural attainments could be appreciated." Does the conclusion follow? Racial barbarians could be culturally Chinese in that other, Confucian world, but this by no means signified that "barbarian cultural attainments could be appreciated," in anything like the reciprocal hellenistic fashion.

It seems, rather, that it was Platonic idealism which eased foreign religious conceptions into hellenistic syncretisms. Why should particulars be resisted when reality was the *noumenon*, the universal which lay beneath them? Zeus here was Jehovah there. Anti-hellenistic Maccabees might fight for the peculiarity of their people, but their Hasmonean descendants were hellenizers. In fact, it is the Jewish experience with hellenism which provides the most complex test of the latter's quality, and Judaism's too. Hadas rises to the occasion with a discussion of the hellenistic age which is fully as much about Jews as Greeks.

Indeed, it is possible to read into this work an anomalous type of Jewish apologetic. I do not mean at all to suggest special pleading, to question the breadth of Hadas' sympathy, or to identify him with such hellenistic Jewish apologetics as he interprets so well: Hadas is worlds away from, say, the picture of Moses as teacher of Orpheus (Moses = Muses). And yet there is something hellenistic about what happens to the meaning of Jewish history in the context Hadas gives it. It is hellenistic in the sense that, while "hellenic" as a term pertains to a specific historical people—the Greeks—the "hellenistic," transnational, and universalist, does not require Greeks to embody it. But Judaism requires Jews, a requirement of particularity which has exasperated universalists ancient and modern, Pasternak as well as the Emperor Hadrian. Hadas notes the requirement, as he juxtaposes Plutarch with the Talmudist, Johanan ben Zakkai. For both, he suggests, a way of life was made into a cult which could command loyalty and receive it when sovereignty was lost—but, "The great difference was that whereas Plutarch's was only metaphorically a cult, Johanan's was one in fact." That is, the Jews gained continuity as a community; the Greeks continued in their intellectual legacy, informing a civilization that followed and transcended the Greek.

Yet, while Hadas keeps this distinction very much in mind, while he duly records that the rabbis who established normative Judaism left Philo ("either Plato Philonizes or Philo Platonizes") strictly alone, his book suggests that Jewish history is rescued from meaninglessness by its disembodied intellectual influence on the central stream of political theory which Rome transmitted to Europe (from Isaiah through the Sybilline Oracles, Vergil, and the Roman imperial ideology), on basic Christianity (from the Septuagint through the Apocrypha), on scholastic theology (from the Bible through Posidonius of Apamea to Seneca and, ultimately, Aquinas), etc. Just as the hellenic can become hellenistic and, by being incapsulated in a universal history, leave the Greeks' history behind, so the Jewish can be incapsulated in the hellenistic, the Christian, the European, and by shaking off the material body claim a triumph of the spirit or the soul.

However, the ultimate Jewish dissociation from hellenism, the final cast for Talmudic law and against Apocryphal apocalypse, was a calculated rejection of just such a typically hellenistic matter-spirit dichotomy as would provide for pleasure of the soul through the bruising—or the forfeiture—of the body. Hadas observes that the Jews' willing subjection to the law was the means of their survival after territory and sovereignty were lost. But the law cannot be vindicated that way, as a means, to those who would devalue the end, ethnic survival, according to hellenistic or Christian criteria. What needs to be seen is that the Jewish will to survival was a religious will, a reaffirmation of the Biblical injunction to "choose life," an acceptance of history and the consequent commitment to action, and thus a rejection of Platonic and neo-Platonic indifference to history and of the antinomian (because antihistorical) Pauline otherworldliness. Whatever hellenistic, post-Biblical elements may be found in rabbinical Judaism, it still kept "the world, universe" and "eternity" together in the Hebrew word *olam* not rent apart in a hellenistic fission. The decision to stay in the world and continue a history was not only a sociological act of resistance to the hellenistic solvent but an intellectual denial of the latter's implications. And the denial was implicit in the act. Or, the thought demanded the survival of the thinker, as a judgment on a universalism so ethereal that bodies, lives, the material world—all particulars of the view and chiliastic deploring of the fact—were consigned to evanescence and in the deepest sense left untouched. Nietzsche was right (and, perhaps paradoxically, *Jewish*) when he claimed vitality for the particular: "and to the eunuch one woman is the same as another, merely a woman, 'woman in herself,' the ever-unapproachable." If the bequeather must vanish in the flesh, the intellectual bequest (from Judaism via hellenism to the "Judeo-Christian tradition") was so transmuted as to belie its name.

Jewish and "Judeo-Christian"

The adjective "Judeo-Christian" is coin of the realm of "interfaith relations." It has an irenic ring, and many Jews accept the combination. Instead of contempt for Jewish values, it seems to promise respect, and a ticket of admission to Western culture. Unfortunately, it is a children's ticket, not an adult's; and admission under these terms dismisses the authenticity of Judaism.

Somehow, the Christian component assimilates, it seems, all the Judaism anyone needs, so that Judaism *tout court* is superfluous. And Jewish identity is watered down so that Jewish survival seems irrelevant. Why not relax with a happy sigh into the great continuum? But the meaning of Jewish survival, Jewish life, is to testify to life—"to life!", *l'hayyim*, is the Jewish toast—and the Hebrew Bible, not the Greek (for all its resurrections), is the testament of life. Whenever Jews complacently echo, with hands across the hyphen, that Christians honor the "Old Testament," they accept themselves as outgrown (and outworn: the "fossil" according to Toynbee). "Old Testament" implies "New Testament," onward and upward—all this and Heaven too—in spurious continuity. But "Old Testament," preempted by Christians to paste it together with "New," is a different book from the Hebrew Bible in solitary splendor (and not merely because of the flaws in the Greek translation from Hebrew). Jews should know the value of the One. It should not be for Jews, of all peple, to mix the meat with the milk and water.

Over the centuries, Jewish apologetics have changed their tone. For normative Christianity, Marcionism (the contention that "New Testament" and "Old Testament" stand for Good and Evil, respectively) is heresy. Therefore, in the officially orthodox middle ages, Christians stressed, as a matter of faith, that the Old Testament flowed into the New. The synagogue was a broken image (*vide* the famous figure in the Strasbourg cathedral), but the Jewish Bible was not broken off. Indeed, the synagogue was supposed to be broken just because it made the break. The great set theme of all those Christian-Jewish disputations, convened under Christian auspices, was the theme of continuity. Christians purported to show, from the Jewish scriptures themselves, that a Christian culmination was expected. It was the Jews who held to the thesis of a radical discontinuity. Christians were welcome to their New Testament, but they should see it for what it was—a radical new departure.

In modern times, when so many liberties began to be taken with Christian orthodoxy, the terms of the argument changed. Liberal Christians tended to convert their New Testament into an edifying document, not a transcendental witness. The Gospels were sublime but not divine, except in a metaphorical sense. And then, so much of the Old Testament was not sublime. So many pages of smite, smote, smitten: over how many liberal pulpits have the Amalekites been littered, and the wretched Israelites, with their tribal Jehovah, shredded! Jews rose to the occasion (in a manner of speaking) with an effort to close the breach. Their Bible (well, maybe not *Judges*) was edifying, too, and rabbinical *Midrash*, the Jews' extension of their Biblical teaching, had all the sweetness that Christians could claim for their extension. If only Christians would stop preening themselves on standing on a higher plane, and realize that the Rabbis matched the Apostles and Fathers in largeness of spirit, we could all be Judeo-Christian together.

This was all very well. No liberal Christian would utter the vulgar epithet, "Christ-killer!" (portions of *John* could be as embarrassing as *Judges*). "Amalekite-killer" was more like it, and even this could be historicized to the childhood of the race. Hillel might be admitted into the club. But he had to be sponsored, patronized. "The Hebrew will turn Christian, he grows kind."

Darwinism, progressive evolutionary theory, could shape religious conviction as well as shake it. Christianity really was on a higher plane. Jews, even still as Jews, could be helped aboard; for liberal theology usually had some psychological link with liberality of spirit. But Judaism, in the last analysis, was pre-Christian and sub-Christian, fossilized and fixed. It was lower than Christianity, really a different and dead species of religion, not just (unrecognized by Jews) the proto-Christian *praeparatio evangelica.*

What had happened in Christianity, essentially, with a Jewish reaction to match, was something ineffably suburban. It was the banishment of revelation (whereby an objective God speaks to the subject) in favor of narcissism (aren't we *nice* to make such a nice God-idea for ourselves?) One of the nice things was a God of love distinctly more spiritual than the God of retributive justice (or even injustice). This sentimental separation has a great deal to do with what Nietzsche saw as the blandness of the "New Testament." In contrast, the strength, the life, of the "Old Testament" is partly in its tension, in its straining correlation of justice *and* mercy. How can mercy exist unless the normal course of justice exists, perhaps in mercy, to be set aside? As the liturgy for Yom Kippur, the Day of Atonement, has it: "If man is judged with perfect justice, who shall stand?" Jonah, the *Haftarah,* the prophetic portion that follows the second and last of the Torah readings on Yom Kippur, tells the quintessential story. Justice for Nineveh would be its destruction; but Jonah fears (with justice), that *t'shuvah,* "turning," atonement, would engage God's mercy, and make Jonah's prophecy of justice abortive. God, who has to be God of justice to be God of mercy, chides Jonah. Jews, in choosing this as the central *Haftarah* of the Jewish year, embrace the principle of the chiding—and reject the justice of any Christian chiding of Jews for allegedly knowing only justice—as though mercy were its confutation instead of its correlative. Mercy exists because man can change, and his fate, too, can change. Where there is one God, fate is not a goddess, man's fate is not inexorably determined. That is why the Hebrew prophets were hortatory, not deterministic. The prophets (at least the prophets of the Books) were moralists, not seers—which is why partisans of the "New Testament," with their commitment to a fanciful exegesis that makes "Old Testament prophecy" seem literally "realized," appear to Jews as partisans of the letter, not the spirit. Jonah's prophecy to Nineveh was not realized. A truly omnipotent God is not bound by a text, so history is not bound to a textual exegesis, as man ("in the image of God"), a creator who can break and refashion the conditions that seem to bind him, is not bound to a fate allegedly prophesied. Prophecy, in the Hebrew Bible, is not so mechanistic.

One might say that the "New Testament" has this correlation: justice (for the Fall) making possible mercy (through the Atonement). But here, truly, is legalism, the abstract weighing of pleasures and pains. God seems Roman-bureaucratic, limited. He provides a channel for redemption and then must go through channels himself, for he can redeem only through the machinery, the apparatus of the Cross. Christian trinitarianism seems to impugn monotheism here, and not just in the literal sense that three is, simply, three, not three-in-one or one-in-three, the famous holy mystery. The crucial damage to monotheism is in the implication that God's power, his flexibility, is impugned. Once God has set up the treasury of grace (filled, enough for all men forever, through the totally undeserved suffering of the vicarious sufferer), all who deserve the suffering of divine punishment can draw on the treasury to pay their debts. The divine books balance, since the crucifixion supplies infinite recompense for the infinite accumulation of human guilt. Men can draw on the treasury, but they must draw, to be saved. That is the law of salvation, the legal obligation of men to pay, in their own substance if not in the blood of the Lamb. It is for Christians, not Jews, that law seems really a yoke that no one can throw off. No one, no One—not man, not God. For God is not free to save when God has to be paid in one specific coin, whether drawn on by faith or paid in the individual destiny of the faith-less individual. Once He has set it up, even God cannot interfere with the abstract legal balance. Far from being the sole Lord, the untrammeled executive of justice and mercy, he seems, with a holy book of *this* sort, an inexorable, impersonal book-keeper.

Paul put God in this situation when he bequeathed to Christianity his idiosyncratic interpretation of man's first disobedience. The fruit was guilt, and its consequence, damnation. The way out was the transfer of debt to Corporation Christi, where there was ample credit with which to pay. In terms of the Hebrew Bible, this is not a biblical faith; this reading of Genesis is Christian, not "Judeo-Christian."

For to Jews, with biblical warranty, the eating of the fruit of the Tree of Knowledge meant, not the impressment into hell, but the expulsion from Eden. That is, man became man, in his actual, historical, human situation—pain, travail, sweat of the brow. "Knowledge" means individuation, discrimination, the break in Edenic continuum of ego and object, the awareness of life which is the awareness of passion (suffering), and of passing time, and death. The fatal flaw in man becomes for Paul the basis of damnation. But for Jews, for a Saul but not a Paul, it becomes the grounds for mercy, since man is not bound to be more than man, and as such his nature must be flawed, which God knows and *excuses:* "Never again (after Noah and the Flood) will I doom the world because of man *since* the inclinations of man's heart (*ki yetzer lev ha-adam*) are evil from his youth (*ra min-urov*)." Thus, man is not condemned for what is of his essence. To have that essence, to be man in the world beyond the Garden, is its own condemnation, and the sole condemnation (to life, not to hell) which the essence implies for man. And this condemnation is not condign, since in life, in history, man can be redeemed. Plunged by the fruit of the Tree of Knowledge (of good and evil) into the midst of life, man may work his way back from time to eternity by way of the (metaphorical) tree of life, from the Sinai of revelation and burning bush. "For I give you good doctrine, foresake ye not my law. It is a tree of life to them who grasp it. . . . Its ways are ways of pleasantness, and all its paths are peace." If knowledge of good and evil made man the man he is, in life, in history, then making history, action, the heeding of commandments (not the assent to propositions), redeems life and assures life by making it good, not evil. The condition of life, the condition of *choice,* is not a curse, for the power to choose is the power to break the conception of life itself, history after Eden, as an invincible curse for the Fall. To choose well in life is nothing less than to choose life itself. "Therefore choose life." This choice is good and sufficient. It is not vitiated by a sin that nothing in life can reach, so that only another's ("Another's") choice of perfect ways and vicarious pain could pay for it.

It is the Jewish inference that man cannot identify with God in substance, but can imitate God (within limits) in action. The Christian inference, for all the variations on "Imitatio Christi" which Christian literature affords, is that the imitation of Christ is not only ultimately impossible, but undesired. Christ is as he is, sinless, not really to inspire men to the same condition, but to compensate for the impossibility of such an inspiration. He cannot remove man's original sin, he can only pay for it. Therefore, the Christian emphasis is on communion, assimilation, one-ness in essence—not action. To Judaism, man can (and must) remain man, not flee to absorption in God (by absorption of God?) in the conviction that man, if only man, is doomed.

And so Jews unequivocally toast, *l'hayyim*. A strong Judaism, one which does not give way to despair, is proof against the fatal Christian tension between life-denying assumptions (antinomian messianism) and inconsistent institutionalization, which make endemic an apocalyptic frenzy.

APPENDIX A: JOSEPH RICHMOND LEVENSON

CHRONOLOGY

6/10/1920	Born Boston, Mass.
1931-1937	Boston Latin School
9/1937-6/1939	Harvard College
6/1939-9/1939	University of Leiden
9/1939-6/1941	Harvard College, A.B., Magna cum laude
6/1941-9/1941	ACLS course in Chinese, Cornell University
9/1941-1/1942	Harvard University, graduate student in History
3/1942	Enlistment, Yeo. 2/C, USNR
3/1942-2/1946	Navy Japanese Language School, Berkeley and Boulder, Colo. Service in Pacific island areas, Washington, D.C. and Japan; action with New Zealand Army and U.S. Navy in Solomons and Philippines campaigns.
3/1946	Honorable discharge, Lieut. s/g.
3/1946-1947	Harvard University, A.M.
1947-2/1949	Harvard University, Ph. D., Teaching Fellow, History
7/1948-7/1951	Junior Fellow, Society of Fellows, Harvard
7/1951-7/1956	University of California, Assistant Professor
7/1956-7/1960	University of California, Associate Professor
7/1960-7/1965	University of California, Berkeley, Professor
7/1965-1969	University of California, Sather Professor of History
April 6, 1969	Death

FELLOWSHIPS;

1954-1955	Fulbright
1958-1959	Center for Advanced Study in the Behavioral Sciences
1962-1963	Guggenheim
1966-1967	American Council of Learned Societies

MEMBERSHIPS:

Association of Asian Studies (Board of Directors 1965-1968)
American Historical Association (Pacific Coast branch prize)

Married, 1950, Rosemary Sebag-Montefiore. Four children: Richard Montefiore, 1952; Irene Anne, 1954; Thomas Montefiore, 1958; Leo Montefiore, 1961.

APPENDIX B: THE WORKS OF JOSEPH R. LEVENSON

PUBLISHED BOOKS

Liang Ch'i-ch'ao and the Mind of Modern China. Cambridge: Harvard University Press, 1953.

Liang Ch'i-ch'ao and the Mind of Modern China. Second edition, revised. Cambridge: Harvard University Press, 1959; London: Thames and Hudson, 1959.

Confucian China and Its Modern Fate: The Problem of Intellectual Continuity. Berkeley: University of California Press; London: Routledge & Kegan Paul, 1958.

Confucian China and Its Confucian Past: The Problem of Monarchical Decay. Berkeley: University of California Press; London: Routledge & Kegan Paul, 1964.

Modern China and Its Confucian Past: The Problem of Intellectual Continuity. New York: Doubleday-Anchor, 1964. Revised and illustrated paperback reprint of *Confucian China and Its Modern Fate: The Problem of Intellectual Continuity*.

Confucian China and Its Modern Fate: The Problem of Historical Significance. Berkeley: University of California Press; London: Routledge & Kegan Paul, 1965.

European Expansion and the Counter-Example of Asia, 1300-1600. Englewood Cliffs, N.J.: Prentice-Hall, 1967.

———and Franz Schurmann. *China: An Interpretive History*. Berkeley and Los Angeles: University of California Press, 1969.

Modern China: An Interpretive Anthology. London: Collier-Macmillan, 1971.

Revolution and Cosmopolitanism: The Western Stage and the Chinese Stages. Berkeley: University of California Press, 1971.

PUBLISHED ARTICLES

1950

"The Breakdown of Confucianism: Liang Ch'i-ch'ao before Exile—1873-1898," *Journal of the History of Ideas*, 11:4 (October 1950), 448-485.

1952

"*T'ien-hsia* and *Kuo* and the 'Transvaluation of Values,'" *Far Eastern Quarterly*, 11:4 (August 1952), 447-451.

1953

"'History' and 'Value': The Tensions of Intellectual Choice in Modern China," in Arthur F. Wright, ed., *Studies in Chinese Thought*. Chicago: University of Chicago Press, 1953. Pp. 146-194.

"Western Powers and Chinese Revolutions: The Pattern of Intervention," *Pacific Affairs*, 26:3 (September 1953), 230-236.

1954

"The Abortiveness of Empiricism in Early Ch'ing Thought," *Far Eastern Quarterly*, 13:2 (February 1954), 155-165.

"Western Religion and the Decay of Traditional China: The Intrusion of History on Judgments of Value," *Sinologica*, 4:1 (1954), 14-20.

1955

"The Attenuation of a Chinese Philosophical Concept: *T'i-yung* in the Nineteenth Century," *Asiatische Studien* (1955), 95-102.

1956

"Redefinition of Ideas in Time: The Chinese Classics and History," *Far Eastern Quarterly*, 15:3 (May 1956), 399-404.

"Western Powers and Chinese Revolutions: The Pattern of Intervention," reprinted in William Appleman Williams, ed., *The Shaping of American Diplomacy*. Chicago: Rand McNally, 1956. Pp. 622-627.

1957

"The Amateur Ideal in Ming and Early Ch'ing Society: Evidence from Painting," in John K. Fairbank, ed., *Chinese Thought and Institutions*. Chicago: University of Chicago Press, 1957. Pp. 320-341.

1958

"History under Chairman Mao," *Soviet Survey*, 24 (April-June 1958), 32-37.

1959

"The Suggestiveness of Vestiges: Confucianism and Monarchy at the Last," in David S. Nivison and Arthur F. Wright, eds., *Confucianism in Action*. Stanford: Stanford University Press, 1959. Pp. 244-267.

1960
"Historical Significance," *Diogenes*, 32 (Winter 1960), 17-27.

"Ill Wind in the Well-Field: The Erosion of the Confucian Ground of Controversy," in Arthur F. Wright, ed., *The Confucian Persuasion*. Stanford: Stanford University Press, 1960. Pp. 268-287.

1961
"The Intellectual Revolution in China," *University of Toronto Quarterly*, 30:3 (April 1961), 258-272.

1962
"Confucian and Taiping 'Heaven': The Political Implications of Clashing Religious Concepts," *Comparative Studies in Society and History*, 4:4 (July 1962), 436-453.

"Liao P'ing and the Confucian Departure from History," in Arthur F. Wright and Denis Twitchett, eds., *Confucian Personalities*. Stanford: Stanford University Press, 1962. Pp. 317-325.

"The Place of Confucius in Communist China," *The China Quarterly*, 12 (October-December 1962), 1-18.

1963
"The Inception and Displacement of Confucianism," *Diogenes*, 42 (Summer 1963), 65-80.

"Origines et itinéraire du Confucianisme; de l'histoire comme fondement de la culture aux sables mouvants de l'historicisme," *Diogene*, 42 (Summer 1963).

1964
"The Humanistic Disciplines: Will Sinology Do?" *Journal of Asian Studies*, 23:4 (August 1964), 507-512.

"The Intellectual Revolution in China," reprinted in Albert Feuerwerker, ed., *Modern China*. Englewood Cliffs, N.J.: Prentice-Hall, 1964. Pp. 154-168.

"The Suggestiveness of Vestiges: Confucianism and Monarchy at the Last," reprinted in Arthur F. Wright, ed., *Confucianism and Chinese Civilization*. New York: Atheneum, 1964. Pp. 291-314.

1965
"The Communist Attitude towards Religion," in Werner Klatt, ed., *The Chinese Model*. Hong Kong: University of Hong Kong Press, 1965. Pp. 19-30.

1966
"Ideas of China," *Times Literary Supplement* (July 28, 1966), pg. 691.

"The Persistence of the Old," *Problems of Communism* (September-October 1966).

"Marxism and the Middle Kingdom," *Diplomat*, XVII, 196 (September 1966), 48-51.

1967

"The Province, the Nation, and the World: The Problem of Chinese Identity," in Albert Feuerwerker, Rhoads Murphey, Mary C. Wright, eds., *Approaches to Modern Chinese History*. Berkeley and Los Angeles: University of California Press, 1967. Pp. 268-288.

———and Franz Schurmann, "What Is Happening in China: An Exchange," *New York Review of Books,* 7:12 (January 12, 1967), 31-34.

"China after World War II," in *Encyclopedia Britannica* (1967), 5:595-598.

"Liang Ch'i-ch'ao," in *Encyclopedia Britannica* (1967), 13:1015-1016.

"Yuan Shih-k'ai," in *Encyclopedia Britannica* (1967), 23:912-913.

1968

"The Past and Future of Nationalism in China," *Survey*, 67 (April 1968), 28-40.

1969

"Communist China in Time and Space: Roots and Rootlessness," *The China Quarterly,* 39 (July-September 1969), 1-11.

"New Trends in History," *Daedalus*, 98:4 (Fall 1969), 903-904, 915-917, 947-948, 961-963, 967-969, 975.

1970

"The Genesis of *Confucian China and Its Modern Fate*" in *The Historian's Workshop*, ed. Perry Curtis (New York: Knopf, 1970).

ABSTRACTS

Revue Bibliographique de Sinologie. Paris: Centre de Recherches Historiques, 1955. Vol. I. Abstracts of two articles in Japanese, one in English; Vol. II, 1956. Abstracts of eight articles in Japanese, one in Chinese.

BOOK REVIEWS

1949

Wen-han Kiang, *The Chinese Student Movement,* in *Pacific Affairs* (March 1949).

1953

H.G. Creel, *Chinese Thought from Confucius to Mao Tse-tung,* in *American Historical Review* (October 1953).

Max Weber, *The Religion of China*, in *Journal of Economic History* (Winter 1953).

1954

H.G. Creel, *Chinese Thought from Confucius to Mao Tse-tung*, in *American Anthropologist* (1954).

1956

Liu Wu-chi, *Confucius: His Life and Time*, in *American Anthropologist* (1956).

Rushton Coulborn, ed., *Feudalism in History*, in *Far Eastern Quarterly* (August 1956).

1958

Carsun Chang, *Development of Neo-Confucian Thought*, and O. Brière, *Fifty Years of Chinese Philosophy, 1898-1950,* in *Pacific Affairs* (December 1958).

"The Heart Has Its Reasons," review of Simone de Beauvoir, *The Long March*, in *The Nation* (June 28, 1958).

Burton Watson, *Ssu-ma Ch'ien, Grand Historian of China*, in *Pacific Historical Review* (November 1958).

1959

Moses Hadas, *Hellenistic Culture: Fusion and Diffusion*, in *The New Leader* (Fall 1959).

Paul A. Varg, *Missionaries, Chinese, and Diplomats: The American Protestant Missionary Movement in China, 1890-1952,* in *Journal of Modern History* (December 1959).

1960

Liang Ch'i-ch'ao, *Intellectual Trends in the Ch'ing Period*, trans. Immanuel Hsu, in *American Hstorical Review* (January 1960).

1961

Wolfgang Franke, *The Reform and Abolition of the Traditional Chinese Examination System*, in *American Historical Review* (October 1961).

"The Day Confucius Died," review of Chow Tse-tsung, *The May Fourth Movement: Intellectual Revolution in Modern China*, in *Journal of Asian Studies* (February 1961).

Theodore H.E. Chen, *Thought Reform of the Chinese Intellectuals*, in *Pacific Historical Review* (February 1961).

Roderick MacFarquhar, *The Hundred Flowers Campaign and the Chinese Intellectuals*, in *The New Leader* (February 13, 1961).

1962

W.G. Beasley and E.G. Pulleyblank, *Historians of China and Japan*, in *Pacific Historical Review* (May 1962).

1964

"The Mind of Mao," review of Robert S. Elegant, *The Center of the World: Communism and the Mind of Mao*; Arthur A. Cohen, *The Communism of Mao Tse-tung*; Stuart R. Schram, *The Political Thought of Mao Tse-tung*, in *New York Review of Books* (September 24, 1964).

1965

Benjamin Schwartz, *In Search of Wealth and Power*, in *Journal of the American Oriental Society* (July-September 1965).

1966

D.W.Y. Kwok, *Scientism in Chinese Thought, 1900-1950*, in *Journal of Asian Studies* (November 1966).

1967

Huang Sang-k'ang, *Li Ta-chao and the Impact of Marxism on Modern Chinese Thinking*, and Maurice Meisner, *Li Ta-chao and the Origins of Chinese Marxism*, in *American Historical Review* (December 1967).

Jonathan Spence, *Ts'ao Yin and the K'ang-hsi Emperor: Bondservant and Master*, in *American Historical Review* (July 1967).

MISCELLANEOUS PAPERS

"Chinese Communist Historiography."

*"The Coronation of Charles X," senior thesis, Harvard University.

"Curators and Creators: Chinese Tradition in the Present Age."

"Curators and Cremators: More Reflections on 'What Is Happening in China.'"

Discussion of Gerhard Masur, "Distinctive Traits of Western Civilization: The Classic Interpretation," American Historical Association, 1960.

"Europe in India and the Far East—Early Contacts by Sea."

"Historical Scholarship as Historical Evidence: The 'Placing' of the Chinese Communists by Their Studies of the Past," paper presented to the Center for Chinese Studies, Berkeley, April 9, 1958.

"History and Cosmopolitanism: East Asia and the Meaning of 'World Classics.'" Unfinished draft, 42 pp. in typescript of Volume 2 of the projected trilogy "Cosmopolitanism, Nationalism, and Provincialism."

"The Hung-hsien Emperor as a Comic Type," paper presented to the Association for Asian Studies, Boston, April 2, 1957.

"The Individual Thinker as a Key to Intellectual History: Liang Ch'i-ch'ao."

"Interpretations of Ch'ing History," paper presented to Society for Ch'ing Studies.

*"Italian Episode—1799."

*"Japan in British Thought in the 1880s."

"Late Ch'ing and Early Republican Politics," panel comment for the Association for Asian Studies, Boston, 1969.

"The No Drama of Japan."

*"The Objective of Columbus."

"On Asian Classics."

*"Religion and the Rise of Capitalism."

"The Tension of Intellectual Choice: 'History' and 'Value' in Modern China."

"Tensions between Monarch and Bureaucrat in the Confucian State," paper presented to the Association for Asian Studies, 1959.

Thoughts for "The Intrusion of History on Judgments of Value."

*Undergraduate papers written for Harvard University.